The North Korean
Communist Leadership,
1945–1965

TO MY MOTHER

The North Korean Communist Leadership, 1945–1965:

A Study of Factionalism and Political Consolidation

by

KOON WOO NAM

The University of Alabama Press
University, Alabama

ACKNOWLEDGMENTS

At various stages in the writing of this manuscript, I received invaluable help from numerous persons, especially from Dr. Franklin W. Houn, Dr. John M. Maki, Dr. Norman Wilson, Mr. Carl J. Mora, and Mr. John Webster. My hearty thanks go to all of them. I am grateful to Mr. George Potter of the Harvard-Yenchin Library and to Mr. Key P. Yang of the Library of Congress for their cooperation in my search for materials for this book. Finally, I owe heartfelt thanks to my wife, Jane, who sustained and encouraged me every step of the way in the completion of this work.

CONTENTS

PREFACE

Ever since its emergence in 1945, North Korean leadership has been characterized by its basic continuity and the regime has been relatively stable. Yet under this continuity of leadership, the regime has undergone a considerable degree of evolution.

Following the liberation of Korea in 1945 after thirty-six years of Japanese colonial rule, three major Korean communist groups emerged in North Korea. They were the native communist group, the Yenan faction, and the Soviet-returned group. The native communist group consisted of communists who had operated inside Korea; the Yenan faction were communists who had come back from Yenan, the communist base in China, after years of exile; and the Soviet-returned group were those who had been in the USSR and came with the Soviet Army that occupied North Korea following the Japanese defeat. Although all three groups had previous anti-Japanese revolutionary records, none had been able to crush the Japanese rule which might have entitled one of them to be the ruling body of liberated Korea. Their emergence itself was primarily the result of the military operation of World War II and beyond their control. None of the three groups had previous administrative experience in national affairs. However, the external conditions for building a communist state were provided by the Russian occupation in North Korea. The immediate problem was forging a workable team out of these three communist groups for the construction of a communist state.

In the early phase of the North Korean regime, power was shared by all three groups and they cooperated with each other because of identity or similarity of ideology. Yet the spirit of cooperation was rather slight and the factional struggle for power within the regime continued from the early days. In the process of this factional struggle, power gravitated towards a subgroup among the Soviet-returned communists and continued to do so until the time when this subgroup, led by one man, emerged as the victor after nearly fifteen years of bitter struggle. This subgroup constitutes the North Korean communist leadership today. In the process of the struggle, the native communist forces and those from China were destroyed and some other individuals eliminated.

Although some English articles have appeared recently in the West on North Korea, each of them has dealt exclusively with one aspect of North Korean life and, in addition to being short and sketchy, they have not shed much light on the evolution of North Korean leadership, particularly the political and social milieu in which the power struggle took place.

The objective of this study then is to trace the process of the emergence of the present leadership. However, unlike the traditional approach in the study of politics, this study does not limit the scope of the investigation to the formal governmental structure. One conclusion of this study is that for several years after the 1945 liberation North Korean officials did not necessarily wield power commensurate with their office. Both in governmental and non-governmental institutions, it was not unusual to find that formally an inferior in a political organ had more influence than his superior during the transition period; that is to say, from the time when all three groups shared power until the time power was monopolized by a subgroup. Further, the real power struggle was staged outside the formal government and within the party, the most powerful political organ in North Korea. At the same time, the factional struggle was greatly influenced by environmental factors such as the division of Korea, the stationing of the Soviet Army in the north and the United States Army in South Korea and their subsequent withdrawal, the Korean War, and the coming of the Chinese communist army to North Korea. Also in evaluating the evolution of North Korean leadership, the social and political backgrounds of the three groups is examined in an effort to understand the factionalism that is so characteristic of them.

The scope of the leadership is treated on the national or central level, since all political power in North Korea has been concentrated on that level. The period covered is from 1945 to the present. However, since the current ruling clique triumphantly emerged from the long and bitter power struggle in 1961 and has been virtually unchanged since that time, the early years of struggle is emphasized. In dealing with the period from the conclusion of the struggle up to the present, the backgrounds of the present leaders, their techniques and policies, is analyzed in an attempt to determine why they have remained in power continuously for so long.

Although as many documents and publications as possible were used to achieve accuracy and objectivity, the research and interpretations were necessarily circumscribed by the available number of source materials as well as by the inherently partisan nature of these sources.

In examining the social backgrounds of the Korean communist leaders, some difficulties arise. North Korea has never published any biographical material on Korean communists except one on their current supreme leader. Some biographical material has been published in South Korea, Japan, and the United States. Yet none of the biographical material—Japanese, English, or South Korean— mentioned the family background, specifically the profession of the father of any communist leader—one of the factors needed to assess the socio-economic status of such individuals before they came to political prominence. None of these biographical sources were consistent in the categories they listed, such as age and education; and some individuals are mentioned only in terms of their recent political activities. Efforts have been made to supplement such biographical data, but the quantity of this information is limited.

There have been wide discrepancies in information regarding many events that took place in North Korea, especially in the causes of drastic events such as the demotion, assassination, or purge of some prominent communists. These discrepancies are especially noticed when comparing North Korean sources and non-communist sources. Since all communications have been under strict governmental censorship in North Korea and only meagre information leaks out, it is extremely difficult to prove the validity of sources. The evaluations and conclusions herein are based upon the writer's own judgment after careful cross-checking of various sources of information.

Almost all the Korean and Japanese materials used for this book are found either at the Harvard-Yenchin Library or the Library of Congress. Some materials were obtained from libraries in the United States through the University of Massachusetts inter-library loan service, and some directly from publishing houses in Japan or South Korea. Numerous Korean and Japanese materials were translated by the writer. Some guidance was received from articles in English on North Korea by several scholars, including Professor Chong-sik Lee of the University of Pennsylvania and Professor Glenn D. Paige of the University of Hawaii. The romanization of Korean names is based on the McCune-Reischauer system, except where the established usage is more familiar to Western readers, and names of Koreans are indicated according to the Korean name order; that is, last name first, with the exception of those who appear to have adopted the Western name order in their English publications.

It is hoped that this book will contribute in a small way to an understanding of North Korean leadership—who the leaders are, how and why they achieved their present position, and why they act as they do now, especially toward the United States of America.

Buffalo, New York   Koon Woo Nam
September 1973

1.

ORIGINS OF THE KOREAN
COMMUNIST MOVEMENT (1918–1945)

Soviet Russia and Early Korean Communist Activities Abroad

THE KOREAN COMMUNIST MOVEMENT HAD ITS START ON RUSSIAN soil among Soviet Koreans and exiled Korean revolutionaries during the period of the October Revolution. The Soviet Koreans were mostly descendants of Korean immigrants who began to migrate to the Martime Provinces in Russia in the mid-nineteenth century for economic reasons. It was those Soviet Koreans, settled in Siberia around Irkutsk, who formed a Korean section of the Russian Communist Party in January, 1918. They participated in the battles against the White Guards in expectation of an improvement in their status under the Bolsheviks. These Koreans later became known as the Irkutsk group. They operated under the direct supervision of the Russian Bolsheviks through the Comintern.[1]

The exiled Korean revolutionaries were those who fled to Siberia following the Japanese annexation of Korea in 1910. While in Siberia, they carried out their anti-Japanese revolutionary activities and, at the same time, sought support from foreign powers for their movement. Eventually, they received assistance from the Russian Bolsheviks, who were eager to chase out the Japanese troops that had advanced into Siberia to aid the White Guards. In June 1918 the exiled Korean revolutionaries gathered near Khabarovsk and founded the Korean Socialist Party (Hanin Sahoedang) with the blessing of

[1]

the Russian Bolsheviks. The new party was headed by Yi Tong-hwi, the acknowledged leader of Korean nationalists in Manchuria and Siberia. Prior to his exile, Yi had been an officer in the royal Korean Army which had been dissolved by the Japanese Regent-General in Korea in 1907.[2]

In August 1919 Yi Tong-hwi and his immediate followers moved to Shanghai in order to take part in the politics of the newly created Korean Provisional Government in exile. Serving as the Premier of the Provisional government under the American-educated President, Syngman Rhee, Yi endeavored to influence the course of that government in politics as well as to disseminate communism among Koreans in China. Encouraged by the successes of the Bolsheviks in Russia, Yi sought to train the Koreans in Manchuria and Siberia for an early military attack on the Japanese. His proposal, however, encountered strong opposition from the nationalist group headed by Syngman Rhee, who advocated negotiation as a means of dealing with the Japanese in Korea. Unable to overcome this opposition, Yi resigned the premiership in January 1921 and began to work exclusively with the communists.[3]

Yi's efforts to propagate communism among Koreans abroad had yielded some fruit, however. In May 1921, when Yi reorganized his old Korean Socialist Party in Shanghai and renamed it the Korean Communist Party (Koryŏ Kongsandang), some of the former nationalists who had been officials of the provisional government in Shanghai joined his new party; and subsequently, many Korean nationalist revolutionaries abroad turned to communism and became members of the Korean Communist Party under him. They did so largely because of Soviet Russia's interest in the Korean independence movement and their profound disappointment with the indifference of other major powers towards their cause.[4] They had come to believe that the "Korean independence movement must be achieved with the assistance of Russia." [5]

The Irkutsk Faction vs The Shanghai Faction

With the emergence of communists led by Yi Tong-hwi, the Korean independence movement now split into two hostile camps: the nationalists and the communists. The Korean communist group under Yi Tong-hwi was later called the Shanghai Faction.

The Korean communist movement that started abroad was beset by factional quarrels from the very beginning. The Irkutsk faction consisted of Soviet Koreans who were members of the Russian Communist Party. Their activities were tightly controlled by their Russian superiors. On the other hand, the majority of the Shanghai Faction were Korean revolutionaries in exile who had initially joined the Korean communist movement to receive aid from Soviet Russians for their anti-Japanese struggle. Unlike the Irkutsk Faction, Yi Tong-hwi's Shanghai group was not under direct Soviet control. Despite the Shanghai Faction's professed belief in communism, their ideological commitment appeared dubious to the Irkutsk Faction and to leaders of the Comintern. For example, Yi Tong-hwi, who had been a military man, did not really understand communism.[6] He became a communist primarily because he wished to gain the aid of the Russian Bolsheviks in achieving independence for Korea. It was not long before Yi became a "disgraced" communist leader in the eyes of the Comintern leaders and his former communist comrades, and he remained so until his death in 1935, in a village in Siberia.

Hoping to put the whole Korean communist movement abroad under its leadership, the Irkutsk Faction, in cooperation with the Comintern authorities, moved to detach members of the Shanghai group from their organization. The efforts of the Irkutsk Faction were facilitated by a rumor that funds had been embezzled by one of Yi Tong-hwi's deputies. These funds had been originally provided by the Comintern in 1919 for the Korean communist movement, but the Shanghai Faction had monopolized them. As the rumor spread, the Irkutsk Faction openly accused the Shanghai Faction of being bourgeois nationalists utilizing communism as a "mere protective color." [7] Such an accusation, along with the rumored embezzlement, caused dissension among the followers of Yi Tong-hwi. Some members of the Shanghai Faction defied their leader and went over to the side of the Irkutsk group. Later, the Irkutsk group, in coordination with the Red Army, even took military action against Yi Tong-hwi's armed groups scattered in Siberia, the largest conflict being the Free City (Alexeyevsk City) Incident of June 1921, in which many of Yi's men were either killed or forced to join the Irkutsk Faction.[8] By early 1922 the position of the Irkutsk Faction *vis-a-vis* the Shanghai group was considerably strengthened. Nonetheless, the Irkutsk group could not absorb all the Korean communists abroad into its ranks. Hence the split of the Korean communists into two hostile groups continued to remain apparent.[9]

The Communist Movement in Korea and Factionalism

Having started their communist movement abroad, both the Shanghai and Irkutsk groups began to infiltrate agents across the border into Korea in the early 1920's. Most of the emissaries of both communist groups were one-time nationalist revolutionaries who had been converted to communism. Upon their secret arrival in Korea, the members of the Irkutsk group formed the Tuesday Association (Hwayo-hoe); and the Shanghai Faction, the Seoul Group. The leading members of the Tuesday Association—Kim Chae-bong, Kim Yak-su, Pak Hŏn-yŏng, and Cho Pong-am—all urged the identification of the Korean communist movement with the international communist movement under the Comintern's control. The Seoul Faction, led by Kim Sa-guk and Yi yŏng, advocated communism that would be "based only on forces within Korea." [10]

While competing for leadership within the Korean communist movement, these two groups infiltrated various Korean youth and labor organizations that had just begun to emerge, especially in cities and towns. The Japanese allowed these Korean organizations to be formed after the Koreans' unsuccessful anti-Japanese demonstrations of March 1, 1919. They were all under the leadership of the national-reformists and their purposes were to heighten the national consciousness of their members and to seek an improvement in the status of the Koreans without advocating immediate independence of Korea from Japanese colonial rule. It was within these organizations that the communist infiltrators began to gather strength clandestinely.[11] The Tuesday Association first recruited enough members to form the First Korean Communist Party secretly in Seoul on April 17, 1925, with the Soviet-trained Kim Chae-bong as its chairman. However, only about six months later the existence of the party was revealed to the Japanese police as some young, zealous, and indiscreet party members waved red flags on the streets and shouted "Long Live Communism in Korea! " The police soon arrested the leaders of the party, including chairman Kim Chae-bong, Pak Hŏn-yŏng, and Kim Yak-su.[12]

After the imprisonment of the leaders of the Tuesday Association, the Seoul Faction moved to form its own party. On December 21, 1925, this faction established the Ch'unkyŏng-wŏn Communist Party at Ch'unkyŏng-wŏn, a restaurant in Seoul. Its leaders were Kim Sa-guk and Yi yŏng. Yet this party was not strong enough to challenge the Tuesday Association even though the latter's prominent leaders were in Japanese prisons. Meanwhile, members of the Tuesday Association who had avoided arrest managed to revitalize the party and named it the Second Korean Communist Party. The new party was headed by a journalist, Kang Tal-yŏng. However, like the First Party, the Second Party did not last long. On June 10, 1926, the funeral day of the last Korean king, members of the Second Korean Communist Party staged demonstrations, carrying red flags, shouting "Long Live Korea!" and demanding immediate independence. The demonstrators, including Kang Tal-yŏng, were immediately arrested. This dealt a heavy blow to the party.[13]

Following the second debacle of the Tuesday Association, a group of Korean communist students returned from Japan. Headed by An Kwang-ch'ŏn, they urged all communists to join hands with nationalists for the cause of independence. Specifically, the students advocated the formation of a united front with national-reformists to "widen the basis of the [revolutionary] struggle, while preserving the class character of the communists." [14] This proposal was opposed by the old guard of the Seoul Faction led by Yi yŏng on the ground that such an action would dilute revolutionary zeal among communists. But the communist students from Japan found supporters of their position among younger members of the Seoul Faction such as Kim Chun-yŏn and Ch'oe Ch'ang-ik as well as a few among the still-remaining members of the Tuesday Association. All those communists who favored a united front with nationalists were called the Marxist-Leninist Group, and they formed the Third Korean Communist Party in December 1926. Now the Korean communists were divided into three groups: the Tuesday Association, the Seoul Group, and the Marxist-Leninist Group. With this tripartite division, factionalism among the Korean communists reached a peak, and acrimonious struggles for power were destined to last well into the mid-1930's.[15] Finally, the Third Korean Communist Party formed a united front with nationalists by joining the nationalist-dominated legal organization known as the Shinkan-hoe (New Trunk Society) in February, 1927. The two groups agreed to subordinate their differences until the goal of Korean independence had been achieved.

Meanwhile, the police detected the existence of the Third Korean Communist Party, largely because of a struggle among leading party members for important party posts, but also because of animosity between the Third Party and its communist antagonists. With the arrest of its leading members, including Kim Chun-yŏn and Ch'oe Ch'ang'ik, the party was greatly weakened.[16] At the same time, Japanese police imprisoned many members of the Seoul Faction who had opposed the united front with the nationalists. Among the victims was Yi yŏng. This marked the demise of the Ch'unkyŏng-wŏn Communist Party.

Immediately after the loss of their prominent leaders, members of the Marxist-Leninist Group still at large managed to form the Fourth Korean Communist Party in February 1928. It was headed by Ch'a Kŭm-bong, a labor leader. However, the party lasted for only a few months and by July of 1928 most of the party members, including Ch'a Kŭm-bong, were jailed.[17] From this point on until V-J Day, there was no formally structured communist party in Korea. The united front between the nationalists and the Marxist-Leninist Group broke up in May 1931 due to unreconciliable differences over tactics to be used in the struggle for national liberation, the communists urging militant action and the nationalists opposing such "precipitous" moves.[18]

After the collapse of the Fourth Korean Communist Party, efforts to revive a national communist party were continued by those communists who were released from their prisons and by communists coming from China, Soviet Russia, and Japan. Due to extremely tight surveillance of the Japanese police, particularly following the Manchurian Incident of 1931, all these attempts ended in failure. Unsuccessful efforts to build a communist party in this period included those made between 1931 and 1934 by the Marxist-Leninist Group under Yi Ki-sŏk, Kwŏn Tae-hyŏng, and Yi Chae-yu,[19] the Party Reestablishment Activity Committee Incident by the Seoul Group in 1933,[20] and the Party Reestablishment Preparatory Committee Incident by the Tuesday Association led by Pak Hŏn-yŏng in early 1933. Pak, who had been arrested in December 1925 in connection with the incident of the First Korean Communist Party, was released temporarily in 1926 during the trial because of illness. But he fled from Korea to Soviet Russia. While in Russia, Pak studied at the Lenin University in Moscow; in January 1933, he entered Korea to contact his comrades and establish a party. But Pak's arrest in the spring of the year of his return to Korea ended the activities of the Party Reestablishment Preparatory Committee.[21]

After a lull of several years, the last and desperate attempt to form a party was made between 1939 and 1941 by a small remaining group of communists. This group, known as the Communist Group (Kom Kurupp), consisted of members of all the three communist groups and it was led by Pak Hŏn-yŏng who had once more been released from prison in early 1939. However, early in 1941, the police began to arrest members of the Communist Group and by late 1941 most members of the Communist Group had been jailed without being able to establish a party. Pak Hŏn-yŏng, this time disguised as a laborer, fled to a brick factory in the town of Kwangju in the southwestern part of Korea and he remained there until the liberation of Korea in 1945.[22]

Effects of the Communist Movement on the Independence Movement in Korea

When the Korean revolutionaries in exile brought communism into Korea in the early 1920's, they found sympathizers for communist doctrines primarily among nationalists. Subsequently Korean political leaders were divided into two antagonistic groups: the national-reformists and the communists. The immediate objective of the national-reformists in the 1920's was the achievement of Korean autonomy within the Japanese Empire, primarily by elevating the cultural and economic status of the Korean people. The slogans raised by the national-reformists mostly read "Heighten National Consciousness!" or "Buy Native Products!" Though the national-reformists were uncompromising towards the Japanese authorities in their efforts to attain their immediate aims and subsequently the independence of Korea, the means adopted by them were peaceful and moderate. Regarding the character of a liberated Korean society, the goal of the national-reformists was essentially capitalistic.[23]

The communists, on the other hand, cherished social ideals drastically different from those of the national-reformists. The communists stood ultimately for the rejection of a private property system and for the establishment of a communist society in a liberated Korea. For the Korean communists, it was Japanese colonial rule that prevented the accomplishment of their social ideals. Thus it was necessary for the communists, like the national-reformists, to win national liberation from the Japanese authorities. As might be expected, in comparison with the national-reformists, the slogans of the communists were both more plentiful and militant in tone, even in connection with the struggle for national independence. Only a few examples of the latter were "Fight for the return of Independence of Korea!", "Overthrow the Tyrannical Rule of the Governor-General!", "Chase All Japanese Out of Korea!" and "Pay No Taxes to the Japanese!" [24] With such slogans, the communists worked for the immediate independence of Korea. It was under the influence of the newly-emerging communist leaders that the native revolutionary movement in Korea took on an increasingly militant stance. Thus the two groups, the communists and the national-reformists often advocated conflicting social goals and tactics for the national liberation movement. The impact of the split of the Korean political leaders that began in the 1920's became apparent in the movement for the national liberation during and after the 1930's.

Following the debacle of the Fourth Korean Communist Party in 1928, the communists, who, until then, had concentrated their activities primarily among intellectuals, moved to the countryside and factories. [25] Up until that time, the factories and particularly the countryside has been relatively calm under the influence of the national-reformists who had been seeking improvement of the lot of peasants and workers through moderate and legal means. [26] With the infiltration of communists, however, the countryside and factories became engulfed in turmoil. In the long run, the communists, with their radical promise to bring about national independence and, perhaps more importantly, a quick improvement in the people's material well-being, were to have more appeal to the poverty-stricken Korean population than the national-reformists, who emphasized political transformation rather than economic or social change.

Throughout the 1930's there occurred numerous peasant disturbances and labor strikes. The striking workers demanded wage increases and recognition of their right to collective bargaining, and they occupied factories in order to obtain concessions from their employers. In the meantime, the peasants demanded reduction of rent and agitated against their landlords' right to eject them from their land. The strong communist influence was most clearly evidenced by the appearance of inscribed slogans reading "No Taxes" and "Land to Farmers." Some striking farmers even went so far as to burn local office buildings and attack Japanese as well as Korean landowners. [27] All these communist-instigated disturbances continued to occur in the face of harsh police measures.

[8]

Peasant uprisings and labor disputes went on to become a major expression of anti-Japanese sentiment in Korea. The number of those who were arrested in connection with communist-instigated incidents far exceeded the number of those who were jailed for other kinds of political offenses.[28] The net effects of the communist activities in Korea were a division of Korean political leaders into national-reformists and communists, the radicalization of the independence movement, and the eventual takeover of that movement by the communists.

Backgrounds of the Communist Leaders[29]

Those persons who led the communist movement in Korea throughout the period of the Japanese domination were predominantly Korean intellectuals. Almost all of them received some sort of college education prior to or during their revolutionary careers—this, at a time when the majority of Koreans could expect, at best, a primary school education. Among sixty prominent communist leaders [30] in Korea during the Japanese occupation, only three had labor backgrounds, while the remainder were middle-school teachers, college professors, journalists, newspaper editors, writers, and lawyers. The family backgrounds of these communist leaders, unlike the mostly upper-class nationalist leaders [31] in Korea, were varied. Some of them came from wealthy landowning families, others from middle-class families, and still others from poor peasant families.

Until the time of the clear division of Korean communist leaders into the Tuesday Association and the Seoul Group, most communist leaders had attended schools in Japan, Korea, or the coastal cities of China. But, with the split of the communists into these two groups, many leaders of the Association went to Soviet Russia for their training, among them being Pak Hŏn-yŏng, Cho Pong-am, and Kim Chae-bong. When the third Korean communist group, the Marxist-Leninist Group, was formed in late 1926, it was led primarily by Korean students from Japan or one-time students in Japan. Among them were An Kwang-ch'ŏn, Yi Chae-yu, Kim Chun-yŏn, and Ch'oe Ch'ang-ik. Kim Chun-yŏn and Ch'oe Ch'ang-ik had previously been members of the Seoul Group, before joining the Marxist-Leninist Group. After the formation of the Marxist-Leninist Group in late 1926, the Seoul Group consisted primarily of "home-made intellectuals," meaning those students who had never been abroad for their studies.

[9]

Although they were from various classes, studied in different regions and were divided into factions, these communist leaders all had one thing in common regarding their backgrounds: they were students or men of considerable learning in a society where men of letters had been traditionally held in high social esteem. It was these Korean intellectuals who took the lead in the communist movement, envisaging the establishment of a proletarian dictatorship in Korea. During the movement, many communists, including Kim Sa-guk, Yi Chae-yu, and Ch'a Kŭm-bong, were arrested and tortured to death.[32] Others renounced their communist allegiance under Japanese police pressure or allurement.[33] Some prominent leaders such as Cho Pong-am, Kim Chun-Yŏn and Kim Yak-su joined the nationalists in South Korea after the liberation of Korea in 1945. Only the most fortunate and unswervingly devoted communists managed to carry on their activities in Korea until V-J Day. They were called "native" communists and most of them were led by Pak Hŏn-yŏng, the son of a poor peasant. Pak was to spearhead efforts in the early 1940's to organize a new communist party.

There were striking similarities in the development of the Korean communist movement of the pre-1945 period and the Chinese communist movement before the emergence of the People's Republic of China in 1949. Communist activities in both countries had their start between the late 1910's and early 1920's, when Korea was under Japanese colonial rule and China was in a similar, semi-colonial status because of foreign intervention. At the time, both countries had predominantly traditional agrarian societies and were in desperate need of modernization of their semifeudal social and political institutions. With these similar national backgrounds, the communist movements in the two Far Eastern countries began after the successful October Revolution in Russia had made an impact upon certain of their leaders. These men came to believe that communism was the key to solving their pressing national problems; and, in both countries, they were able to turn to their own advantage the pre-existent dissatisfaction of certain segments of population with the moderate nationalist leaderships and, eventually, to seize power for themselves.

In both Korea and China, it was the intellectuals who introduced communism to their countries and it was they who led the communist movements.[34] In doing so, the intellectuals carried out extensive but largely clandestine propaganda and agitation activities among the youth, the workers, and the peasants in order to develop their "consciousness" and organize them into revolutionary forces. In this respect, they proved Lenin's theory that "professional revolutionaries" [35] were essential for the success of any revolutionary communist movement. In performing the role of "professional revolutionaries," these intellectuals directed and guided the masses who were economically and socially discontented but politically inarticulate.

Chart of the Korean Communist Factions, 1918–1945

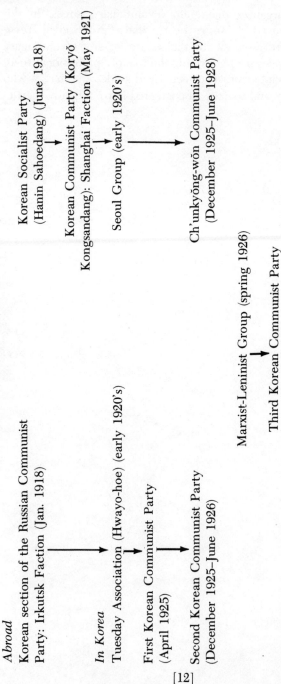

Abroad

Korean section of the Russian Communist
Party: Irkutsk Faction (Jan. 1918)

Korean Socialist Party
(Hanin Sahoedang) (June 1918)

Korean Communist Party (Koryŏ
Kongsandang): Shanghai Faction (May 1921)

Seoul Group (early 1920's)

Ch'unkyŏng-wŏn Communist Party
(December 1925–June 1928)

In Korea

Tuesday Association (Hwayo-hoe) (early 1920's)

First Korean Communist Party
(April 1925)

Second Korean Communist Party
(December 1925–June 1926)

Marxist-Leninist Group (spring 1926)

Third Korean Communist Party
(December 1926)

Fourth Korean Communist Party
(Feb. 1928–July 1928)

The Communist Group (Kom Kurupp) (1939–1941)

[12]

2.

KOREA'S LIBERATION AND
THE COMMUNISTS IN THE NORTH
(AUGUST–DECEMBER 1945)

THE SOVIET UNION DECLARED WAR AGAINST JAPAN ON AUGUST 8, 1945. Within a few days Russian troops began to enter North Korea and by August 15, the day of Japan's formal declaration of surrender to the Allied Forces, substantial Russian forces were already in the northern part of Korea. With the arrival of the Soviet Army, old "native" Korean revolutionaries emerged to resume their political activities openly. Following the collapse of the Japanese administrative apparatus, these revolutionaries proceeded to organize people's councils in their localities and made an effort to maintain law and order with the assistance of Soviet troops. At the beginning, these people's councils were mostly composed of "native" nationalists and communists.[1] These nationalists and communists were referred to as "native" because they, unlike many Korean revolutionaries who had engaged in anti-Japanese activities abroad, had operated in Korea during the period of Japanese rule.

On August 24, 1945 the Russian occupation forces entered P'yŏngyang, the future capital of the Democratic People's Republic of Korea (North Korea). To their displeasure, the Russian authorities found that the people's council in P'yŏngyang was composed of 18 nationalists and of only a few native communists. It was headed by Cho Man-sik, an old conservative nationalist. The Russian authorities ordered a reorganization of the council so that equal representation on that body could be achieved between communists and nationalists. The council was reorganized between August 26 and September 8, 1945 to include 16 nationalists and 16 native communists. Soviet occupation authorities elsewhere in North Korea also reportedly caused the reorganization of the people's councils with the objective of strengthening the position of the communists at the expense of the nationalists.[2]

On October 8, 1945 representatives of five provincial people's councils in North Korea met in P'yŏngyang. They formed an administrative body known as the Five Provinces' Administrative Bureau. The bureau, headed by Cho Man-sik, a nationalist, had "executive power to govern the entire area occupied by Soviet troops." Responsibilities in the bureau were evenly divided between native nationalists and native communists.[3] With the formation of the bureau, the first step toward creation of the future central North Korean government was completed. For awhile, Russian authorities at least feigned cooperation with the bureau and Cho Man-sik, although they covertly sought to dominate it indirectly through those Koreans who were sympathetic to their policies.

On October 12, 1945, two months after the arrival of Soviet forces, I. M. Chistiakov, Commander of the 25th Soviet Army issued his first public statement:

> Korea has become a free state, but this is only the first page in the history of new Korea. The happiness of Korea can be achieved only through the efforts and steadfast struggle of the Korean people. The Soviet Army has provided all the conditions for the free and inventive efforts of the Korean people [for building of a new nation]. The Korean people themselves must become the creators of their own happiness.[4]

This statement reminded the Koreans of the vital role of the Soviet armed forces in the liberation of Korea, but also indicated some sensitivity on the part of the Soviets to the Korean people's aspiration for national independence. Although they refrained from prescribing that North Korea follow the path of communism, perhaps it was unnecessary, since that had become inevitable because of the presence of the Red Army. Still, lest this statement alone be taken as insufficient evidence that the Red Army would not interfere with North Korean internal affairs, the Soviet occupation authorities issued another statement on the same day:

The Soviet Army has not come to Korea to gain territory or to establish a Soviet system on the Korean territory. The Red Army has come to Korea [solely]to protect the ownership of all Korean enterprises and help them resume normal operation in every way.[5]

In the meantime news spread among Koreans that General Kim Il-sŏng had arrived in P'yŏngyang on October 10, 1945 and that a mass meeting would be held in the city in order to welcome him. Prior to this, General Kim had been known to many Koreans as a brilliant and heroic anti-Japanese leader, even though few knew anything more about him, including his age. Most people, however, believed that he was a man of advanced age and great experience.[6] Thus when the 34-year-old General Kim Il-sŏng appeared at the mass rally on October 14, some people could not believe their eyes and there were sudden murmurs in the audience. When they saw that their hero was only a young man, they suspected that the hero presented to them was a fake.[7] To these unbelieving people the young man made a speech. Having deeply thanked the Soviet Army that had "smashed" the Japanese imperialism and had brought "freedom and liberation" to the Korean people, he urged not only peasants and workers but also intellectuals and even rich people to make the utmost effort to build a new "democratic, autonomous, and independent" Korea.[8] He did not mention communism but appealed only to the fervent aspiration of Koreans for independence. The fact that he was introduced by a Russian general at the rally immediately convinced observers that the Red Army was supporting him as the future leader of Korea.

As noted above, on October 12, 1945, the Commander of the Russian occupation forces pledged that Koreans would become "the creators of their own happiness." Yet, two days later, the Russians presented Kim as the leader of the Korean people. The occupation authorities, contrary to their pledge, were not keeping their hands off North Korean internal affairs.

Unlike the United States Army in South Korea, which set up a military government upon its arrival,[9] the Soviet Army dealt directly with people's councils, some of which had been already in existence when the Russians arrived in the north. Though the Soviet Army gave "full support" to these people's councils at various levels, they did not give Koreans real political authority. Actually the Red Army controlled these seemingly indigenous organs through their own military and political personnel as well as through the use of

Soviet-trained Koreans who returned to North Korea with the Red Army. The Russian personnel engaged in this task belonged to the so-called "Romanenko Command." [10]

Separate from the supreme Chistiakov Command and headed by Major General Romanenko, the Romanenko Command was a "political command" with vast powers over North Korean affairs during the period prior to the establishment of a formal regime in the north. Through its political advisers, the Romanenko Command directed the affairs of all the people's councils from local to national levels. It censored newspapers, radio broadcasting, books and other publications and controlled all political, economic and cultural organizations. It also seized all transportation and communications facilities in the north.[11]

Transmitting the directives of the Romanenko Command to the various North Korean organizations was the task of the Soviet Koreans who came to North Korea with the Red Army. According to one source,[12] a group of Soviet Koreans, called the Special Military Operation Corps arrived in North Korea early in September, 1945. Consisting of some 300 members and acting in accordance with instructions emanating from the Soviet authorities in the north, the corps was to help carry out the task of sovietization of North Korea through political and cultural indoctrination of the masses. It was also to make secret preparation for the establishment of a communist party in the north. Members of the corps were quick to infiltrate local and regional governments. Since many of these Korean returnees possessed Soviet citizenship and were familiar with Soviet ideology, they were effective liason agents between Soviet occupation authorities and native North Korean leaders.[13]

Though all the members of the corps were called Soviet Koreans, they can be classified into two different elements in terms of their political and social backgrounds: 1) long-term residents of the Soviet Union and 2) former Korean partisans who had fled to the Soviet Union from Manchuria around 1940. The former elements consisted of descendants of Korean immigrants in the Soviet Union,[14] drawn mostly from the Korean colonies in the Soviet Central Asian regions. They had attended leading political and technical schools in the Soviet Union, had worked in their local governments and were members of the Soviet communist party. Of the 300-man Special Military Operation Corps some 250 were Soviet Koreans of this type. They had no previous records of anti-Japanese guerrilla activities. (Hereafter the term Soviet Koreans will be used to designate these

[16]

men.) Leading figures among them were Hŏ Kai, Pak Ch'ang-ek and Nam Il. Hŏ Kai, a graduate of KUTV (University of the Toilers of the East) and said also to have attended the Moscow University, was formerly secretary of the communist party in the Tashkent Republic.[15] After his return, Hŏ was primarily in charge of building a new communist party in North Korea. He was perhaps the most powerful Soviet Korean. Pak Ch'ang-ok's responsibility lay in the affairs of press, publications and propaganda. Nam Il, later North Korean senior delegate to the Panmunjŏm Truce Conference, was in charge of directing educational institutions in North Korea.

The latter group in the Special Military Operation Corps consisted of remnants of former Korean communist partisan fighters, numbering no more than 50 men.[16] Among them were Kim Il-sŏng, Kim Ch'aek, Ch'oe Yong-kŏn, Kim Il, Ch'oe Hyŏn and Im Ch'un-ch'u. The Soviet Koreans among themselves reportedly called these former guerrillas "ignorant and boorish guys," and they even made fun of Kim Il-sŏng. In turn, the former partisans were contemptuous of the Soviet Koreans who had no experience in anti-Japanese guerrilla activities. This antagonism between the two subgroups in the corps, however, remained latent until they had eliminated their common enemies: nationalists and some recalcitrant native communists.

What was the social and military background of these "ignorant and boorish" partisan fighters? Kim Il-sŏng, the leader of this group, was born Kim Sŏng-ju in P'yŏngan Namdo, a province in the north-western part of Korea in 1912, the year when the legendary Kim was presumably active. As did many other families after the Japanese annexation of Korea in 1910, Kim's parents migrated to Manchuria in 1924. In Manchuria, Kim's father ran a drugstore, and he also had some connection with the Korean nationalist movement, which was fashionable among Korean immigrants.[17] However, the senior Kim died unknown within a few years.

North Korean sources have given different accounts of Kim's family background.[18] They describe him as a man born to an extremely poor peasant family. They claim that when Kim was young his father taught him Korean history thoroughly and inculcated patriotism in him. They also assert that while in Manchuria his father ran a hospital treating the poor free of charge. What the North Korean sources attempt to convey is that the senior Kim was a poor peasant, an intellectual, and also a physician. The reason for this interpretation would appear to be the following: first, since Kim Il-sŏng was the son of a poor farmer, he and his family were not members of the

[17]

bourgeoisie who were "enemies of people"; second, the North Koreans apparently attempted to make their leader seem to be a man who had been conscious of the plight of Korea since his childhood; and third, they wanted to emphasize the fact that members of Kim's family were all patriotic.

If the North Korean version of the family background may be disregarded, Kim Il-sŏng, the son of a lower middle class family, managed to go to school in Manchuria until 1930, completing ten grades. The following year Japan invaded Manchuria touching off a wave of anti-Japanese sentiment among the Chinese. In the countryside of Manchuria numerous Chinese guerrilla units emerged. These "bandit" units came gradually under the control of the Chinese Communist Party. In 1932, Kim joined one of these guerrilla units. It was also about this time that Kim changed his name from Sŏng-ju to Il-sŏng. In January, 1936, the Chinese Communist Party finally managed to unify most of these scattered guerrilla forces. The newly amalgamated forces were called the Northeast Anti-Japanese United Army, headed by a Chinese supreme commander. At the time Kim had some 160 men under his control, and they operated primarily in the southeastern part of Manchuria, heavily settled by Korean immigrants.[19] Among his men were Im Ch'un-ch'u (appointed North Korean Ambassador to Bulgaria in 1958) and Kim Sŏng-guk (as of 1966 Lieutenant General in command of body guard troops for Kim Il-sŏng), both of whom were sons of indigent Korean immigrants. In the same area there were other Korean guerrillas such as Soviet Russian-educated Kim Il (Vice Premier in 1954, Vice Chairman of the North Korean Workers' Party in 1961), Ch'oe Hyŏn (Commander of a North Korean division in June 1950, Minister of Communications in 1958) who had no formal education, and a Chinese communist military academy graduate named Kim Kwang-hyŏp (Vice Premier and member of the Politburo of the North Korean Workers' Party as of 1966).

In northern Manchuria, Ch'oe Yong-kŏn (President of the Presidium of the North Korean Supreme People's Assembly in 1957), a graduate of a Chinese nationalist military academy, was leading some 100 communist fighters and Kim Ch'aek (Vice Premier in 1948, killed during the Korean War while commanding North Korean forces), son of Korean immigrants in Soviet Russia, was serving as a political commissar in a unit of the Northeast Anti-Japanese United Army.[20] It is not known what was the relation between the Korean

[18]

guerrillas in northern Manchuria and those in southern Manchuria or why later Korean partisans acknowledged Kim as their leader. On this question North Korean sources merely mention that "Comrade Kim Il-sŏng . . . during the winter of 1934–35 carried on a northern Manchurian expedition . . . and solidified the unity of comrades in the region." Despite this claim, there was still no effective coordination between the various guerrilla units, and Kim apparently was not yet a leader who could direct all the Korean communist activities in Manchuria.

Kim's reputation as a guerrilla leader spread after his attack on June 4, 1937 on Poch'ŏnbo, a Korean town located right across the Korean-Manchurian border. This was prearranged with the cooperation of local communists such as Pak Tal and Pak kŭm-ch'ŏl, the latter being a migratory peasant. During the assault, some 100 guerrillas under Kim Il-sŏng and Ch'oe Hyŏn destroyed Japanese and pro-Japanese Korean installations and also killed several Japanese officials. After this they retreated to Manchuria.[21] It is believed that the result of the attack was reported along with Kim's name to the Soviet Military Headquarters in Khabarovsk through Isram and Teinof, Soviet agents in the Northeast Anti-Japanese United Army.[22] This was the beginning of Kim's connection with the Soviet authorities. However, the attack was the peak of Kim's guerrilla activities. Thereafter, his partisans along with other units of the Northeast Anti-Japanese United Army rapidly declined in strength, as the Japanese and Manchukuo armies intensified their mopping-up campaigns. Finally, in 1942, Kim, along with other surviving guerrillas, fled Manchuria to the Soviet Union. Later, Kim's comrades, as well as those inside Korea, were called the Kapsan Faction after a North Korean town near the Korean-Manchurian border. It was in the area of Kapsan that the local communists such as Pak Tal (died of an ailment in 1960 at no more than the age of 51) and Pak Kŭm-ch'ŏl, (Vice Chairman of the North Korean Workers' Party as well as of the Presidium of the North Korean Supreme People's Assembly as of 1966), who supported Kim's attack on Poch'ŏnbo, operated in the 1930's.

North Koreans today consistently claim that their leader remained in Manchuria until the very moment of the liberation of Korea. Their intention is obviously to depict their leader as a man of unbreakable will who fought persistently against great odds for the independence of his motherland. Yet such a claim is unconvincing in view of the fact that Kim was a Major in the Soviet Red Army when he arrived in Korea. More important is that the Soviet authorities would not have installed Kim as the leader of the newly occupied North Korea if they had not known him for a reasonable length of time. It is more plausible to believe that Kim and some of his comrades served in a military unit under the Soviet Command in Khabarovsk later entering the Soviet Union in 1942, there to receive political training for future activities in North Korea.

Kim Il-sŏng and his surviving partisan fighters, numbering no more than 50 men, arrived in North Korea early in September 1945 with the Soviet Army. They changed from their Soviet military uniforms into civilian clothes and settled in an unmarked former Japanese house in P'yŏngyang. Occasionally they were visited by unidentified Russians. For more than a month, until October 14, when Kim was introduced at the mass meeting as a national hero by his Russian sponsor, they were quietly observing political developments in North Korea, particularly the activities of native Korean communists.

At the time of liberation it was estimated that there were about 6,000 native communists in North Korea.[23] Up until then, some of them had been imprisoned while others had led a clandestine existence. They now resumed political activities openly in "liberated" North Korea. Operating mainly in their own localities or provinces the first two months after the liberation, none of these native communists had the power to assume leadership of the Korean communist movement in the north. At this juncture, Kim, with the support of the Soviet occupation authorities, sought to unify and direct the diverse native Korean communist forces. The first step taken towards this end was to build a new communist party. One of Kim's tactics to gain the support of local communists was to dispatch his immediate followers to various provinces to contact these leaders.[24]

It was said that Kim Ch'aek was sent to the eastern part of North Korea, Kim Il to the northwestern part, and Ch'oe Hyŏn to the central part of the Korean-Manchurian border region. Kim Il-sŏng, Ch'oe Yong-kŏn and Im Ch'un-ch'u remained in the future capital of North Korea, taking care of the affairs of the surrounding area. During this time Kim used the names "Kim Sŏng-ju" or "Kim Yŏng-hwan," and few North Koreans recognized who he was. At the same time, Kim also sent his personal agents across the 38th Parallel into South Korea to contact Pak Hŏn-yŏng, an old native communist leader who was leading the South Korean communist movement.

Kim's agents in North Korea were said to have met native communist leaders secretly and individually, and to have persuaded them to cooperate in establishing a "Marxist-Leninist party of a new type." [25]

The tasks of Kim's agents were made more difficult due to the opposition of many native communists, prominent ones being, O Ki-sŏp, Chang Sun-myŏng, Chŏn Tal-hyŏn, Yi Chu-ha [26] and Hyŏn Chun-hyŏk, and this in spite of constant pressure from the Soviet authorities stationed in various localities of North Korea. These native communists were the veterans who had remained inside Korea during the difficult period of Japanese rule. Most of them had been in Japanese prisons at some time during their revolutionary careers. Each was a leader of a newly formed party in his own locality, though none could muster much strength beyond the local level. For these communists one of the most obvious consequences of founding a new central communist party under the then prevailing circumstances in North Korea would mean loss of influence and the necessity of subjugating themselves to a group of returnees who, after long absence from Korea, appeared suddenly with the Soviet Army. Particularly strong resistance came from O Ki-sŏp in Hamkyŏng Nando (the province in the southeastern part of North Korea) and Hyŏn Chun-hyŏk in P'yŏngan Namdo (the province in the southwestern part of North Korea).

O, a graduate of the University of the Toilers of the East (KUTV) at Sverdlovsk in the Soviet Union, joined the Korean communist movement late in the 1920's. From then on, he worked among laborers and poor peasants in his native province inciting them to strike and establishing communist cells. His activities were interrupted only by his occasional arrests by the Japanese police. After the liberation O came forward openly in his native province and began to establish local and provincial communist parties in cooperation with other local leaders. In August and September of 1945, O was not only the leading figure in his home province but also, apparently, directing communist leaders throughout the eastern part of North Korea.

Kim Ch'aek, the Soviet-returnee, met O early in September and discussed the plan to form a unified central party in North Korea by merging native communists with the Soviet-returnees. Pressure was also brought upon O from the Romanenko Command through a Russian political adviser who was attached to the Russian Defense Headquarters stationed in O's province. O, however, refused to yield

[21]

on the ground that there was already a Korean communist party in Seoul, and that formation of a new party in the north would result in dividing Korean communists into two groups.[27] O reportedly added that "there cannot be two parties within one country." [28] Confronted by this opposition, Kim Ch'aek was hard pressed to achieve his mission.

While O was refusing to accept the plan in order not to divide Korean communist forces, Hyŏn Chun-hyŏk was opposing the plan on other grounds. Hyŏn, born of a peasant family, was a graduate of Keijō Imperial University (now Seoul National University) and a one-time normal school teacher. He had operated primarily among student bodies prior to the defeat of Japan, forming various study centers for social science where young Koreans learned Marxism-Leninism. He was more an idealistic communist than a practical one and was often called a "living-room communist." Yet Hyŏn was a man of independent thought and action. Shortly after August 15, 1945 he emerged in his native province, P'yŏngan Namdo, and formed the P'yŏngan Namdo District Committee of the Korean Communist Party, establishing himself as Chairman.

Though communist, Hyŏn reasoned that Korea was still undergoing a "bourgeois democratic revolution" and that the leadership of the revolution at that stage should be assumed by the bourgeois-oriented nationalist leaders. He advocated that hegemony by proletariat in the Korean revolution should be taken only after the completion of that bourgeois democratic revolution, not by violence, but by "democratic and exemplary" practices. Because of this belief, Hyŏn ignored the proposals of those who were bent upon establishing a "Marxist-Leninist party of a new type." Thus, while serving as Vice-Chairman in the P'yŏngan Namdo People's Council, he fully supported Chairman Cho Man-sik, a nationalist.[29] Hyŏn's ideology was popular not only among his immediate communist circles but also in the overall political arena in the western part of North Korea. Hyŏn was a dangerous person in the eyes of the Russians who were planning to perform their own version of "democratic reform," based upon the proletariat.

While Hyŏn's popularity was increasing, Kim Il-sŏng reportedly met secretly with some native communist leaders in P'yŏngyang and succeeded in detaching a few extremists from Hyŏn. They were Chang Shi-u, Kim Yong-bŏm and Pak Chŏng-ae, a woman. Chang, a student in Korea and Japan and a veteran communist since the early 1920's, was an open advocate of violence as the means to achieve an end. Kim and Pak (man and wife), both of whom were Russian-trained communists, had infiltrated into Korea from Soviet Russia in the early 1930's and worked among laborers to establish communist cells. After several secret meetings Kim Il-sŏng (still Kim Yŏng-hwan or Kim Sŏng-ju) and the extremists were believed to have come to a conclusion that Hyŏn was a "nationalist in communist disguise." [30] Kim Il-sŏng informed the Romanenko Command of his conclusion, and, finally, on the morning of September 28, 1945, Hyŏn was called into the office of General Romanenko for a conference with other communist leaders. On his way back from the conference, however, Hyŏn was shot to death. It was near the center of the city and around noontime. The assassin was allegedly directed by Chang Shi-u who was then the head of the Justice Department of P'yŏngan Namdo People's Council.[31] The killer was not apprehended. Thus one of the most formidable native rivals of Kim Il-sŏng was eliminated by native communists—a procedure that Kim Il-sŏng conveniently used in his attempt to weaken native forces. At the same time "this action, obviously condoned by the Russians, served effective notice on the local communists that they were not to be the chosen leaders of the future communist regime." [32] After the assassination, native leaders began to show a conciliatory attitude to the proposal to establish a new party. It took about a month for Kim Il-sŏng to eliminate or persuade native communists who stood in his way to form a new communist party in North Korea.

Finally on October 10, 1945, a meeting, called the Conference of Communist Representatives and Enthusiasts of the Five Provinces of North Korea and attended by some 70 persons, was held in P'yŏngyang to establish a party.[33] The conference however was said to have been held in secrecy and a Russian political adviser Colonel Ignachev was there. During the four-day meeting the participants discussed and decided various matters regarding the new party. The Kim Il-sŏng group and the Soviet Koreans proposed to name the new organ the North Korean Communist Party. But the native communists opposed it on the ground that such a title would imply an existence of two communists parties, one in the south and another in the north.[34] After bitter argument, they reached an agreement that the new organ should be called the North Korean Central Bureau of the Korean Communist Party, which appeared to acknowledge the party in Seoul as the central communist organ as insisted upon by native communists. It was also agreed that Kim Yong-bŏm, a native communist, should serve as the Acting Secretary of the bureau.

The fact that the North Korean Central Bureau of the Korean Communist Party was formed after overcoming resistance from various native opponents was an indication that at last the Soviet-returnees were provided with an open domestic instrument whereby they could make attempt to control native communist leaders. The newly formed bureau gradually became the actual center of all North Korean political activities in spite of the absence of legal provisions to that effect. After having established this domestic base of power, Kim Il-sŏng emerged publicly on October 14, 1945 at the mass meeting in P'yŏngyang and he was introduced as a "nationalist hero" of the Korean people. Thereafter, Kim and his comrades devoted much energy to the task of consolidating their positions in the new central bureau. Meanwhile, they infiltrated their agents into various local communist parties, recruited new members who were loyal to them, and made efforts to detach allegiance of local communists from their former leaders. In all this time, Kim Il-sŏng did not participate in the Five Provinces' Administrative Bureau, the joint body of nationalists and communists, supposedly having the executive power to govern the entire area occupied by Soviet troops.

In the midst of these activities the Second Enlarged Conference of the Executive Committee of the North Korean Central Bureau of the Korean Communist Party was held in mid-November 1945. To this conference Kim Il-sŏng gave reports on past activities of the central bureau as well as future programs, even though he was an ordinary member of the central bureau. During his reports, Kim attacked native communist leaders, branding them as "separatists" and urging other communists to "struggle against the evil intentions of these destructive forces." [35] Such denunciation was an indication that there was still a substantial number of veteran native communists who were trying to resist the encroachment of the Soviet-returnees. It was after another month's busy effort on the part of Soviet-returnees who had been infiltrating the provincial and local communist party establishments that the position of the native veteran communists as a whole became utterly untenable.

When the Third Enlarged Conference of the Executive Committee of the Central Bureau was held in P'yŏngyang on December 17, 1945, the Soviet-returnees were assured of their position apparently with the support of new recruits. At the conference they changed the name of the central bureau to the North Korean Communist Party. Kim Il-sŏng was "elected" the First Secretary of the party.[36] Hŏ Kai, the Soviet Korean, became the head of the Organization Department of the party. O Ki-sŏp, the native communist, was made Second Secretary of the party. However, O was later to reap the consequences of his earlier opposition to the formation of the party. After hard and bitter struggles for more than three months, the Soviet-returnees finally achieved their initial objective, and Kim Il-sŏng appeared to have established his footing for the eventual monopolization of political power in North Korea.

3.

NON-COMMUNIST LEADERS
AND POLITICAL EFFECTS OF
THE "DEMOCRATIC REFORMS"

> Everyone regardless of whether he is a member of the Korean Workers'
> Party or not must be loyal to the Korean Workers' Party.[1]

Non-Communist Leaders and their Political Parties

WITH THE LIBERATION, MOST OF THE WELL-KNOWN FORMER PRO-
Japanese Korean collaborators in North Korea who were not caught
and executed, fled to the south where they were left unmolested
by the Americans.[2] Though there still remained in North Korea some
former pro-Japanese Korean functionaries, they were of the minor
sort and became politically impotent in "liberated" North Korea.
The possibility of opposition from these people to the communists
was almost nil.

At the time of liberation there were at least two non-communist
groups potentially capable of opposing the communists in the north.
They were the Korean Christians and the believers of the Teaching
of the Way of Heaven (Ch'ŏndogyo), the extremely nationalistic
native religious sect. Both groups had been anti-Japanese revolutionary forces. With such a political past they now emerged openly
in the "liberated" North Korea and made attempts to rally their
followers in competition with the communists.

However, local communists, supported by Soviet occupation
troops, invariably interfered with the activities of these non-communist groups on the pretext of "erasing subversive elements" hidden
within them.[3] All this time the Soviet authorities did not, or perhaps

[26]

could not, outlaw these non-communist leaders as "reactionaries" or "pro-Japanese reactionaries" in order to stop their activities. Instead, the Russians relied primarily upon local communists to hamper the activities of the non-communist leaders while making no formal announcement regarding the status of these potential anti-communist forces. Due to the absence of declared Soviet policies, the non-communist leaders, in spite of the harassment by local communists, continued their covert attempts to form political parties.

On October 12, 1945, nearly two months after the arrival of the Soviet Army, the Chistiakov Command issued the "Order of the Commander" which, among other things, included regulations regarding political activities in the north. Section 4, Article II of the order provided:

> . . . as pointed out all anti-Japanese political parties and democratic groups will register themselves with the Soviet Army Commander as well as the local self-government concerned, along with their platforms and regulations, and submit a list of their members.[4]

The issuance of this order by the Soviet Command appeared to permit any groups to engage in political activities as long as they were anti-Japanese and democratic. Soon a group of Koreans, mostly Christians were moving to form a political party.

Because of their anti-Japanese revolutionary activities, as well as their Western democratic ideas, the Korean Christians had been constantly punished by the Japanese authorities, however, despite the persecutions and the Japanese efforts for "de-Christianization," [5] the number of Christians increased steadily. It was estimated that there were some 700,000 Korean Christians at the time of liberation.[6] Among them some 200,000 were in the north.[7] When the Christians in the north were preparing for the establishment of a party, the Russians not only condoned their activities but even appeared to encourage them.[8]

The Russians may have chosen this policy in order to avoid being compared unfavorably with the American Military Government, which was then maintaining a relatively free political atmosphere in South Korea, at least to the extent of allowing communists to engage openly in political activities. Perhaps of more practical interest to the Russians, however, might have been the fact that local anti-communist elements, by engaging openly in political activities, would expose their methods and identities that much more quickly. Support for the latter consideration may be found in the all-out anti-nationalist extermination campaigns carried out shortly afterwards by North Korean communists throughout the area controlled by the Soviets.

On November 3, 1945 the first non-communist party, known as the North Korean Democratic Party (Puk Chosŏn Minjudang) was formed in P'yŏngyang. The party's platform consisted of the following major points.[9]

1. Efforts shall be made for the development of Korea and for guaranteeing people's basic rights.
2. New political and economic institutions shall be established that will promote the welfare of all people.
3. Friendly relationship shall be maintained with all democratic nations.
4. Freedom of speech, press, assembly, association and religious belief shall be guaranteed.
5. Two congressional houses shall be established and separation of powers shall be observed.
6. An appropriate election system shall be established.
7. The livelihood of the working class shall be guaranteed.
8. A land reform shall be accomplished in the interest of farmers.
9. Planned economic policies and rationalization of distribution of products shall be established.

The Democratic Party was headed by Cho Man-sik, an uncompromising anti-Japanese nationalist, one-time school teacher and a Christian.[10] He was often called the "Gandhi of Korea." Serving under him in the central headquarters of the party were his nationalist followers. Soon, branch party offices at provincial and local levels were opened throughout North Korea. The party derived its support mainly from Christians, businessmen, intellectuals, comparatively well-to-do workers and peasants. This party, which was the rallying point of all North Korean nationalist groups, claimed some 200,000 members within a few months after its inception.[11] What disturbed the communists most were the anti-communist and anti-Soviet demonstrations that broke out shortly after the formation of the Democratic Party.

Though the Soviet Army was somewhat successful during its initial period of occupation in promoting their image as "liberators" of Korea, they failed utterly in their economic policies. Perhaps the Russians had no economic policies at all. They demanded a regular supply of food at North Koreans' expense. They printed and put into circulation a large amount of occupation rubles, which aggravated the inflation that had been under way for some time. They removed some industrial equipment from North Korean factories causing the populace some concern. Through their tight control of the food supply in North Korea, they managed to alienate many farmers who wanted a free market for their produce. In addition to these economic practices, or lack of practices, the undisciplined conduct of Russians also antagonized Koreans.[12] At the same time, North Korean communists were dutifully carrying out these Russian policies, and in so doing they alienated local non-communist elements. All these hitherto seething anti-communist feelings erupted into sudden outbursts of revolt, led largely by students and other youth groups, after the formation of the Democratic Party.

On November 23, a few weeks after the establishment of the Democratic Party, some 3,000 students in the town of Shinŭiju, after disputes and fistfights with local communists who ordered students to attend a mass meeting, began to attack local communist organizations. The attacking students carried banners reading "Communists, Go Away!" and "We Oppose Communist Education." During the ensuing clash with local communists who were supported by armed Russian soldiers, some 30 students were said to have been shot to death and more than 100 wounded. This was a signal for youths in other North Korean towns to rise up. Throughout the winter and the following spring, there occurred numerous clashes between nationalists and local communists in many North Korean cities and towns, and each time the demonstrators sustained casualties. It was only after the incident in the city of Hamhŭng in March in which many demonstrators were shot by Russian soldiers that revolts began to subside. All those who had participated in the uprisings, particularly the leaders, were given heavy punishment by local communists and the Russian authorities.[13]

All these anti-communist outbursts were followed by communist retaliation. Communists, supported by the Soviet Army, openly attacked local offices of the Democratic Party and often imprisoned party officials who were suspected of having instigated student action. Churches also became the objects of communist attacks and harassment.

> [The Russian authorities] although nominally tolerant of religion, probably showed neither special respect for the Christian churches nor offerred them protection from the attacks of militant Korean opponents.[14]

Fearful of their personal safety and repelled by communist rule, some nationalist leaders, as well as other persons who were marked because of their anti-communist activities, began to flee across the 38th Parallel to the south, where they joined South Korean nationalist groups in the carrying out of anti-communist activities.

In communist parlance, "the ringleader of these North Korean reactionaries who consisted of pro-Japanese elements, people's traitors, landlords and lackeys of American missionaries" was Cho Man-sik.[15] While the Chairman of the Five Provinces' Administrative Bureau, Cho was in constant disagreement with the Russians, opposing vigorously their grain procurement program and their removal of industrial equipment from North Korea. From the earliest days of the Russian occupation, Cho had been distrusted by the occupation authorities. He was not given any real power even though he was allowed to occupy the chairmanship of the Five Provinces' Administrative Bureau that had "executive power to govern the entire area occupied by Soviet troops." The Kim Il-sŏng group which was then gradually moving into the political arena somewhat openly began to make efforts to bring about the complete downfall of Cho and his nationalist followers.

When the Democratic Party was founded on November 3, 1945, there were among its 33 central officials two and possibly more communist agents who were disguised as nationalists. The two agents who have since revealed their true identity were Ch'oe Yong-kŏn and Kim Ch'aek (alias Kim Jae-min), the most trusted associates of Kim Il-sŏng.[16] Ch'oe and another nationalist leader became vice-chairmen of the Democratic Party, and Kim became a member of the political bureau of the Democratic Party. These communist agents immediately began to make efforts to convert some party officials, watched moves of other nationalist leaders, and attempted to disrupt the operation of the Democratic Party, whose very existence under a predominantly nationalist leadership was a constant stimulus for anti-communist incidents. From the very beginning, the internal situation within the Democratic Party was extremely "tense," [17] and because of the communist agents' constant subversive activities, Chairman Cho Man-sik's grip on the party itself was gradually slipping away. Cho's loss of position. became final at the end of 1945 following his refusal to support the provisions for Korean trusteeship agreed upon at the Moscow Foreign Ministers' Conference.

In order to prevent the permanent division of Korea into the United States-occupied south and Soviet-controlled north and to specify definite plans for the future of Korea, the foreign ministers of the United States, the Soviet Union and the United Kingdom met in Moscow on December 16, 1945. After ten days of negotiations, they announced the agreement concerning Korea. The Moscow Agreement of December 27, 1945 provided for a Joint Commission to consist of representatives of the United States Command in the south and the Soviet Command in the north. The Joint Commission was to make recommendations for implementing the proposed four-power trusteeship of Korea for a period up to five years under the supervision of the United States, the Soviet Union, United Kingdom, and China.[18] The trusteeship plan for Korea was arranged on the assumption that Korea needed a preparatory period during which her leaders would obtain experience and training for self-government.

When the news of the proposed trusteeship plan reached Korea on the morning of December 29, 1945, reactions of Koreans, including communists in both North and South Korea, were immediate and hostile. The Koreans reasoned that any trusteeship, no matter how temporary, would mean an unnecessary postponement of immediate independence. While in the Soviet zone where the Soviet Army was already on special alert against any anti-trusteeship demonstrations the opposition was generally expressed in grumbles, in the American zone political parties of all shades, including communists, vehemently denounced the Moscow decision. Thus for a few days public opinion in Korea appeared to be unanimous in opposing the proposed trusteeship. During these few days Kim Il-sŏng and his immediate associates were said to have kept silent. It was on January 2 of the next year that they, in the name of the North Korean Communist Party, came out with a decision in support of the Moscow Agreement:

> The Moscow Agreement made by three foreign ministers of the Soviet Union, the United States and the United Kingdom is the expression of justice and sincerity. Therefore, we shall support the agreement with our whole hearts and shall make our utmost efforts to establish an independent and democratic Korea based upon the agreement.[19]

Having made the decision, the North Korean Communist Party immediately dispatched instructions to the South Korean Communist Party. The instructions which were believed to have reached the south before noon of January 3, 1946 asked all South Korean communists to reverse their stand and to come out publicly for trusteeship.[20]

[31]

The South Korean Communist Party's response to the instruction was instant. The attitude of leftists in both the south and the north abruptly changed.[21] Hereafter the rift between the nationalists who continued to denounce the trusteeship and the communists who now supported it became even more obvious and irreparable. In North Korea, the leader of the anti-trusteeship movement was Cho Man-sik.

Perhaps from the very moment of their arrival in North Korea, the Russians may have endeavored to eliminate Cho Man-sik, the leader of indigenous nationalists in the north. But Cho enjoyed great popularity among the North Koreans. The Soviet authorities apparently found it expedient to appoint him head of the Five Provinces' Administrative Bureau and through him carry out their programs rather than to antagonize the nationalists by eliminating Cho immediately. It was perhaps because of such Russian considerations that in November, 1945, the Soviet authorities even allowed Cho to form the Democratic Party which received substantial support from middle-class people, including Christians and intellectuals. Although the relationship between the Soviet authorities and Cho was marked from the beginning by an air of distrust, the Russians were outwardly polite to Cho even though he was not meeting their expectations. But with the trusteeship issue, the Russians' attitude changed markedly.

On December 30, 1945, while the whole of Korea was seething with indignation over the trusteeship proposal, Cho Man-sik was summoned to the headquarters of General Chistiakov, and he was asked to accept the Moscow Agreement. Cho did not yield his original position. After the meeting with General Chistiakov in which the two antagonists reportedly exchanged heated arguments, Cho immediately gathered some officials of the Democratic Party and, with their support, decided to continue to oppose the trusteeship plan. Because they were fearful of possible communist agents or the presence of traitors in the party, the decision of the party was said to have been made at a secretly held conference and was not announced publicly.[22]

Beginning to lose his followers to the communists and pressed hard by the Russians, Cho Man-sik gradually became an isolated man. Russians and Korean communists were now moving fast to force "the old obstinate guy"[23] to accept the Moscow Agreement or to eliminate him altogether. Two days later, on January 1, 1946, Cho Man-sik was asked to appear at the Romanenko Command. In the office of General Romanenko there were said to have been a few Korean communists, including Kim Il-sŏng. The Russian general was reportedly to have told Cho bluntly: "Support the trusteeship plan! Then you shall become a Stalin of Korea, or your personal safety shall not be guaranteed." [24] However, Cho was said to have retorted defiantly to the Russian's threat. The next day, on January 2, the North Korean Communist Party announced its support of the trusteeship, allegedly going along with "all political parties and all social organizations" in North Korea, [25] although the chairman and some officials of the Democratic Party were still in opposition.

In order to make the North Koreans' support of the trusteeship plan really unanimous the communists made one last effort to change Cho's stand on the issue. The attempt was made at a committee meeting of the Five Provinces' Administrative Bureau, which was held for that purpose on January 4, 1946. The committee originally was composed of 16 native communists and 16 nationalists. But when the session opened there were only six nationalists, including Cho Man-sik, whereas all 16 communists were there. The conference table was reportedly surrounded by Soviet political advisers and by the Soviet-returned Koreans. The communist members of the committee argued that the stand of the Five Provinces' Administrative Bureau on the question of trusteeship should be decided by a vote of majority of the committee members. The nationalists were said to have refused to go along with the communists on the ground that a matter of critical importance for Korea should not be decided merely by casting a vote. Unable to block the move of the communists, Cho announced his resignation from the chairmanship of the administrative bureau and left the conference with his fellow nationalists. When Cho came out of the meeting he was instantly arrested by Russian soldiers and was confined in the Korea Hotel in P'yŏngyang, never to be seen again. [26]

With the elimination of Cho Man-sik, North Koreans began their pre-trusteeship mass demonstrations on January 6, in cooperation with their communist fellows in South Korea, denouncing the nationalist "reactionary groups" that were staging anti-trusteeship demonstrations and strikes in the south throughout that month. As a result, the differences between the communist "democratic camp" and the rightist "reactionary forces" sharpened further. [27]

The arrest of Cho Man-sik was immediately followed by an exodus [28] of a large number of nationalists, Christians and most officials of the Democratic Party, leaving the central party apparatus in the hands of communists and signalling a severe curtailment of the nationalist movement in the north.[29] In February, communists hidden in the Democratic Party convoked a party congress in order to select new party officials. Though at the congress nationalists made an attempt to block such a move, "victory went to the genuine democratic elements," [30] who "exposed the anti-people's policy [of Cho Man-sik and his group], expelled the traitors, and organized a new central committee around Ch'oe Yong-kŏn, [the new chairman of the party]." [31]

After emasculating the major elements of anti-communist forces through the take-over of the Democratic Party, the Soviet authorities and North Korean communists allowed another group of non-communist leaders to amass their followers and to form the North Korean Youth Fraternal Party (Ch'ŏndogyo Ch'ŏng-u-dang) on February 8, 1946 in P'yŏngyang. The new party was headed by Kim Tal-hyŏn, a preacher of the Teaching of the Way of Heaven (Ch'ŏndogyo). Kim, born in 1884 in a farming village in the northern part of Korea, graduated from a veterinary college in Japan in 1918. Arrested by Japanese authorities in 1921 following the Koreans' anti-Japanese uprising of 1919, he spent 14 months in prison. After his release, Kim joined leftist organizations, carrying out his activities among tenant-peasants in his native village. Under this chairman, Pak Yun-kil and Kim Chŏng-ju became vice chairmen of the newly formed party. The party membership consisted primarily of believers of the Teaching of the Way of Heaven.

The Teaching of the Way of Heaven was founded as a new indigenous religious movement in the latter part of the 19th century by disgruntled Korean scholars who refused to accept any foreign teachings such as Confucianism, Buddhism, and Taoism and Christianity. The new religion taught that everyone, regardless of his social origin, could become "a good man" and communicate with heaven directly by observing simple rituals as prescribed by its founders. When everyone became "a good man," there would emerge "a new state," guided by the Preacher of the teaching in which all men are equal and blessed without having to endure worldly sufferings.[32] Because of its equalitarianism and implicit anti-foreign bias, the new religion strongly appealed to the oppressed segments of the population in the then decaying Kingdom of Korea, ruled over, as they were, by aristocratic officials who followed the Confucian precepts.

In turn, the followers of the Teaching of the Way of Heaven were persecuted by Court officials because of the danger inherent to the preservation of the Kingdom of Korea. The new religious movement now began to take on a political tone. Following the Japanese annexation of Korea in 1910, the nationalistic element in the teaching asserted itself strongly. Encouraged by the preachers, believers formed the Youth Fraternal Party on September 2, 1919 and carried on anti-Japanese activities in order to establish the "new state" as envisaged by the founders of the teaching.[33] Throughout the period of Japanese rule they constituted a major Korean nationalist force, although their political strength gradually declined and their party subsequently faded away. With the coming of liberation in 1945, the Youth Fraternal Party was revived in Seoul on September 14, 1945. In a declaration, the party reviewed its past at great length but made only a vague short statement on its new objectives:

> We endeavor to contribute to the establishment of a new nation and also try to revive local party offices as soon as possible.[34]

Though nothing concrete was said in terms of party policies, obviously the ultimate objective of the party was to found a theocratic state headed by the Preacher of the Teaching of the Way of Heaven.

Perhaps it was partly because of its religious nature that the communists in North Korea delayed until February, 1946 the reorganization of the North Korean Youth Fraternal Party. When the North Korean Youth Fraternal Party was formed on February 8, 1946, it was considered of "liberal persuasion" [35] in the North Korean political context, meaning anti-communist or non-communist. As Kim Il-sŏng candidly acknowledged, the party had strong influence among the farming population,[36] as peasants accounted for about 95 per cent of the total 200,000 party members.[37] These peasants were mostly believers of the Teaching of the Way of Heaven and they were attracted neither to communism nor to Christianity. Due to the indigenous quality of the Youth Fraternal Party, communists in the north did not interfere with the affairs of this non-communist organization as much as they did in the case of the Democratic Party. And in its initial period, the party was "treated well" by the communists, although the communists adopted the policy of "giving correct guidance" to the Youth Fraternal Party in "the political sphere." [38]

Both the Democratic Party, whose party leadership organ was reorganized in February, 1946, and the Youth Fraternal Party joined the communist-dominated North Korean Democratic United Front on July 22, 1946 along with various social organizations to support "all the democratic measures" initiated by the communists and to "fight against pro-Japanese Koreans and people's traitors." Subsequently, the North Korean Democratic United Front established its branch organizations at provincial and local levels, and all the local branches of the Democratic Party and the North Korean Youth Fraternal Party joined with other North Korean organizations.[39] Under these circumstances the two originally non-communist parties lost their independent status and became instruments of the communists for the execution of their "democratic reforms."

The Political Effects of the "Democratic Reforms"

In addition to their efforts to emasculate non-communist organizations, the North Korean communists simultaneously launched various "democratic reforms," whose quick and relatively successful implementation significantly weakened the social basis of the non-communist organizations. Following the arrest of Cho Man-sik, the nationalist leader, in early January 1946, the Five Provinces' Administrative Bureau quickly faded away. In order to establish a new central governmental organ "representatives of North Korean local people's councils, social organizations and political parties" met on February 8, 1946, in P'yŏngyang. The conference founded the North Korean Interim People's Council. This new Council was headed by Kim Il-sŏng and virtually all the important posts on the council were occupied by communists. The Interim People's Council was to "unify and direct the work of all local people's councils" and guide them in solving urgent political and economic problems facing the nation and people.[40]

The Japanese, during the 36-year colonial rule of Korea, excluded the Koreans from every aspect of policy-making. Some 75 per cent of the total Korean population was engaged in farming, and over half of the peasants worked as tenants paying high rent.[41] As a result, when the country was liberated, the majority of the Koreans still held to their traditional ways of doing things and appeared unprepared for the task of establishing a new and modern nation. The urgent task facing the North Korean communists was to restore the political and economic order that had been dislocated by the hasty departure of the experienced Japanese administrators, teachers, policemen, industrial managers and technicians who fled the north before the advancing Soviet Army.[42] After its formation, the North Korean Interim People's Council immediately addressed itself to this task.

[36]

In agriculture, the communist policy in 1945 was merely to reduce the rental payment of tenant farmer from 50 per cent of his harvest to 30 per cent.[43] The relatively moderate policy appeared to be in part a concession to the nationalists in the defunct Five Provinces' Administrative Bureau who were strongly opposed to outright confiscation of land without compensation and free land redistribution. It was only after the establishment of the Interim People's Council that communists initiated drastic land reform measures along with other "democratic reforms."

The first decree ever promulgated by the Interim People's Council was the "Land Reform Decree" of March 5, 1946[44] which indicated the urgent concern of the communists for the farming situation. Article 1 of the decree stated that:

> Land reform in North Korea is necessitated by both historical and economic reasons. The task of land reforms lies in the abolition of land-ownership of Japanese and Korean landlords as well as land tenancy and thus giving the right of the use of the land to those who till it. The agricultural system in North Korea shall be based on a farm economy which does not subject farmers to landlords, while *recognizing the farmers' permanent private ownership of land.* (italics mine)

The ordinance provided for the confiscation of the following categories of land without compensation:

> a) land owned by the Japanese Government and individuals and organizations; b) land owned by traitors to the Korean people, persons who collaborated with the Japanese, and those who fled their native places at the time of liberation; c) land owned by Korean landlords in excess of five chungbo [one chungbo is 2.45 acres] per a farming family; d) land not personally tilled by the owner but rented out; e) land, regardless of size, continuously rented out; and f) land owned by churches, monasteries, and other religious organizations in excess of five chungbo [12.25 acres].

The decree stipulated that the land confiscated would be redistributed without charge to landless peasants or persons with insufficient land. The law further stipulated that all debts owed by peasants to landlords would become void and that all farm animals, farm machinery, and houses formerly owned by landlords should be confiscated and then distributed among the peasants. The decree which was signed by Kim Il-sŏng, the Chairman of the Interim People's Council, was effective from the moment of its promulgation.[45] The law was carried out quickly by local people's councils under the direction of the

North Korean People's Council, and the work was completed before the end of March. The portion of land which each of landless peasants received was on the average less than 1.5 chungbo (less than four acres).[46]

According to North Korean sources, some 750,000 North Korean households that had had little or no land previously were given land free of charge.[47] Counting the North Korean population at the time of liberation of some 6,500,000 [48] and counting each family size as four persons, approximately half of the total North Korean population were beneficiaries of the land reform. Though the new owners of lands were prohibited from selling, renting, or mortgaging their newly acquired lands, they now became owners of land, emerging from long servitude to their landlords. The communists themselves claimed that the purpose of the land reform was to abolish a "feudalistic" agricultural system and to establish a "democratic" farming system, without even hinting at the future collectivization movement which might have changed the attitude of the peasants. In any event, land reform was carried out with "little bloodshed." It proved "extremely popular" with the peasants and was accepted "favourably" by most other elements in North Korea.[49] Beneficiaries of the land reform who, as noted above, accounted for nearly half of the total North Korean population, now had a "vested interest in the stability of the new regime," [50] and, at the same time, the North Korean government gained an important propaganda weapon in its campaign to drive its potential opponents from the political arena.

Following the accomplishment of the land reform, the communists mounted an active campaign to detach members of poor peasant origin from the Democratic Party and Youth Fraternal Party.[51] Meanwhile, the religious organizations that had been affiliated with these two parties lost all their land under the land reform law,[52] and thus their economic foundation was weakened. Though there was no active anti-religious propaganda carried on by the communists during the early stage of the North Korean regime, the two parties gradually became isolated from the North Korean populace under the impact of the popular land reform measures, and their ideological and organizational sources of resistance to the regime dwindled. The isolation of the two parties indicated the basic weakness of religious beliefs of the Koreans at that time, and their general disinclination to devote themselves to any religious cause. Thus under the pressure of the communist three-fold campaign—organizational infiltration,

[38]

destruction of the economic base and erosion of ideological commitment through "democratic reform"—the strength of the two non-
communist parties progressively declined.

In the midst of the execution of the land reform law, the North
Korean Interim People's Council on March 23, 1946, announced
its 20-point platform [53] which became the basic program of the North
Korean regime until the promulgation of the Constitution of the
Democratic People's Republic of Korea in July, 1948. The platform
stated, among other things, that the North Korean regime would:

1. Purge all the remnants of pro-Japanese elements;
2. Prohibit political activities of the reactionaries and anti-democrats;
3. Guarantee to all the people freedom of speech, press, assembly,
   association and religious beliefs;
4. Nationalize big industrial and commercial enterprises;
5. Guarantee and encourage private handicraft industry and freedom
   of commerce;
6. Confiscate lands of traitors and of landlords.

Not one of the 20 points mentioned socialism or communism. Instead,
the purpose of the Interim People's Council in announcing the
platform was to express the "truly democratic" wishes of all Koreans
for establishing an independent nation and a democratic government.
Generally speaking, the platform catered to poor peasants, workers,
and the lower-middle class. The 20-point platform was later translated
into a series of laws and decrees promulgated by the Interim People's
Council.

On June 24 a labor law was proclaimed. Designed to bring about
"a fundamental change in the working conditions of the Korean
workers and to improve their living standard," the law provided
an eight-hour working day and other labor regulations, including
social security benefits for the workers. It was the first labor law
ever enacted in Korean history.[54] However, it is very doubtful
whether the workers immediately benefitted from the law, because
in 1946 North Korean factories were still recovering from war damage
and the workers were forced to work more than eight hours a day
under various pretexts of the communist regime. Perhaps the impact
of the law at that time was more psychological and political than
economic and social. Be that as it may, it did make clear that there
was at last to be a regime that cared for the laborers who had been
long neglected.

Human relations in factories changed immediately. Instead of the old repressive Japanese ownership and management, all factories from the top down were now in the hands of Koreans,[55] who were quickly trained, though not sufficiently, at night schools set up by factories and labor unions.[56] All Korean managers and workers were now working for the restoration of their country's industry.

The labor law was shortly followed by the promulgation on July 30 of "the decree on equal rights for men and women." [57] The decree "liberated" North Korean women from "medieval shackles" and gave them equal rights with men to participate in political, economic, and cultural life in the north. The decree banned polygamy and public prostitution. Less than two weeks after the promulgation of the decree, the North Korean Interim People's Council enacted a law on August 10 on the nationalization of basic industry. As a result, all industrial enterprises, banks, and transportation facilities, comprising 90 per cent of all the North Korean industry [58] which formerly belonged to the Japanese and "traitors" to the Korean people were confiscated and nationalized.[59] The process of nationalization was relatively smooth, because 96 per cent of the North Korean enterprises were formerly owned by the Japanese,[60] and after V-J Day their operations were placed under the supervision of the Soviet Army. The nationalization of these enterprises actually affected the private interest of very few Korean citizens. Small wonder that the reaction of North Koreans to the nationalization law was minimal or perhaps neutral as it entailed "the disappropriation of only a few members of the former Korean elite." [61]

The nationalization decree was followed on October 4 by a "decree on private property and private enterprises." Its purpose was to "preserve the rights of private property in plants and factories which belonged to Korean citizens of good standing" and also to "encourage the private initiative of manufacturers and traders for the development of industry and trade." [62] The private sector protected by the decree comprised about 10 per cent of all the North Korean plants and factories, and it consisted mostly of small handicraft and trading firms. Thus the North Korean regime in its initial stage did not antagonize small businessmen to the extent that they would revolt, though there was some extra-legal interference with the private business sector.

Among all the "anti-imperialist," "anti-feudal," and "democratic reforms" which were carried out to build "a democratic base" in

North Korea, perhaps the most crucial one was the communist policy of manning their new bureaucracy. Unlike South Korea, where former pro-Japanese Korean officials, policemen, and teachers found positions of authority along with nationalist revolutionaries,[63] in the north, all former Korean officials working under the Japanese were purged. This sweeping purge in North Korea served a double purpose. It "appeased the Korean public" and also "removed from positions of authority men with questionable loyalty" to the regime.[64] Thus senior governmental posts in North Korea were filled mostly by former native communist revolutionaries as well as by Korean communists who returned from abroad.[65] The lower bureaucrats were drawn almost exclusively from workers and peasants who had no pro-Japanese records and who had positive interests in the stability of the new communist regime. Though the newly created elite was administratively inexperienced, its political reliability served to consolidate the communist government.[66]

By November 1946, the North Korean regime had apparently consolidated its power sufficiently to hold elections on the third day of the month for provincial, county, and city people's councils. According to North Korean sources, the elections were held to "choose people's representatives by the people themselves" and to "stabilize legally" all local people's councils that had "emerged spontaneously." The elections were conducted by "democratic methods" such as "direct," "equal," and "secret" voting.[67] Except "pro-Japanese elements" and "people's traitors," all men and women over twenty years of age were given the right to vote.

However, the communists actually controlled the "democratic elections." As one North Korean source admitted, the right to nominate candidates was given only to "democratic" political parties, public organizations, and societies that had joined the communist-controlled North Korean Democratic United Front.[68] In almost all cases only one candidate was nominated for each post. At each polling place there were provided two ballot boxes, white and black, which were guarded and watched by election committee members who were chosen by the communist party. Each elector received a ballot which he dropped into the white box for "Yes" and the black box for "No." [69]

Communist sources claimed that approximately 96 per cent of the 4,500,000 registered voters participated in the "democratic elections," and about 97 per cent of these cast their ballots for the designated candidates. Only three per cent voted "No." As a result,

[41]

some 3,500 officials of the local people's councils were elected, including 453 women. The party composition of the newlyelected officials was 31 per cent for the communist party (then the North Korean Workers' Party); [70] one per cent for the Democratic Party; 0.8 per cent for the North Korean Youth Fraternal Party, and 67.2 per cent for candidates with no party affiliation. The social composition of the newly elected was as follows: 94 per cent were workers, peasants, and "progressive" intelligentsia who were sympathetic to the communist party and six per cent were manufacturers, representatives of religious cults, and former landlords. [71] As can be seen, the overwhelming majority of posts in the people's councils went to members of the communist party or its sympathizers, and noncommunists were given only a token number of posts. As a result, North Korea was assured of moving "along the path of genuine democratic development." [72]

By the time the elections were completed, the North Korean communists had been well assured of their positions thanks especially to land reform. The elections themselves, though carried out under dubious circumstances, gave to the North Koreans a sense of being participants in the political process of their country, a privilege which they had not been previously allowed. Perhaps even the least popular measure, the nationalization of industry, did not antagonize businessmen as a whole. The quick execution of these measures successfully eclipsed all the non-communist leaders.

4.

THE THREE-WAY
COMMUNIST COALITION

IN LATE SEPTEMBER 1945, WHILE THE SOVIET-RETURNED KO-
reans were secretly preparing plans for establishing a communist
party in North Korea, a new group of Korean communists arrived
in Antung Prefecture in Manchuria right across from Korean territory.
This group sought early permission from the Soviet Command to
enter North Korea in order to participate in political activities going
on there, but the Soviet authorities were deliberately delaying the
granting of such permission.[1] This new group of Korean communists,
led by Kim Ho and Kim Kang, was a detachment of the Korean
Volunteer Corps, the military arm of the North China Korean Independence League (Hwapuk Chosŏn Tongnip Tong-maeng).

The Independence League, formed in North China with the blessing of the Chinese Communist Party, was a product of several years'
struggle between Korean communists and Korean nationalists for
leadership in the Korean independence movement in China. Encouraged by China's gradually mounting anti-Japanese sentiment in
the early 1930's, various Korean revolutionary groups began to reac-
tivate, and they moved to unify all their scattered fellow-countrymen
in China. They finally managed to amalgamate most Korean organizations in China and formed the Korean National Revolutionary Party
(KNRP) in Nanking in July 1935. The party was headed by Kim
Wŏn-bong,[2] a moderate leftist, and had as its military arm the Korean
Volunteer Corps. The party platform adopted at the amalgamation
meeting showed a strong leftist or even communist tendency without
mentioning communism. The platform mentioned not only the ur-

[43]

gency of immediate and complete independence of Korea from Japanese colonial rule but the elimination of feudalistic institutions and the establishment of a "democratic" regime in Korea. For the eventual building of a "democratic" Korea, the platform specifically spoke, among other things, of the necessity of distributing land to peasants, eventual nationalization of land and large-scale industries, and confiscation of all property of the "national traitors" and public and private property of the Japanese in Korea.[3]

Partly due to the strong leftist orientation of the party in its economic policy, the new party, formed mainly for strengthening the resistance movement against Japan, failed to achieve unity, and, by 1937, had been divided into leftist and rightist wings.[4] The left wing formed the Korean National Front, headed by Ch'oe Ch'ang-ik and Han Pin, and the rightists formed the Korean Independence Party, led by Kim Ku. Following the outbreak of the Sino-Japanese War in July, 1937, the Korean Independence Party retreated to Chungking and its members closely cooperated with the Chinese Nationalists. On the other hand, the members of the Korean National Front moved northward, near Yenan, and dissolved their organization to form the North China Korean Youth Federation in January 1941, in cooperation with Korean communists who had been in North China. The youth federation, formed with the blessing of the Chinese Communist Party and headed by an extreme-leftist Korean communist, Mu-Jŏng, who had long been associated with the Chinese communist leaders, revived the Korean Volunteer Corps in North China.

The declaration of the youth federation, issued immediately following its formation, urged all Koreans to join, regardless of ideology. It appealed to patriotism and emphasized the opportunities for Korean liberation presented by the Sino-Japanese War. Though the declaration did not mention communism as an ultimate goal, there was little doubt about the federation's ideological commitment. The communist orientation of the youth federation also was indirectly revealed in its platform which referred to Great Britain and the United States as "imperialist" nations, while presenting the Soviet Union as a country striving for the emancipation of the oppressed nations.[5]

Although the original membership of the youth federation was not more than 300 persons,[6] and its activities somewhat limited, the establishment of the youth federation was an event of great importance. It signified the polarization of the Korean revolutionary camp in China between right and left wings, motivated largely by ideological factors. It also portended the eventual division of Korea between the south and the north. While its armed forces were waging battles against Japanese troops, the youth federation endeavoured to induce Kim Ku's followers in Chungking to go to North China. Their efforts were successful, and many nationalists deserted their original organization in order to join the Korean communist group. Eventually, the nationalist leaders in Chungking were left almost without followers. The youth federation, in order to absorb these former nationalists, was reorganized in August 1942, and renamed the North China Korean Independence League (NCKIL) (Hwapuk Chosŏn Tongnip Tong-maeng).[7]

The newly-formed league was headed by Kim Tu-tong with Ch'oe Ch'ang-ik and Han Pin as its vice chairmen. Mu-Jŏng became the supreme commander of the military arm of the league, the Korean Volunteer Corps in North China. With its headquarters in Yenan, the military units of the NCKIL battled against Japanese forces in North China. At the same time the NCKIL sent its agents into Japanese-occupied areas, including the southwestern part of Manchuria, to do espionage and to induce Korean soldiers in the Japanese armies to defect. When the war ended the NCKIL had more than 5,000 members,[8] and it was the strongest among the various surviving Korean communist groups. Subsequently known as the Yenan Faction, it played an important role in North Korean politics of the early post-liberation period. Following are brief sketches of the social and political backgrounds of thirteen leading members of the Yenan Faction until their return to Korea.[9]

Kim Tu-bong (55 years of age as of 1945) Born in a fishing village in South Korea, Kim was a renowned Korean linguist. Once he taught at a middle school in Seoul but was dismissed by a Korean nationalist principal. The Japanese imprisoned him. In 1919, Kim fled from Korea to Shanghai, where he joined the Korean communist movement under the leadership of Yi Tong-hwi. From that time on he continued his revolutionary career in China.

Ch'oe Ch'ang-ik (47 years of age in 1945) Son of a poor peasant in North Korea, Ch'oe attended college in Japan and became a communist in the early 1920's. He was imprisoned for six years because of his communist activities. In 1936, he fled from Korea to China and then became an instructor at the Anti-Japanese Military and Political University in Yenan.

Han Pin (42 years of age in 1945) Born the son of a Korean revolutionary in Vladivostok, Han attended colleges in Russia. He began to engage in communist activities in Korea in the 1920's and was imprisoned for five years. He left Korea for China in 1936.

Mu-Jŏng (41 years of age in 1945) A northerner, Mu-Jŏng attended a middle school in Seoul. In 1923, he left Korea for China where he studied at a military academy before becoming an officer in the Chinese Nationalist Army. Later, he joined the Chinese Red Army, participated in the Long March and then took charge of training Korean youths in Yenan.

Hŏ Chŏng-suk (37 years of age in 1945) Daughter of a lawyer in northern Korea, Hŏ studied at a middle school in Seoul before attending colleges in Japan and the United States. She then served as a reporter for the Korean newspaper *Tong-A Ilbo* in Seoul. The Japanese imprisoned her. In 1936, she left Korea for China, where she studied and taught at the Anti-Japanese Military and Political University in Yenan.

Kim Ch'ang-man (33 years of age in 1945) A northerner, Kim studied at a middle school in Seoul and then participated in the peasant movement before leaving Korea for China in 1934. While in China, he attended the Central Military Academy in Nanking.

Yang Min-san (32 years of age in 1945) A southerner, Yang left Korea for China in 1929, where he received middle school and college training. Subsequently, he served as an instructor at the Anti-Japanese Military and Political University in Yenan.

Kim Han-jung (34 years of age in 1945) A northerner, Kim attended a middle school in Korea and participated in the anti-Japanese student movement in 1929. He left Korea for China in 1935 and then attended the Central Military Academy in Nanking.

Pak Hyŏ-sam (34 years of age in 1945) A northerner, Pak studied at a middle school in Korea and then went to China in 1924. Upon graduating from the Whampoa Military Academy, he first became an officer of the Chinese Nationalist Army, and then, following the outbreak of the Sino-Japanese War in 1937, he joined the Korean communist group in North China and finally became a deputy commander of the Korean Volunteer Corps.

Yi Ch'un-am (40 years of age in 1945) Born in the central part of Korea, Yi studied in a middle school in Korea before going to China in 1925. He became a communist while studying at the Whampoa Military Academy.

Pak Il-u (34 years of age in 1945) Born in Manchuria, Pak studied at a middle school in Manchuria. In 1940 he graduated from the Anti-Japanese Military and Political University in Yenan. Later he operated in Manchuria as a deputy commander of the Korean Volunteer Corps.

Yi Yu-min (33 years of age in 1945) A southerner, Yi attended a college in Shanghai. After the outbreak of the Sino-Japanese War in July 1937, he went to Yenan where he studied at the Anti-Japanese Military and Political University.

Chang Chin-kwang (34 years of age in 1945) Born in the United States of America, Chang went to Shanghai as a youth. In 1938, he went to Yenan, where he studied at the Anti-Japanese Military and Political University.

In short, all but three of these leading members of the Independence League were born in Korea and received at least part of their schooling there. Only one studied in the Soviet Union. The social and educational background of these leaders was in sharp contrast with the Soviet-returnees, all of whom were either raised or trained in Soviet Russia. Several leading figures of the Independence League had longer revolutionary careers and were even better known among Koreans than Kim Il-sŏng. But the Yenan Faction's affiliation with the Chinese Communists put it in an extremely disadvantageous position to compete for power in North Korea with the Soviet-returnees, in whom quite naturally, the Soviet occupation authorities had more confidence.

After the Japanese surrender, all Korean Volunteer Corps forces under Mu-Jŏng immediately moved to Manchuria from North China and were augmented by a significant number of Korean youths who had deserted from the Japanese Army. The first detachment of the Volunteer Corps, reportedly consisting of about 1,500 persons, moved toward Korea and reached the Yalu River Bridge late in September 1945.[10] At the bridge, which spanned the Yalu between the Manchurian town of Antung and the Korean town of Shinŭiju, they were halted by the local Soviet authorities who would not permit them to enter Korea. The official Soviet reason for this action was that, since Korea was under occupation by the United States and the Soviet Union, and since there was no Korean government, there could be no armed forces in Korea other than those of the United States and Soviet Russia.[11] However, the Yenan Koreans insisted on being admitted. They were said to have pointed out that there were already remnants of Kim Il-sŏng's former guerrillas in the occupied north, a fact which the Soviet authorities attempted to disclaim.[12] After bickering for nearly two months, the Soviet authorities changed their original position, and the Soviet Command in P'yŏngyang allowed the armed Yenan Koreans to enter the border city of Shinŭiju. In order to understand the nature of this delayed permission of the Soviet Command it is necessary to note the events that had taken place inside North Korea in the previous two months.

In the months of September and October, Kim Il-sŏng and his comrades worked busily but secretly to form a communist party and succeeded in establishing it on October 13, this in spite of the native communists' opposition. The next day, Kim Il-sŏng, with the backing of the Soviet authorities, made his political debut at a mass meeting in P'yŏngyang. Following this, he and his comrades endeavoured to infiltrate their men into various local communist parties and people's councils. For example, early in November, Kim Il, Kim Il-sŏng's comrade-in-arms from Manchuria, became the first secretary of the P'yŏngan Pukto provincial communist party.[13] While the Yenan Koreans were anxiously awaiting entry at the Yalu River Bridge, Kim Il-sŏng and Kim Il were reportedly in constant contact with the Soviet authorities regarding the Yenan group's request to enter Korea.

It was only after a series of maneuvers that the detachment of the Korean Volunteer Corps was finally admitted into Shinŭiju, in the province of P'yŏngan Pukto, in late November. They were put up for the night in a high school building. Before dawn, the detachment was surrounded and disarmed by local self-defense forces led by Han Ung, a local communist who allegedly acted under the instructions of Kim Il. All members of the disarmed detachment were "chased" back across the Yalu River into Manchuria.[14] Apparently the Soviet-returnees felt that their newly-acquired positions would be threatened by the Yenan Faction if they failed to take precautionary measures against the latter at the very beginning. The incident was also the first of a series of conflicts between the Yenan Faction and the native communists because the treacherous disarmament was carried out by the latter. Thus, the incident signified that future relations between the three communist groups in North Korea would not be harmonious and that there would be vicious struggles for political power.

The Yenan Koreans, deprived of an early chance to join the political competition, returned to North Korea a few months later. They did so, however, by way of South Korea since that border was not yet closed. Though several leading figures of this group were better known than any of the Soviet-returnees, their arrival in the north was hardly noticed by the public. There was no mass rally to welcome them, and all North Korean press and communication media were mute on their return.[15] Occasional bills pasted on walls reading "Long Live Kim Tu-bong and Mu-Jŏng!" were perhaps the only public signs indicating the return of the Yenan Faction.[16] Despite the fact that Kim Tu-bong joined the North Korean Interim People's Council as vice-chairman [17] under chairman Kim Il-sŏng and that other Yenan-returnees worked with the North Korean communist party that Kim Il-sŏng had organized, the cooperation between the Yenan Faction and the Soviet-returnees was more apparent than real. Furthermore, the Yenan-returnees refused to join the North Korean communist party. Instead, they revived the North China Korean Independence League in P'yŏngyang on March 30, 1946, renaming it the Shinmin-tang (The New People's Party) in opposition to Kim Il-sŏng's communist party.[18] The newly established New People's Party was headed by Kim Tu-bong with Ch'oe Ch'ang-ik and Han Pin serving under him as vice-chairmen of the party. The party quickly established a branch organization in Seoul.

The New People's Party declared that its objective was to contribute to the creation of "a democratic regime," "a democratic economic system," and "a new Korean democratic culture." The political and economic policies of the party included the following major points: [19]

1. The creation of a new democratic regime with universal and equal suffrage.
2. Guarantee of freedom of speech, press, assembly, association and religious beliefs.
3. Confiscation and nationalization of all large-scale industries that formerly belonged to the Japanese and pro-Japanese Koreans.
4. Redistribution of the lands confiscated and the abolition of the tenancy system.
5. Suppression of all reactionary thoughts.

The economic and agricultural policies of the New People's Party appeared more moderate than those envisaged by the North Korean Communist Party.[20] While the latter was moving to nationalize virtually all industries except small-scale plants, the former planned to nationalize only large-scale enterprises, leaving medium and small ones in the hands of private businessmen. In agriculture, while the

[49]

North Korean Communist Party was carrying out confiscation of land without compensation and free distribution of land to landless farmers through the Interim People's Council, the New People's Party did not specifically mention how to execute the needed land reform. It is possible that the party's agricultural reform measures might not have been as drastic as those of the communist party. In spite of the absence of any open refutation of the communist party's policies, the New People's Party seemed to be in favor of a more strict interpretation of such terms as "reactionaries" and "pro-Japanese," [21] whose broad and often indiscriminate interpretation by the communist party brought about not only the downfall of the upper class and pro-Japanese elements but also many middle class landowners, as well as religious organizations. [22]

Unlike the communist party that espoused Marxism-Leninism and recruited new members primarily from the working class and poor peasants, the New People's Party did not explicitly mention Marxism-Leninism as its organizational principle. Instead, the party urged all people of "democratic classes" to join the party, defining the immediate task of the party as a "bougeois-democratic" transformation of Korea. [23]

Due to its implicitly mild policies as well as its non-Marxian-Leninist tenets, the New People's Party won the support of former landowning farmers and men of middle-class background, all of whom were dissatisfied because of the land reform of March 1946. The party also succeeded in recruiting intellectuals, teachers, and even ex-Korean bureaucrats in the Japanese government, all of whom found the communist party leadership repugnant. [24] The stance of the New People's Party could have been, in part, a reflection of the personality of the party's chairman Kim-Tu-bong, the middle-aged and affable intellectual who was an "unreliable" person in the eyes of the Russians.

At the time of its formation, the New People's Party claimed some 120,000 members against the 30,000 members of the communist party. [25] The membership of the New People's Party clearly indicated that a substantial number of people were alienated by a communist party membership consisting mainly of the illiterate and indigent. There were even among non-communist elements rumors that the communist party was made up of "thugs" and "terrorists." Thus—as admitted in a recent North Korean source—throughout April and May, the activities of the New People's Party were of major concern to the Soviet returnees [26] as well as to the Soviet authorities. The

Soviet response to the expanding strength of the New People's Party was to discontinue the communist party, which was then a minority party, and to merge it with the New People's Party in order to absorb the Yenan communists and their followers in a more broadly based party, the North Korean Workers' Party. Throughout June and July, Kim Il-sŏng and other Soviet-returnees, under the instruction of General Romanenko, endeavored to make plans for the merger, succeeding in having "the joint conference of the central officials of the two parties" proclaim their willingness for the merger.[27] Another month elapsed during which local officials of the two parties discussed the plan and 821 "representatives" were chosen to attend the meeting of the formal amalgamation of the two parties. These preparatory measures were carried out in the face of considerable opposition from certain segments of both parties.[28]

Finally, on August 28, the formal amalgamation conference opened in P'yŏngyang. According to a South Korean source, a Russian army officer, Colonel Ignachev, came to the meeting as a "guest." [29] But on the very first day of the meeting some representatives made attempts to block the plan for the merger. Some native communists, who held a "leftist, self-righteous and haughty attitude" toward the New People's Party, objected to the merger on the ground that a new party would become petit-bourgeois in its outlook. On the other hand, some "rightist" elements in the New People's Party attempted to resist the merger on the belief that the amalgamation was a communist scheme to submerge them in a new communist-controlled party.[30] Other "rightists" maintained that they would join the new party if the new party did not adopt the Marxist-Leninist tenets. Despite these objections and fear of the consequences of the merger, it was announced that the two parties were formally "dissolved" and the North Korean Workers' Party was formed. Next day, on the 29th, Kim Il-sŏng delivered a speech at the conference, explaining the necessity for forming the North Korean Workers' Party, expounding its character and stating its purpose. Defining the members of the two dissolved parties as "working masses," Kim asserted:

At the present historical stage, the power of our working masses must not be splintered. In order to accomplish the great democratic task before the Korean people, a united power of the working masses—a strong vanguard party—is necessary.[31]

Regarding the nature of the North Korean Workers' Party, Kim defined it as a "combat unit and the vanguard of the working masses."

Here Kim was apparently referring to the Leninist principle that a communist party is the vanguard of the proletariat. Yet Kim also defined the new party as a "party of all united working masses," implying that the new party was a mass party and not a party based upon the Leninist organizational principle.[32] Thus it was practically impossible to foresee the exact type of party that Kim was envisaging, except that he was attempting to form a broader type of political organization than a party which consisted only of workers and poverty-stricken peasants. In spite of this somewhat ambiguous definition of the new party, Kim warned both "leftists" and "rightists" not to cause further trouble. He apparently was addressing his remarks to those native communists and former members of the New People's Party who had opposed the merger on various grounds. Then Kim went on to proclaim the goal of the North Korean Workers' Party as being "the building of a strong and democratic state," which, according to Kim, was "in complete harmony" with the stated objectives of the Interim People's Council.[33] As he refrained from defining the new party as a Marxist-Leninist Party, Kim's program stressed "national" and "democratic" aims and it was as yet silent on the "building of socialism."

In contrast to the lengthy speech of Kim Il-sŏng, Kim Tu-bong made a short speech which could be construed as evidence of his contemptuous attitude towards the merger. Kim Tu-bong asserted that the formation of the North Korean Workers' Party was necessitated not only by the "tactical need for unity" but also by the lack of intellectual leadership in the communist party. He made it clear that the merger did not mean an absorption of one party into another, thus indicating the existence of two different groups in the same party and a consequent troublesome future course for the party.[34]

The last part of the three-day amalgamation conference was spent on the selection of the leadership of the newly amalgamated party. It was generally expected that Kim Il-sŏng, by virtue of his position as the chairman of the Interim People's Council, would become the chairman of the newly formed party. But unexpectedly the conference chose Kim Tu-bong, the vice-chairman of the Interim People's Council, as the chairman of the North Korean Workers' Party.[35] Kim Il-sŏng was relegated to the vice-chairmanship along with a native communist leader Chu Nyŏng-ha. Chu, the son of a wealthy landowner, was a graduate of Keijō Imperial University (now Seoul National University). Under these three, the party's new central committee of 43 members was to serve as the executive organ of the party with the responsibility for administering party affairs between party congresses. Among the 43 members on the central committee, 29 were from the old communist party and 14 from the former New People's Party.[36]

After accomplishing all these tasks the meeting closed on August 30. Since then, the meeting has been referred to as the First Congress of the (North) Korean Workers' Party. Immediately after the adjournment of the Congress, the first plenary session of the central committee of the new party was held to choose officials for various posts in the party. Those who were elected to the five-man Politburo, the decision-making organ of the party, were Kim Tu-bong (Yenan Korean), Kim Il-sŏng, Chu Nyŏng-ha (native communist), Ch'oe Ch'ang-ik (Yenan Korean) and Hŏ Kai (Soviet Korean). Kim Tu-bong, by virtue of his chairmanship of the party, became the chairman of the Politburo, and Kim Il-sŏng and Chu Nyŏng-ha became its vice-chairmen. The newly-created ten departments of the central party were headed by three Soviet returnees, four Yenan Koreans, and three native communists.[37] Out of the 14 central party officials who became either members of the Politburo or heads of departments or both, four were Soviet-returnees, six were Yenan Koreans and four were native communists. In terms of previous party affiliations, eight were from the communist party and six were members of the New People's Party. On the whole, the distribution of positions within the new party seemed fairly even for the component groups.[38]

5.

NORTH KOREA
AND HER LEADERS
IN 1947 AND 1948

The Establishment of a Permanent Governmental Structure

THE FORMATION OF THE NORTH KOREAN WORKERS' PARTY AND its subsequent growth as the ruling party were paralleled by the institutional development of the North Korean regime and by its expanding activities. As an additional step toward formalizing the governmental structure "the Congress of People's Councils of Provincial, County and City Levels," consisting of 1,186 members of local people's councils, convened in P'yŏngyang from the 17th to 20th of February 1947.[1] During the four-day meeting the representatives, on the motion of Ch'oe Yong-kŏn who was the chairman of the Democratic Party, elected 237 persons from among themselves to form the People's Assembly as the "supreme legislative organ" of North Korea.[2] The 237-member People's Assembly was composed of 89 members of the North Korean Workers' Party, 29 members of the Democratic Party, 29 members of the Youth Fraternal Party and 90 non-party members.[3] Thus the People's Assembly appeared to represent all parties and all strata of the population. Immediately on February 21, the newly-formed People's Assembly held its first meeting, lasting for only two days. During this brief session, the assembly "unanimously" confirmed the legislative acts of the former Interim People's Council, elected an 11-member Presidium of the

People's Assembly with Kim Tu-bong as its chairman and chose Kim Il-sŏng as chairman of the 22-member People's Council. As chairman, Kim Il-sŏng was empowered to select other members of the People's Council.[4] The new People's Council was to replace the Interim People's Council as the "highest executive organ" in North Korea.[5]

Unlike the People's Assembly which was believed to have had no real power, the People's Council was dominated by members of the North Korean Workers' Party. Specifically, the Workers' Party held 16 of the 22 seats on the Council.[6] In terms of their original group affiliations, two of the 16 Workers' Party members were Soviet-returnees, three were Yenan Koreans, and the remainder were native communists.[7] Although it appeared that the native communists were the largest group heading the departments of the central People's Council, their actual power and influence were carefully circumscribed by their deputy-heads, who were Soviet Koreans or trusted lieutenants of Kim Il-sŏng. Furthermore, Soviet advisors, who appeared to have "more power than an ordinary advisor would enjoy," were assigned to most of the departments of the People's Council.[8]

In early March, within less than a month after the reorganization of the central People's Council, elections were held for village people's councils and district councils in towns and cities.[9] By March, 1947 people's councils were established from provinces down to villages—all, ultimately subordinate to the control of the central People's Council.[10] Besides the local people's councils, the central People's Council was rapidly developing other such control mechanisms as courts, procurators, and a police force, all, not coincidently, modeled after the Soviet pattern. At the same time, the central People's Council was rapidly building its armed forces,[11] and carrying out economic, social, and cultural reforms.

Efforts for the Establishment of a "Democratic and Independent Nation"

Immediately after the formation of a permanent governmental structure, the North Korean regime unfolded its One-Year People's Economic Plan For 1947 which affected practically every aspect of North Korean life.[12] The plan for 1947 was followed by one for 1948.[13] The first one-year economic plan stressed the rehabilitation of the North Korean economy that had been dislocated both by

[55]

the war and by the subsequent departure of Japanese managers and technicians, whereas the second one-year economic plan emphasized "expansion."

In the field of industry the North Korean government made efforts to correct the "lopsidedness" of the North Korean industrial structure, which was a legacy of Korea's former dependence upon the Japanese economic system.[14] Although some industrial plants were left in the hands of private businessmen after the nationalization of industry, private enterprise was brought under close governmental supervision and control.[15] As a result of such control, the private sector began to diminish while the state sector was increasing its scope of activities.[16]

In agriculture, the regime had to correct its "lopsidedness" which stemmed from North Korea's former dependence upon South Korea for agricultural products, textiles, and other consumer goods. In order to increase agricultural products, the regime opened up virgin lands by compulsory labor. To increase per capita productivity the regime started to organize "brigades of mutual aid" among peasants as early as in the spring of 1946 so that peasants could give reciprocal help in seeding and could jointly utilize draft animals and farm instruments.

Besides participating in such group farming, peasants were also obliged to contribute donations of "patriotic rice" to the regime, in addition to paying their regular tax in kind from 10 to 27 per cent of their land productivity as stipulated in a law enacted in May 1947. As a result, it was said that peasants seldom paid less than 50 per cent of their crops to the regime either in tax or in the name of "patriotic rice." [17] All those who did not comply positively with governmental requirements lost their lands in 1948 when the North Korean government reissued certificates of landownership only to those who cooperated with the regime. Under such a situation the peasant's new status as a landowner became insecure and the initial enthusiasm for the land reform gradually faded away. Many peasants now felt that they were "production units of the State." [18]

Along with the inauguration of a state-controlled economy, the regime initiated intensive programs for ideological reorientation of the masses. The programs were purported to root out "undesirable" and "reactionary" concepts in the minds of the people, and to reeducate them along the line set by the regime. To this end, the regime monopolized all the communications media and took control of the schools. The regime also sponsored professional meetings, mass meetings, and community meetings for mobilizing public support and remolding the people's outlook. Through these government-sponsored meetings and the governmental control over the communications media, the North Korean regime was able to insulate the masses from ideas and information that ran counter to its own.[19]

With the economy and people's thought under its firm control, the North Korean regime effectively stamped out all organized opposition in the territory under its rule. In the absence of organized opposition, the regime was able to implement its programs without the use of violence. And the relatively peaceful reforms contributed to the regime's consolidation of power and strengthened its ability to mobilize the population for other tasks.[20]

Intra-Party Politics

The real moving force behind all the activities of the North Korean government and various social organizations was the North Korean Workers' Party. Members of the Workers' Party held key positions in government and economic and cultural organizations. It was through these members that the party exercised central direction of all political, economic and cultural activities in the north, despite the party's lack of constitutional standing.

On August 28, 1947, exactly one year after the formation of the North Korean Workers' Party, Kim Il-sŏng defined the party's operational principle and its over-all standing in the North Korean political scene. According to Kim, the party operated in accordance with democratic centralism,[21] which requires lower organs to obey higher organs, the minority to obey the majority, and individual members to obey the organizations.[22] Regarding the party's relationship with the government and various social organizations, Kim explained:

1. Our party must carry out propaganda and educational works in people's councils in order to achieve ideological and political unity among the members of the people's councils.
2. Our party must further strengthen social organizations, [and] must educate masses through these organizations and rally them firmly around our party.[23]

Thus, according to Kim, it was not the government but the North Korean Workers' Party that played the leading role in all political and social activities in North Korea. In fact the party had been the most powerful organization, and it was through the party that various governmental and ostensibly non-governmental activities were coordinated. It was because of the important role of the party that Kim and his comrades lost no time in attempting to control its apparatus. In doing this, their initial efforts were primarily concentrated on weakening the position of the native communist leaders in the party.

Kim's first target in his battle to control the party in the north was the native communist leader Hyŏn Chun-hyŏk, who was assassinated in September 1945 by an agent allegedly sent by Kim and acting with the connivance of the Soviet occupation authorities. According to a South Korean source and a non-communist Japanese source, Yu Chae-il, who had served as an interpreter for the Korean and Russian conspirators plotting the assassination, was banished to Siberia following his inadvertent disclosure of the plot.[24] Hyŏn's elimination was shortly followed by the disappearance of two more native communist leaders, Han Ung and Kim Yong-bŏm. Han Ung, head of the peace preservation department of the provincial people's council in P'yŏngan Pukto, was said to have been the man who led the local communist forces in disarming the Korean Volunteer Corps in November 1945. Han was also believed to be the man who directed local communists in cooperation with Soviet armed forces in the suppression of the student uprising in the town of Shinŭiju in late November of that year.

Kim Il-sŏng was said to have summarily attributed the cause of the student unrest to "errors" and "mistakes" of local communist leaders in carrying out the "correct" policies of the Soviet occupation authorities. Among the local communists Han Ung was singled out for execution.[25] However, under the then prevailing North Korean circumstances, no Koreans could or would act as Han Ung did in such serious incidents without explicit direction of the Soviet-returnees, who in turn were acting under orders of the Soviet Command. The charges against him were no more than a convenient pretext to eliminate him since he had shown considerable military capacity during the disarmament incident.

Han's elimination was followed shortly by the untimely death of Kim Yong-bŏm, one of those native communists who first cooperated with Kim Il-sŏng in the establishment of the North Korean communist bureau in October 1945. It was perhaps because of his initial cooperation with the Soviet-returnees that Kim Yong-bŏm became the first

[58]

acting secretary of that bureau. However, he lost his secretaryship to Kim Il-sŏng when the bureau was reorganized that December. Afterwards it was rumored that the relationship between the two Kims cooled. When the North Korean Workers' Party was formed in August 1946, Kim Yong-bŏm was not given any post, nor was he assigned to any office when the central People's Council was reorganized in February 1947. Thereafter, the unhappy Kim Yong-bŏm was said to have constantly complained about the high-handed manner of the Soviet-returnees until September 1947, when he died after an operation in hospital.[26]

The disappearance of the top native communist leaders were shortly followed by the central party officials' efforts to strengthen the party's organization and to increase its membership. Immediately after the formation of the North Korean Workers' Party in August 1946, the leaders of the new party chose a policy of rapid expansion of rank and file members. However, according to Kim Il-sŏng, in the process of recruiting new members for the party, "errors" occurred. Some local party officials, presumably those who had been members of the defunct New People's Party, committed "rightist errors" by admitting into the party numerous "undesirable" elements. Other local party leaders, presumably native communists from the dissolved North Korean Communist Party, made "leftist mistakes" by becoming overly selective in choosing new members, thus preventing the party from developing into a "mass party."[27]

Kim's denunciation spearheaded a new Soviet-returnee policy, that of excluding followers of the Yenan faction from the party on one hand, while, on the other hand, admitting new elements who had been unable to join due to the selective approach of the native communists. With the support of the new recruits, the Soviet-returnees were planning to move to dominate their opponents, and possibly to liquidate them altogether. In spite of the implications of the party's new policy regarding membership admittance, there has been no evidence to date of any joint effort undertaken on the part of the Yenan faction and the native communists as a counter-measure. The lack of any such sign, in fact, no actions at all, was apparently not the result of their ignorance of Kim's strategy, but was most likely the result of their inability to resolve feuds among themselves, even temporarily. For instance, in the pre-1945 period, Ch'oe Ch'ang-ik, the leading figure of the Yenan faction, had been a member of the Seoul Group until he joined the Marxist-Leninist group in 1927. The native communists, on the other hand, for some time after 1945 were followers of Pak Hŏn-yŏng, who had been a member of the Tuesday Association in the 1920's, when the association had competed acrimoniously with the Seoul Group for the hegemony of the Korean communist movement. When the northern native communists were professing their allegiance to Pak Hŏn-yŏng following Korea's liberation, Pak had been leading the Korean Communist Party in Seoul since September 1945. Thus, possibly, an old feud between Ch'oe Ch'ang-ik and Pak Hŏn-yŏng may have inhibited any efforts towards cooperation between the Yenan faction and the native communists. In this connection, too, Kim Il-sŏng's relative newness in the Korean communist movement was an advantage which he fully utilized. Also, it must not be forgotten that the treacherous disarming of the homecoming Yenan force in November 1945 was carried out by the native communists, an action hardly the basis for future cooperation between the two factions. And, as if this were not enough, as will be seen in this manuscript, the Yenan faction opened a branch of their New People's Party in Seoul in the spring of 1946 and competed with Pak Hŏn-yŏng's Korean Communist Party in Seoul for the allegiance of South Korean leftists. Altogether, the Yenan-returnees and the Soviet-returnees were from abroad, and they apparently shared a common fear of the native communists whose strength, it should be remembered, was considerable at the time of the liberation.

Finally, though, were not the foregoing reasons enough to preclude any cooperative effort between the two factions to combat Kim's bid for power, it appears that there was a feeling of futility and a sense of resignation among the native communists and the Yenan returnees which prevented, on their part, any efforts to subvert the policy of the Soviet authorities backing Kim Il-sŏng. It was these complicated factors and ramified relations which were accountable for the failure of Kim's opponents to take timely countermeasures. Kim capitalized on their failure, utilized it to his own ends, and eventually was able to eliminate the opposition altogether.

In order to "correct the rightist and leftist errors" and to expand the party in quantity while raising its quality,[28] the central Politburo on December 3, 1946 issued a directive entitled "Regulations Regarding the Issuance of Party Certificates and Registrations." According to the directive, local party leaders were urged to recruit new members rapidly, but primarily from peasants, office, and factory workers. At the same time, local parties were required to submit to the central headquarters detailed biographical data on party members.[29] As a result of this policy, party membership increased from 366,000 in August 1946, to 680,000 in August 1947,[30] and finally reached 708,000 in January 1948.[31] The increase was accompanied by a change in the social composition of the party members. Whereas in August 1946, less than 50 per cent of the total membership were persons of worker and peasant origin, in January 1948, over 60 per cent were workers and poor peasants. Because of such a growth of the party membership, by late 1947 party cells had been established in all places of work as well as in all villages in North Korea.[32] On the other hand, the party in 1947 alone expelled from 40,000 to 60,000 members of heterogeneous backgrounds such as "landlords, industrialists, profiteers, and lagging elements of the laboring class," [33] probably the majority of these purgees being followers of the Yenan returnees.

Though the majority of the new recruits were desirable in terms of their social origin, they had no previous experience in organizational life and lacked revolutionary discipline. This was acknowledged by Pak Ch'ang-ok, the Soviet Korean "party theoretician." In order to raise the quality of the party by transforming its undisciplined members into an "iron-like solid organization," new members were indoctrinated in Marxism-Leninism and were trained to act in accordance with the Leninist organizational principle.[34] To provide educational material for the "arming" of the new members with Marxism-Leninism, the central party by late 1947 had translated Russian works on the Soviet communist party, published the central party organ *Nodong Shinmum* (Worker's Daily), and the party theoretical monthly periodical *Kŭlloja* (Worker). Each provincial party organization had its own press.[35] According to Kim Il-sŏng, due to careful recruitment, purges, and political training, the party by early 1948 had been strengthened organizationally and had made "great advancement in maintaining its purity." [36] After one and a half year's efforts to consolidate the new party, the Second Congress of the North Korean Workers' Party was held in P'yŏngyang from March 27 to March 30 in 1948.[37]

By the time the Second Party Congress was held, the hope for Korean unification had faded further. Attempts made by the Soviet and American occupation authorities to achieve agreement had ended in failure by July 1947. The United States put the Korean problem to the United Nations in September of that year. In November 1947, the United Nations appointed a "Temporary Commission on Korea," entrusting it with the mission to oversee elections for an all-Korea constituent assembly that would form an independent Korean government and bring about the unification of the country. The formation of the United Nations Temporary Commission on Korea was a U. S. diplomatic victory over the Soviet Union, which opposed its formation. However, when the Temporary Commission arrived in Seoul in January 1948 and asked permission to enter North Korea, the Soviet occupation authorities and the North Korean regime refused to grant permission. Therefore, the Commission was instructed by the "Little Assembly" of the United Nations to restrict its efforts to the south of the 38th Parallel.[38] At the time, North Korea was moving rapidly to execute its "democratic reforms," and Kim Il-sŏng was well on his way to consolidating his newly acquired position both in the government and the party.

Kim Il-sŏng's firm political position was well reflected by the events that took place at the Second Congress of the North Korean Workers' Party which was attended by 999 delegates representing some 750,000 party members.[39] In his opening speech Chairman Kim Tu-bong duly acknowledged the role played by vice-chairman Kim Il-sŏng in the rapid growth of the party. According to Kim Tu-bong, the North Korean Workers' Party had become a "great mass party because of the correct guidance of Comrade Kim Il-sŏng and the Central Committee."[40] On the second day of the meeting, Vice-Chairman Kim Il-sŏng gave a "Report on the Work of the Central Committee." The report consisted of three parts: the international situation, domestic affairs, and party problems.

Surveying international problems, Kim Il-sŏng concluded that "international democratic forces" led by the Soviet Union would grow stronger day by day in contrast to the eventual downfall of the "international reactionary forces" headed by the United States. On domestic matters, the speaker made it clear that North Korea would not tolerate the "illegitimate" activities of the Temporary Commission on Korea in Korea. Furthermore, Kim expressed the determination of the party to further strengthen the "people's regime" which had been formed under the guidance of the party in the north and to extend the political form of the "people's regime" to South Korea as the basis for the achievement of the unification of Korea.[41]

The most important part of Kim Il-sŏng's speech, in terms of further consolidation of his position in the party, was the one on party problems. It was divided into three sections: "Struggle for Strengthening of the Party," "Expansion of the Party Influence and Party Organizational Activities," and "Party Propaganda and Ideological Education." It was during his address on the first section that Kim Il-sŏng, in the name of party unity, made his charge against native communist leaders who had once opposed him. Reminding the party representatives of the native communist leaders' past opposition to the establishment of the North Korean Central Bureau of the Korean Communist Party, Kim said:

> In spite of the clear necessity for the formation of the bureau at the time, some comrades in our party who were enslaved by past sectarianism, narrow localism, and lives of egocentricity and self-importance, opposed it, on the excuse that they were 'supporting the central headquarters [in Seoul]. [However,] their [real] intention was to prolong the sectarianism of the past and the outmoded localism. For instance, Comrade O Ki-sŏp was a typical person among them.[42]

Because of his early recalcitrant attitude toward Kim Il-sŏng, the political position of O Ki-sŏp had been constantly weakened. Though elected the second secretary of the party under the first secretary Kim Il-sŏng in December 1945, O Ki-sŏp lost the post the following January after holding it less than two months. When the Interim People's Council was formed in February 1946 with Kim Il-sŏng as its chairman, O Ki-sŏp was made chief of the propaganda department, but within a few months he was transferred to head the insignificant labor department.[43] After these downgrading measures, Kim Il-sŏng now openly attacked O at the Congress for his past "mistakes" with the object of further weakening the latter politically. Other leaders of the native communists vaguely referred to by Kim Il-sŏng in his denunciation were believed to include Chŏn Tal-hyon, Ch'oe Yong-dal, Yi Pong-su, Yi Sung-kūm, and Chang Sun-myŏng.[44]

Kim Il-sŏng's charge against his native communist opponents was instantly followed by debates of delegates who held important posts in the party, all in "strong support" of Kim Il-sŏng.[45] They were Chu Nyŏng-ha (native communist and vice-chairman of the party),[46] Hŏ Kai (Soviet Korean and chief of the organization department of the party), Kim Yŏl (Soviet Korean), and Han Mu-il (Soviet Korean and chairman of the Kangwŏndo provincial party).[47] Kim Yŏl's attack was said to have been particularly vociferous.

[63]

According to Kim Yŏl, the opposition to the establishment of the bureau, in spite of "the favorable condition" created by the stationing of the Soviet Army, constituted a "rightist opportunistic tendency." Kim Yŏl also accused the native communists of having made "leftist errors" by advocating the immediate implementation of "socialism," instead of supporting the execution of "democratic reforms" which were the "correct" policy of the party. Kim Yŏl continued, because of such "leftist" and "self-centered" behavior of "some comrades," the party alienated the masses for a while.[48] It should be noted that these charges were made at the Congress even though O Ki-sŏp previously "confessed" his errors.[49] Overwhelmed by the severity of attacks and hostile debates, all the accused native communists made "self-criticism," expressing regrets for their past mistakes and pledging to correct them. O Ki-sŏp, however, in his self-criticism made attempts at passive resistance. After duly admitting all his "criminal activities which paralyzed and weakened party activities" O added:

> Believing that it is not correct behavior not to point out errors of other comrades who owe self-criticism, I urge Comrade Mu-Jŏng who was called 'the great father' in the Hwanghae province to do self-criticism.[50]

Mu-Jŏng, the veteran communist soldier, was perhaps the most powerful among the Yenan Koreans. He was Kim Il-sŏng's potential rival for political power. In order to prevent Mu-Jŏng from gaining more power, Kim made certain he was not given a suitable post on the Interim People's Council when it was formed. Later, when the Peace Preservation Corps (forerunner of the North Korean People's Army) was formed in July 1946, Mu-Jŏng was given the position of artillery commander under the general commander of the corps, Ch'oe Yong-kŏn, who was a trusted comrade of Kim Il-sŏng. At the same time, Kim Il, another trusted lieutenant of Kim Il-sŏng, became cultural commander of the corps to take charge of political, information, and personnel affairs in the corps. Thus the Soviet-returnees did wield real power not only in the government but also in the army. Because of his relatively impotent position in the army as well as his relatively insignificant status as the chief of the training department in the party, Mu-Jŏng was said to have complained often about Kim Il-sŏng, accusing him of being bent on establishing his own political influence by placing his men in key posts of various organizations.[51] Han Pin was another unhappy Yenan Korean. Upon his arrival in North Korea, Han Pin was said to have been branded as an "anti-Soviet person" along with a few other Yenan Koreans because of his criticism of Soviet-returnees. Subsequently, Han Pin, in spite of his long revolutionary career, was given the post of curatorship of P'yŏngyang Library.[52]

Despite their anti-Kim Il-sŏng attitude and consequently "anti-Soviet" behavior, these Yenan Koreans were not publicly denounced at the Second Party Congress by Kim Il-sŏng and his followers, who concentrated their attacks upon their native enemies and deliberately avoided offending the Yenan Koreans in order to isolate the native opponents at the Congress. Thus O Ki-sŏp's remark that Mu-Jŏng owed self-criticism was an insinuating remark upon the tactics of his attackers. Or perhaps it was a trap whereby O Ki-sŏp intended to turn the attention of his attackers toward some Yenan Koreans and possibly bring to the surface the latent hostility existing between the Yenan Koreans and Soviet-returnees. However, O Ki-sŏp's attempt was smothered by Kim Il-sŏng, who replied to O:

> Comrade O Ki-sŏp is trying to drag another person into his case, saying why should he alone stand for self-criticism when there is such a man like Mu-Jŏng. O Ki-sŏp's attitude for self-criticism is not proper and sincere.[53]

Kim Il-sŏng implied that Mu-Jŏng's case should be overlooked, saying that "it should be remembered that everyone can make a mistake once in a while." While putting aside the problems of Mu-Jŏng, Kim Il-sŏng went further to insult O Ki-sŏp:

> There are persons who obey orders in one's presence but oppose them behind one's back. In the past Comrade O Ki-sŏp frequently played this kind of naughty trick.
> Comrade O Ki-sŏp, while pretending to follow [the policies of the party], complained about them among his relatives, his schoolmates, among those with whom he worked, and among those with whom he served prison terms.
> In order to curry favor with people, O Ki-sŏp invited them to his house and entertained them with wine. This is a handicraftman's method for organizing factions. (loud laughter) At present we have our party schools where annually several thousand cadets graduate.
> How can the pre-modern handicraftman's method match our modern party schools [in training factionalists]? (loud laughter)
> Thus Comrade O Ki-sŏp did not engage in large-scale factionalism but did in trivial factionalism, by using the handicraftman's method to raise his followers.[54]

[65]

With Kim Il-sŏng's insulting accusation, the debate regarding the "Struggle for Strengthening of the Party" was concluded. The attempts of the recalcitrant native communists to resist passively through their leader O Ki-sŏp were blocked. They were duly branded as "sectarians" who committed "leftist and rightist errors" (without, however, being expelled from the party).

While reporting on the "Expansion of the Party Influence and Party Organizational Activities" and on "Party Propaganda and Ideological Education," Kim once more emphasized the importance of educating the rank-and-file membership with the "advanced theory" of Marxism-Leninism. According to Kim, arming party members with Marxism-Leninism was the most powerful weapon to combat "formalism and bureaucratism" among some local party officials, to strengthen the party organizationally, and to maintain ideological solidarity among the party membership. Kim mentioned that the majority of the new members did not understand the party and the meaning of communism when they joined it. It was only afterwards that they could be educated.

In spite of the party leaders's effort to instruct the large number of new recruits in communism and to train them in the principle of democratic centralism, the new members, predominantly peasants and laborers, proved later to be less than dependable students, as will be seen herein. The majority of them were to sever their relations with the party and were to act as a fifth column for the South Korean army when it occupied North Korea during the winter of 1950–1951, thus bringing about the total disintegration of the party. The same failure of a mass communist party was to be repeated by the Indonesian Communist Party (PKI) following its abortive coup attempt in 1965. The members of peasant origin, who had previously joined the party in large numbers not only failed to resist the Indonesian army but also disowned their leaders and cooperated with the army in searching out their former comrades, thus bringing about the rapid and total collapse of the PKI.[55] It should be remembered that, in North Korea, the North Korean Workers' Party was the ruling party, and also, in Indonesia immediately prior to the 1965 incident, the PKI appeared to be about to grasp power largely due to the favorable (albeit deplorable) conditions in the country under Sukarno. Apparently peasants and workers in the two countries were allured by the communist practice of upgrading the social status of workers and farmers as well as by the promise of other material benefits that were believed to accrue to members of the parties in power. The decision of the communist elites in the two countries to recruit peasants, in spite of their lack of ideological commitment, proved to be fatal to the preservation of the parties at the critical moment. Both in Korea and Indonesia, Lenin's precept that a revolutionary communist party should be a conspiratorial cadre party and not a mass party, proved once more valid.

Next on the agenda of the Congress after Kim Il-sŏng's lengthy speech was the revision of the rules of the party. Regarding the recruitment of the new members, the Second Congress decided that stricter procedures had to be adopted in order to prevent the infiltration of "undesirable elements" into the party.[56] Such a stringent measure, however, apparently was taken on the belief that the party with its 750,000 members had to devote more attention to the task of strengthening the party qualitatively. The Congress also decided to establish a seven-member inspection committee to check party work. Then the Congress decided to enlarge the central committee of the party from 43 to 67 regular members and to add 20 alternate members.

The last part of the Second Party Congress was devoted to the selection of central party officials. Prior to the selection of new party officials, Hŏ Kai, a Soviet Korean, was said to have proposed that candidates for party offices should be recommended by the Politburo and by the chairmen of provincial parties, instead of being recommended by individual delegates. Hŏ's proposal was accepted. Thereupon, Chu Nyŏng-ha, the native communist and vice-chairman of the party, reportedly requested all those in the hall who were not delegates to leave the meeting so that the selection could be made by the representatives in closed session.[57] When the representatives were left alone in the closed conference room it was again Kim Il-sŏng, vice-chairman, and not the chairman Kim Tu-bong, who offered guidelines for the selection of central party officials. The vice-chairman warned against any tendency to select officials on the basis of "private consideration, friendship or sectarian relationship." He urged the delegates to choose their leaders in the light of the nominees' "dedication to the party and people and their abilities for practical work." [58]

It should be remembered that Kim's assertion was made to the delegates, the majority of whom had no right to recommend any candidates to party offices. These individuals could only vote on those candidates recommended by the Politburo and the chairmen of provincial parties. Thus the primary interest was whether or not the former native opponents of the Soviet-returnees would be recommended and reelected. On this important question Kim Il-sŏng apparently deemed it wise to show leniency. He said:

Some comrades among the central party officials, such as O Ki-sŏp, made mistakes in the past. But since the party has already criticized them enough in order to encourage and to keep them in the party, the party shall continue to treat them generously by leaving them in the party as officials.[59]

This "generous" policy was adopted perhaps in consideration of the anti-Japanese activities of the comrades concerned. For example, O Ki-sŏp, one-time student in the Soviet Union was imprisoned by the Japanese for thirteen years. Yet when the result of the election was announced, only three of the six native communists who were on the old central committee were kept on the new central committee. The three lucky ones were O Ki-sŏp, Yi Sung-kŭm, and Chang Sun-myŏng. However, their reelection did little to bolster their political fortune, since they had been formally branded as "sectarian" and their political influence upon rank-and-file members of the party had reached a vanishing point.[60]

Though none of the Yenan Koreans was officially disgraced at the Second Party Congress, the election of the new central committee reduced their strength. Two of the younger leaders of the Yenan Faction on the old central committee, Yun Kong-hŭm and Kim Ch'ang-man, failed to be reelected to the new central committee reportedly because of their previous "anti-Soviet" attitude.[61] The majority of the new central committee members consisted of Soviet-returnees and newly emerging native communists who were pro-Kim Il-sŏng.[62]

The 67 members of the new central committee, in turn, elected a 15-man presidium that was to work in the place of the central committee between the latter's plenary sessions.[63] Factional affiliations of the members of the new presidium were as follows: [64]

1. *Partisan comrades of Kim Il-sŏng.*
   Kim Il-sŏng
   Kim Ch'aek
   Kim Il

2. *Soviet Koreans*
   Hŏ Kai
   Pak Ch'ang-ok
   Ki Sŏk-Pok
   Kim Chae-uk
   Chin Ban-su

3. *Pro-Kim Il-sŏng native leaders*
   Chu Nyŏng-ha (a veteran communist)
   Pak Chŏng-ae (a veteran woman communist)
   Chŏng Il-yong (a newly emerging man)
   Chŏng Chun-t'aek (a newly emerging man)

4. *The Yenan Faction*
   Kim Tu-bong
   Ch'oe Ch'ang-ik
   Pak Il-u

The 15 members of the new presidium elected a new seven-man Politburo among themselves. They were Kim Tu-bong, Kim Il-sŏng, Chu Nyŏng-ha; Hŏ Kai, Kim Ch'aek, Ch'oe Ch'ang-ik, and Pak Il-u.[65] It was from the seven members of the Politburo that the party's chairman and vice-chairmen were chosen. Kim Tu-bong was again elected to the chairmanship and Kim Il-sŏng, Chu Nyŏng-ha and Hŏ Kai were made vice chairmen.[66] The Soviet Korean, Hŏ Kai, was elected to the vice-chairmanship for the first time, whereas Kim Il-sŏng and Chu Nyŏng-ha had served as vice-chairmen previously.

By the time the Second Party Congress adjourned, virtually all important central party posts had been taken by those communists who returned home from abroad after the liberation of the country. The chairmanship, two vice-chairmanship out of the three, six posts on the seven-man Politburo, and 11 posts on the 15-member Presidium were occupied by Soviet-returnees and the Yenan-returnees. Of the four native communists who were elected to the Presidium, only two were old renowned communists, and the other two were newly emerging leaders who owed their positions to their cooperation with the foreign returnees. The veteran native communists in the northern half of the country had lost their early political influence, the fruit of their long persistent struggle inside Korea. Furthermore, they appeared to be on the verge of extinction.

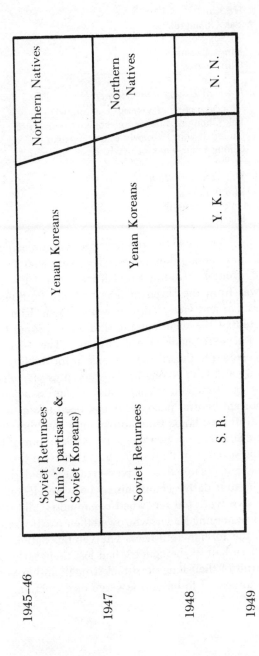

Chart of North Korean Communist Factionalism, 1945–1949
(Dwindling of space indicates decline of influence)

6.

SOUTHERN COMMUNISTS vs NORTHERN COMMUNISTS IN THE KOREAN WORKERS' PARTY

The Emergence of Old Korean Communists in South Korea and their Activities

ON AUGUST 16, 1945, ONE DAY AFTER THE LIBERATION OF Korea, a group of old communists, consisting mostly of former members of the Seoul Group and the Marxist-Leninist Group, met in Seoul to establish a party. This new party, led by Yi Yŏng, was called the Chang-an Faction after the name of the building where the meeting took place. Besides including former members of the Seoul Group and the Marxist-Leninist Group, there were a few former members of the Tuesday Association in the new party as well. It appeared that the members of the newly-formed group wished to disregard their past factional affiliations.[1]

Another rival group of old communists was also moving to establish a communist party. Led by Pak Hŏn-yŏng, this group consisted mostly of those communists who, in the late 1930's and early 1940's, made attempts to reorganize a Korean communist party. When they re-emerged in August 1945, they were called the Party Reestablishment Faction (Chae Kŏn-p'a).[2] Thus there emerged two separate and mutually opposed communist groups in South Korea shortly after the liberation.

It was, however, the group led by Pak that succeeded in forming the Korean Communist Party on September 11, 1945 by absorbing the group led by Yi Yŏng. Pak became the chairman of the party, and most of the other party posts were occupied by members of his faction. The purpose of the party was proclaimed to be the ultimate establishment of a communist society in Korea through a proletarian dictatorship.[3] There was some dissidence from Yi Yŏng's group over the distribution of party posts, yet the party under Pak managed to contain the dissidents and to control communist activities throughout South Korea. The new party made abundant use of the political freedom then existing in South Korea where communist newspapers were permitted to appear and communist meetings were tolerated by the American Military Government.[4] Under such favorable conditions the party membership increased rapidly, reportedly reaching about 20,000 persons in the summer of 1946.[5] The party strove to establish front organizations primarily among workers, peasants and youth groups in order to strengthen its position against nationalists in South Korea.[6]

Besides the Korean Communist Party under Pak Hŏn-yŏng, there were two other major leftist parties in the south. They were the New People's Party (Shinmin-tang) and the People's Party (Inmin-tang). The New People's Party in Seoul was formed in the spring of 1946 as a branch of the New People's Party in the north. It was headed by the leftist, Paek Nam-un, formerly a college professor.[7]

The People's Party was formed on November 12, 1945, headed by the moderate leftist Yŏ Un-hyŏng. Though some communists penetrated his party, it was not a communist group. At the outset Yŏ stated that the party purported to become a mass party representing the interests of all classes, including some capitalists and landlords, and excluding only "reactionary elements." The core of the party leadership was tightly organized around Chairman Yŏ. Although they were sympathetic to the communists and willing to cooperate in the formation of a workable coalition, they were also willing to work with right-wing nationalist groups. Thus the People's Party remained a middle-of-the-road group.[8]

Leaders of the Korean Communist Party apparently believed that a united front of all the leftist groups in the south under the leadership of communists was necessary for them to achieve any sort of political success. As early as November 29, 1945, Pak Hŏn-yŏng urged all leftist groups to rally around the Korean Communist Party.[9] However, a tentative united front of leftist forces in South Korea was not achieved until the spring of 1946, largely stimulated by the hostility of the American Military Government toward leftists as well as by the move on the part of right-wing forces to form a joint organ.

The first American hostility towards the leftists was shown on October 10, 1945 when the Military Government ordered the dissolution of the "Korean People's Republic" and people's councils that had been organized since September 6, 1945 by leftists in the south. The American decision was supported by leaders of right-wing groups such as Syngman Rhee and Kim Ku. The attitude of Rhee and Kim immediately provoked hostile reaction from the leftists.[10] On February 14, 1946 when the military government selected a group of Koreans to form an advisory organ known as the "Korean Democratic Council," it chose only right-wing nationalists.[11]

The cleavage between the rightists who were supported by the military government and the leftists thus came to the fore. Soon the division of the two camps became irreparable over the trusteeship issue. When it was first announced on December 27, 1945 that a plan for a five-year trusteeship of Korea had been decided upon at the Moscow Foreign Ministers' Conference, both right-wing groups and leftists all united in denouncing the decision. But on January 3, 1946, the communists, on instructions from North Korea, suddenly changed their position and declared their support of the trusteeship. The communists now explained that the proposed trusteeship was not an "imperialist mandate rule" but instead "friendly assistance" offered by the foreign nations concerned for the independence of Korea.[12] The People's Party under Yŏ Un-hyŏng and all other leftist groups quickly decided to support the communist stand, whereas the right-wing forces continued their opposition to the trusteeship. In the face of the apparent solidarity of the nationalists in the Korean Democratic Council, some 40 leftist organizations in South Korea, led by the communists, formed the "Korean Democratic People's Front" (Minchuchu'i Minjok Chŏnsŏn) on February 16, 1946.[13] This was not an amalgamation of the leftist groups but rather a loose alliance against the nationalists. The People's Front conducted propaganda in support of the trusteeship plan, while the nationalists staged anti-trusteeship demonstrations.

Meanwhile, the U.S.-Soviet Joint Commission opened its first session at the Dŏksu Palace in Seoul on March 20, 1946 to discuss the formation of an all-Korean provisional government that would be put under the four-power trusteeship as agreed upon in Moscow in December 1945. However, the negotiations in Seoul were deadlocked on the question of consultation with "Korean democratic parties and social organizations." The Soviet delegation, led by Colonel General T. F. Shtikov, argued that any party representatives who had expressed criticism of the trusteeship plan should be considered ineligible for consultation in the formation of a new Korean provisional government. The United States delegation, led by Major General A. V. Arnold, on the other hand, contended that the Soviet interpretation would deny the right of free speech and insisted that all "democratic" groups should be consulted and should be able to participate in the provisional government, regardless of their view on the trusteeship. In effect, the Soviet position was that only leftists should be consulted, while the United States argued that this would exclude all nationalists from the new provisional government. Neither the Soviet representatives nor the United States delegation were willing to compromise on this crucial issue, and, unable to overcome the impasse, they abruptly adjourned the conference on May 6, 1946.[14]

Attributing the failure of the Joint Commission to reach some form of agreement to a scheme of the American occupation authorities and the Korean right-wingers, and, in the face of the increasing hostility of the Military Government, the communists began to show their anti-American stance publicly. This further stiffened the American attitude towards the communists and other leftist groups. Open suppression of the communists by the American Military Government was prompted by a counterfeiting episode known as the Chŏngp'an-sa Incident, in which 16 alleged communist counterfeiters were arrested by the police between May 4 and July 6, 1946.[15]

In June of 1946, the American Military Government ordered the closure of the Soviet consulate in Seoul which had served as an intermediary between North Korea and the southern communists.[16] At the same time the military government began to arrest local communists who were secretly preparing terrorist activities. On August 21, 1946 the Military Governor, Lieutenant General John R. Hodge, warned all political groups, presumably meaning the communists, not to attempt "to sabotage Military Government activities." [17] Finally, on September 6, 1946, General Hodge ordered suspension of publication of three leftist newspapers, *Inmin-Ilbo* (People's Daily), *Chungang-Ilbo* (Central Daily), and *Haebang-Ilbo* (Emancipation Daily), on the ground that the publication of the three newspapers was "conducive to disorder." [18] On the same day

General Hodge ordered the arrest of the major officials of the Korean Communist Party, including Chairman Pak Hŏn-yŏng, Yi Chu-ha, and Yi Kang-kuk on the ground that their activities were "prejudicial to law and order." [19] Thus, by early September of 1946, the communists in South Korea were forced to go underground.

Hitherto, the communist party, though critical of the policies of the American Military Government, had been relatively reserved in its criticism. Now, exasperated by a series of anti-communist suppressive measures, the party began its public denunciation of the Korean nationalists as well as Americans. The communists maintained that the Chŏngp'an-sa Incident was "fabricated" by the Americans and the Korean right-wingers to disgrace the communist party in the eyes of the public. [20] Accusing the American policies of being "aggressive" and branding the Korean nationalists as "native reactionary lackeys," the communists cried out for the "downfall of American imperialism" and the "destruction of the anti-trusteeship camp."

On September 14, 1946, railroad workers in Seoul, instigated by the communists, went on strike demanding wage increases and improvement in working conditions. The strike immediately expanded to other major cities, and, before the end of the month, all the railroad workers and employees in the rest of the transport industry throughout South Korea joined the strike. While the disturbances were spreading, the workers' earlier demands for economic improvement were supplanted by those of a more political tone. Communist influence and the political rather than economic nature of the general strike could be seen from the following demands of the strikers:

1) Reopen the U.S.-Soviet Joint Commission; 2) Cancel the order for the arrest of communist leaders; 3) Transfer governmental functions to the people's councils; 4) Execute land reform and nationalize basic industries; and 5) Guarantee the stabilization of livelihood. [21]

The strike, however, subsided in early October and the paralyzed transport system began to function once again.

As soon as the strike of the transport workers subsided, there broke out a series of mass uprisings against the authorities beginning in the southeastern part of South Korea. They spread immediately westwards and then northwards by mid-October. By late in the month most of the provinces in South Korea were plagued by disorder and violence. Martial law was soon proclaimed. Pak Hŏn-yŏng, unable to evade pursuing authorities any longer, fled in mid-October to the town of Haeju, north of the 38th Parallel, where he continued to direct uprisings in the south. The strikers raided police stations, local governmental offices, and the homes of landlords, destroyed bridges and cut other communications lines throughout the whole South Korean countryside, and struck a series of blows against the nationalists and finally brought the American Military Government activities to a standstill in the fall of 1946. There were many casualties both among the strikers and those who attempted to suppress the uprisings. During the month of October in the city of Taegue alone, 44 policemen were killed and 153 were seriously wounded, and among rioters, 39 were killed and 148 were injured.[22]

There were also a series of attempts on the part of the leftists to assassinate prominent nationalists. As early as September 12, 1946, two youths, allegedly sent by North Korean communists, made an unsuccessful attempt on the life of Syngman Rhee in Seoul. In the same city on October 16, 1946, communist terrorists attempted to assassinate Cho Pyŏng-ok, chief of the South Korean national police, and on November 13, communists tried to kill Chang T'aek-sang, chief of the Seoul police force.[23] The uprisings lasted for three months until late December of the year. Throughout this turbulent period, the right-wing groups closely cooperated with the authorities in suppressing the rioters.

The Formation of the South Korean Workers' Party

While the strikes and uprisings were occurring in the fall of 1946, leaders of the three major leftist parties in South Korea were reportedly instructed by the North Korean Workers' Party to attempt the formation of a single unified party of all leftist groups in the south.[24] However, there were, in all the three parties, supporters as well as opponents of the proposed amalgamation. Within the Korean Communist Party, Pak Hŏn-yŏng led the majority of the central party officials in favor of the coalition. Pak set up a committee in his party for conducting negotiations for the merger. The committee consisted only of Pak's immediate followers. The decision for merger was challenged by the "Congress Group," formerly the Chang-an Faction, led by Yi Yŏng and Kang Chin, who had been excluded from the party's important posts and now again were excluded from the committee in charge of negotiations on the merger.

Subsequently, the Congress Group withdrew from the Korean Communist Party.[25] For Pak, the move to merge was partially to reduce American hostility towards his communist party since American suppressive measures against the People's Party and the New People's Party were not as harsh as to the communist party.

On the other hand, for the People's Party and the New People's Party, the proposed coalition with the communist party apparently meant a permanent loss of their independence. The two parties had already suffered a partial loss of independence when they joined the "Korean Democratic People's Front" with the communist party in February 1946. Furthermore, many officials of the People's Party and the New People's Party apparently feared that a unification with the communist party might increase the American occupation authorities's hostile measures against themselves. Thus, in the People's Party, the majority of the leaders, including Yŏ Un-hyŏng, opposed the suggested unification in order to maintain the "party's independent status" and to bring about cooperation with the American Military Government and the more moderate right-wing groups—the very thing the communists opposed. But communist agents in the party managed to carry the problem of merging to an "enlarged conference of party officials," where the majority voted in favor of the coalition in order to take concerted actions with the communists.[26]

In the New People's Party, Chairman Paek Nam-un opposed the merger, not because of his hope for cooperation with moderate right-wing groups, but because of his fear that the merger would result in the subordination of his party to the communist party. As in the case of the People's Party, however, the majority of party officials, including Hŏ Hŏn, persuaded by communist agents, decided in favor of unification in order to take joint action with the communists.[27] By late September, 1946, the proponents of unification in the three parties were well on their way to the formation of a new party. The opponents of this move in all the three parties, however, rallied behind Yŏ Un-hyŏng in order to obstruct the merger, which, they claimed, was "a dogmatic act" of Pak Hŏn-yŏng. They formed the Socialist Workers' Party (Sahoe Nodong-tang) on October 14, 1946, thus defeating the very purpose of the unification of leftists in South Korea. Yŏ Un-hyŏng was elected to the chairmanship of the party, and Kang Chin (Korean Communist Party) and Paek Nam-un (New People's Party) became vice-chairmen.[28]

Unable to prevent the formation of the Socialist Workers' Party the proponents of the unification finally, on November 23, 1946, announced the formation of the South Korean Workers' Party (Nam Chosŏn Nodongdang). The purpose of the party was declared to be the establishment of a "strong democratic and independent Korea" by carrying out "democratic reforms," [29] which strongly resembled the policies of the then North Korean Workers' Party and, for that matter, the policies of the then North Korean Interim People's Council. Hŏ Hŏn (New People's Party) was elected chairman of the party with Pak Hŏn-yŏng (Korean Communist Party) and Yi Ki-sŏk (People's Party) as vice-chairmen. Most of the other central party posts were occupied by former members of the communist party. [30]

While directing uprisings in late 1946, Pak Hŏn-yŏng's lieutenants presumably with support from the north, constantly put pressure on the leadership of the Socialist Workers' Party to join the South Korean Workers' Party. At the end of January 1947, Kang Chin and a few others of the anti-Pak communist faction in the Socialist Workers' Party left their party and joined the South Korean Workers' Party. Eventually, so did many other members of the Socialist Workers' Party. [31]

On May 24, 1947, Yŏ Un-hyŏng reorganized his gradually dwindling party and renamed it the Working People's Party (Kŭllo Inmintang). Yo became chairman of the reorganized party and Paek Nam-un and Yi Yŏng were made vice-chairmen. The party with its moderate leftist program made some efforts to cooperate with the American military government as well as with moderate right-wing groups. [32] But on July 19, 1947, Yŏ was assassinated in Seoul by a 19-year-old youth, whose political convictions have yet to be confirmed. Thereafter, the party leadership, attacked by both extreme right wing groups and the communists, disappeared from the South Korean political scene, and its rank-and-file members either abandoned political activities altogether or were absorbed into the South Korean Workers' Party. [33]

By this time almost all the leftists in South Korea had joined the South Korean Workers' Party. At the height of its strength in 1947 the party boasted 370,000 members. [34] The American Military Government's hostility towards the new communist-dominated party was as strong as it was towards the former Korean Communist Party. On August 11, 1947, some 100 leading members of the South Korean

Workers' Party, including vice-chairman, Yi Ki-sŏk, were arrested while preparing for a large-scale uprising on August 15, the day of the second anniversary of the liberation of Korea.[35] Due to a subsequent series of arrests and generally harsh measures taken by the military government, the party's membership rapidly dwindled, reaching 50,000 in late 1947.[36]

Meanwhile, the second session of U.S.-Soviet Commission opened on May 21, 1947, again in Seoul. But it broke down on October 21, 1947, deadlocked over the same question that had caused a stalemate in session in the spring of 1946. This time, however, it was the end. On September 17, 1947 the United States had already put the Korean problem to the United Nations where the Temporary Commission on Korea was appointed in November of that year to oversee elections for an all-Korea constituent assembly. However, when the Temporary Commission on Korea arrived in Seoul in January 1948, they found it was impossible for them to enter North Korea. Consequently the commission had to restrict its role to the elections scheduled to be held in South Korea on May 10, 1948. Now, members of the South Korean Workers' Party moved to obstruct the elections in the name of the "Struggle to Save the Country." From February 7 to May 1948 they staged strikes and demonstrations and carried out terrorist activities against election officials, candidates, and policemen.[37] However, the elections were carried out as scheduled and the Republic of Korea (South Korea) was born on August 15, 1948. Realizing the futility of further opposition in the south, most of the leading members of the South Korean Workers' Party, along with other minor leftist groups, fled to the north to participate in North Korean politics.

Those communists who remained in the south continued guerrilla activities now sporadically and in a declining degree, the most serious one being the brief successful revolt of a regimental unit of the South Korean Army stationed in the town of Yŏsu between October 19 and 26 of 1948. For a week, rebellious soldiers, in cooperation with local communists, murdered numerous policemen and local nationalist leaders in the town of Yŏsu and the surrounding area. Thereafter communist activities began to decline rapidly because of large-scale "mopping-up operations" launched by the combined forces of the South Korean Army and the police against "communist bandits." Beginning the seizure of the communist apparatus in Seoul in September 1949, the authorities had destroyed most of the communist underground bases scattered in South Korea by March of the next year.[38] During the campaigns, the army arrested 196 leading members of the South Korean Workers' Party and dispersed most of their followers. Among those 196 arrested were Kim Sam-yong, the head of the party's underground organization, and his assistant, Yi Chu-ha. Kim Sam-yong, a one-time factory worker, had been a follower of Pak Hŏn-yŏng since the late 1930's. Yi Chu-ha, an old native communist, came to Seoul from North Korea sometime between late 1945 and early 1946, discontented with the Soviet-returnees in the north. The two men were among the most trusted lieutenants of Pak Hŏn-yŏng. During their "mopping-up operations" the police uncovered an apparatus operated exclusively by North Korean communists, whose growing influence in the communist movement of South Korea had been well confirmed by the authorities by late 1947. As a result, all the communist organizations, except a few in the mountainous southwestern corner of South Korea, had collapsed by the time the Korean War broke out.[39]

The Formation of the Korean Workers' Party

The most prominent of the South Korean communists who fled to North Korea was Pak Hŏn-yŏng. Ever since he had first joined the Korean communist movement in the early 1920's, Pak's career had been devoted to revolutionary activities inside Korea, interrupted only by occasional local imprisonments, and some periods of training in Soviet Russia. It was largely because of his persistence in, and devotion to, the cause of communism, that Pak was able to form the Korean Communist Party in Seoul in September 1945 and establish himself as its head.[40]

According to the declaration of the Korean Communist Party issued on September 14, 1945, it was Pak Hŏn-yŏng and his comrades who had led the communist movement in Korea during the Japanese occupation of Korea. Significantly enough, no names of the Yenan Koreans or Soviet-returnees, including Kim Il-sŏng, were mentioned in connection with the origin of the Korean communist movement and its subsequent development within Korea.[41] Thus for Pak Hŏn-yŏng and his colleagues, the Korean communists from Yenan and Soviet Russia were outside the mainstream of the Korean communist movement. Although most of the central posts of the Korean Communist Party had been occupied by Pak Hŏn-yŏng's followers, Kim

Il-sŏng and two Yenan Koreans (Ch'oe Ch'ang-ik and Han Pin) were named to its eight-man Politburo in absentia.[42] Though this had been no more than a gesture, it had at least expressed the ambition of Pak to be the leader of the Korean communist movement in both parts of the country.

Immediately following the establishment of its headquarters in Seoul in September 1945, the Korean Communist Party directed most of the communist activities in the south. The party also extended its influence to the north through agents such as Ch'oe Yong-dal [43] and Chang Sun-myŏng, both of whom were to be condemned as "sectarians" at the Second Congress of the North Korean Workers' Party. Besides these two, Pak Hŏn-yŏng was believed to have had several other agents in the north. Thus, immediately after the liberation, Pak's party in Seoul maintained a semblance of a national communist party for all parts of Korea, and Pak conducted himself as if he were the supreme leader. It was because of such an ambition that Pak went to North Korea in October 1945 and unsuccessfully tried to dissuade Kim Il-sŏng from forming the North Korean central (communist) bureau.[44] Failing in his attempt, Pak returned to the south to lead communist forces there.

In the meantime, political developments in Korea rapidly moved to force the Korean Communist Party in the south to subordinate itself to the North Korean Communist Party. It was under instructions from the north that, in January 1946, communists in the south suddenly changed their attitude on the question of the proposed trusteeship. Again, it was after they had received suggestions from the north that the communists in the south moved to form the South Korean Workers' Party. Although Pak Hŏn-yŏng still directed the communist movement in the south after his escape to the north in October 1946, Pak had to rely heavily upon the North Korean Workers' Party for funds and propaganda material.[45] Meanwhile, most of the active communists who remained in the south were arrested and their followers were dispersed by the South Korean authorities. When the leaders of the South Korean Workers' Party gathered in North Korea in late 1948, they were very much leaders *sans* followers.[46] In contrast, the North Korean Workers' Party had been growing steadily both in membership and organizational strength. Those native communists who were suspected of being agents of Pak Hŏn-yŏng were losing their political influence, and the bulk of the new party members professed their allegiance to

[81]

Kim Il-sŏng. With its growing strength, the North Korean Communist Party was extending its activities across the 38th Parallel. While the South Korean Workers' Party first developed and then collapsed amidst the revolutionary struggles against the American Military Government, the North Korean Workers' Party grew as a ruling party in relatively peaceful circumstances thanks to the support of the Soviet forces. The different circumstances in which the two parties operated were aptly expressed by a South Korean communist comedian:

O! North Korean Workers' Party is carrying out revolution with *words*, whereas the South Korean Workers' Party is doing revolutionary work with *deeds*.[47]

It was then that the different policies of the two occupation authorities ultimately decided the relative strength of the two parties.

When the government of the Democratic People's Republic of Korea (North Korea) was formed on September 9, 1948, all members of the South Korean Workers' Party in the north joined it. The establishment of the Democratic People's Republic of Korea was preceded by a series of final preparations. Already a constitution drafting committee headed by a Soviet Korean, Kim T'aek-yŏng, had drawn up a constitution following the example of the Soviet Constitution of 1936. The draft constitution was adopted by the People's Assembly on May 1, 1948. On August 25, 1948, an election was held to form a Supreme People's Assembly consisting of 572 deputies. The new Supreme People's Assembly was to replace the People's Assembly as the "supreme legislative organ" in North Korea. Of the 572 seats, 360 were awarded to South Korean leftists.[48] In the Cabinet headed by Prime Minister Kim Il-sŏng, four members of the South Korean Workers' Party were given ministerial posts. The two highest posts of the four were a vice-premiership and the foreign ministership and both posts were occupied by Pak Hŏn-yŏng. But the influence of the cabinet members from the south was carefully circumscribed by their vice-ministers who were members of the North Korean Workers' Party. For instance, it was the Vice-Foreign Minister Pak Tong-ch'o (Soviet Korean) who really ran the affairs of the Foreign Ministry.[49]

Having given leaders of the South Korean Workers' Party offices in the North Korean government, Kim Il-sŏng reportedly forced them to join his party in order to take over the leadership of the communist movement in the south from the then virtually defunct South Korean

Workers' Party and thus to provide "unified leadership" to all communist forces both in the south and the north.[50] Kim's move was accompanied by a mild purge of North Korean officials in the people's councils and branch organizations of the North Korean Workers' Party who were still suspected of their connection with the South Korean Workers' Party. Approximately 15 per cent of local officials were removed from their posts.[51] Finally in June 1949, a "conference of joint central committees" of the South and North Korean Workers' Parties was held in P'yŏngyang reportedly without disclosing the nature of the meeting to the followers of Pak Hŏn-yŏng in the south. A new amalgamated party, the Korean Workers' Party, emerged from the conference.[52] It was now Kim Il-şŏng who became the chairman of the newly formed party, superseding Kim Tu-bong, the nominal chairman of the North Korean Workers' Party.[53] Pak Hŏn-yŏng was made a vice-chairman of the new party along with the Soviet Korean Hŏ Kai.[54]

Since the South Korean Workers' Party had actually become defunct prior to the formation of the Korean Workers' Party, the new party was established by the absorption of the remaining South Korean communists into the North Korean Workers' Party rather than by merger of two independent parties. The formation of the new party put an end to the struggle for the location of a central Korean communist headquarters between P'yŏngyang and Seoul. In this initial battle for power, North Korean communists won because they formed the Korean Workers' Party under circumstances which put all South Korean communists under their discipline. From now on, both in name and in actuality, the entire Korean communist movement was to be directed from the north. In this respect the formation of the Korean Workers' Party also meant the realization of a much cherished dream to form a unified Korean communist movement, which ever since its inception in the late 1910's had been plagued by factionalism. The dream, however, became a reality not under the leadership of an old veteran communist but under that of a relatively new figure in the Korean communist movement—Kim Il-sŏng.

In spite of all this, the leadership of the Korean Workers' Party was far from being solidified, being an alliance of leaders of contending groups within the party. In the subsequent chapters we shall deal with a series of purges and the description of the varying fortunes of groups and prominent individuals until a tightly-knit leadership around one acknowledged leader emerges.

[83]

7.

EFFECTS OF
THE KOREAN WAR
ON FACTIONALISM

THE ESTABLISHMENT OF THE DEMOCRATIC PEOPLE'S REPUBLIC of Korea (North Korea) on September 9, 1948, was followed by the withdrawal of the Soviet occupation forces by December of that year.[1] In South Korea, following the birth of the Republic of Korea on August 15, 1948, the American forces had also withdrawn by June 1949, leaving behind only its 500-man Military Advisory Group to train armed forces of South Korea. Under these conditions, the North Korean government continued its military buildup, presumably its prime objective being to unify the divided country by military force.[2] Finally, on June 25, 1950, the North Korean armed forces began a massive invasion of South Korea across the 38th Parallel. This was the beginning of a war that lasted for three years and one month, involving not only the North and South Korean armies but also foreign troops.

The morning after the outbreak of the war, the North Korean Premier, over the P'yŏngyang radio, appealed to the Korean people to cooperate fully with North Korea's military campaign:

> All Korean people must stand up and join our struggle to destroy the puppet government of the traitor Syngman Rhee and its army . . . pay every sacrifice to achieve victory in our struggle . . . [and] execute traitors everywhere. The time has come to unify our country. Forward![3]

Kim Il-sŏng made it clear that the war would not stop short of the unification of Korea under the direction of his regime. In order to achieve victory, the Premier urged people to kill those who were deemed "traitors," a term which could mean virtually anyone who would not positively support North Korea's war aims. On the same day, a Seven-Man Military Committee was organized to coordinate all operational, administrative, and ordinance activities relating to the army. This committee was vested with authority to mobilize "the entire forces of the country" and all citizens, organs of power, political parties and social organizations were "obliged to submit themselves completely" to it. The military committee was headed by Kim Il-sŏng, Premier and Chairman of the Party. The other six members on the committee were: Pak Hŏn-yŏng, a Vice-Premier, Foreign Minister and a Vice-Chairman of the Party; Kim Ch'aek, a Vice-Premier and Minister of Industry; Ch'oe Yong-kŏn, Minister of National Defense; Pak Il-u, Minister of the Interior and a Yenan returnee; Hong Myŏng-hi, a Vice-Premier and Chairman of the Democratic Independence Party (from South Korea); and Chŏng Chun-t'aek, a native communist.[4]

On July 4, 1950, the Presidium of the Supreme People's Assembly appointed Kim Il-sŏng the Supreme Commander-in-Chief of the North Korean People's Army. Thus within less than two weeks after the outbreak of the war, the whole of North Korea came under a tight wartime control. On July 8, 1950, Kim Il-sŏng again appealed over the radio to the Korean people to support the war. Calling the war a "Great Liberation War of the Korean People for Freedom and Independence," he declared that the war should end in "complete victory" in order to "raise the glorious flags of the Democratic People's Republic of Korea" throughout the southern part of Korea.[5] Kim once more made it explicit that the war would be continued until the whole of Korea became unified under communism. The war progressed well for North Korea. Within six weeks the North Korean armies "liberated" some ninety per cent of the South Korean territory, including its capital, Seoul, and ninety-two per cent of the population of South Korea.[6] And the South Korean government had been on the verge of a "complete collapse." [7] It appeared momentarily that the North Korean communists would be able to conquer the remaining part of South Korea and would establish a communist system throughout Korea. However, the subsequent massive counterattacks launched in mid-September, 1950, by the combined forces of the South Korean armies and the United Nations forces (consisting mostly of United States troops) changed the war situation. By late September, the North Korean forces had been driven back across the 38th Parallel. From October 1, South Korean troops and U.N. forces began to cross the demarcation line and moved northwards. For nearly a month afterwards North Koreans were continuously in rout or retreat and the opposing forces penetrated deep into their territory.

Foreseeing the inevitability of retreat, Kim Il-sŏng, on October 11, 1950, over the radio asked North Korean armies and the members of the Korean Workers' Party to:

> 1) Defend your area to the death by disturbing the rear of the enemy; and 2) Pick up, arrest, and decimate uncompromisingly spies, destructive elements, melancholic elements, disheartened elements, cowards, and those who spread wild rumors.[8]

Thus Kim urged the North Korean soldiers and communists to organize guerrillas in the enemy-occupied area and also to execute diehard non-communist elements relentlessly. Following this speech, Kim Il-sŏng fled P'yŏngyang northwards, entrusting the defense of the capital of North Korea to General Mu-Jŏng. Mu-Jŏng, the Yenan-returnee and Kim's previously formidable rival was then the Commander of the Second Army Corps. Like most of the other North Korean army leaders, he fled in the face of advancing enemy forces. At the same time, grave damage was done to the Korean Workers' Party. The rank-and-file members of the Party had been recruited in peaceful circumstances, and they had no previous revolutionary experience. When the enemy troops advanced into their localities, the majority of them, instead of putting up a fight, either fled or hid. They threw away their party identification cards to save their lives, and some even cooperated with the advancing enemy troops.[9] Furthermore, many members of the two North Korean non-communist parties (Democratic Party and Youth Fraternal Party) joined the South Korean army in its efforts to pursue the retreating communist troops and to search out hidden members of the Korean Workers' Party. Under such circumstances the party faced almost complete disintegration, and the North Korean regime was on the verge of collapse toward the end of 1950. It was only through the massive intervention of Chinese Communist "Volunteers," which began late in October of the year, that the North Korean regime avoided extinction.[10]

Although its existence was saved, the regime now openly became a target of discontent for a certain segment of its inhabitants. Encouraged by official sanction announced over radio by Kim Il-sŏng on October 11 as well as reported secret orders from above, North Korean communists and soldiers executed all political prisoners whom they could not take with them in their hurried retreat. Dissatisfied with the communists and/or wishing to avoid persecution, some 685,000 North Koreans fled to South Korea with the retreating South Korean and U. N. forces between the late 1950 and early next year. Those who still remained in the north and were deemed "reactionaries" were duly punished by the communists in "people's courts," following the recovery of their territory.[11]

Although the position of Kim Il-sŏng and his immediate associates had been continuously strengthened, they still shared power with various communist factions. In order to maintain his position Kim Il-sŏng had utilized Russian support whenever necessary to counter those communists who challenged his position, but he had also courted the reluctant communists for the support of his position. The posts in leading organs of both the government and the party had been occupied by all the major communist groups, though the proportion of influence was by no means equal. Thus the party and the government were run, in fact, by a coalition of factions. However, with the war situation changed adversely and the possibility of victory appearing remote, there occurred a series of events inside the North Korean leadership that resulted in the alteration of the positions of the factions.

While the Chinese Communist forces were pushing the enemy troops successfully southwards in the winter of 1950–51, the Third Plenum of the Central Committee of the Korean Workers' Party was held from December 21 to 23, 1950 at Kang'ke, a Korean town located on the Manchurian border. The meeting was held in order to take measures against "defects" shown in the army and the party during the retreat of North Korean forces. The occasion was also used by Kim Il-sŏng to eliminate his rival, Mu-Jŏng. In the opening part of his speech, Kim, in spite of the uncertainty of the outcome of the war, again expressed the determination of the party to unify Korea under communist domination:

> Our party would not connive and tolerate or so contradict the wishes of the Korean people as to allow the 38th Parallel to separate our territory into two parts.[12]

This was followed by a lengthy analysis of the changed military and political situation due to the intervention of foreign troops.

Throughout the analysis Kim accused a number of army leaders, who "busied themselves during the time of the retreat with their egoistic personal life and displayed cowardice" as well as some party leaders at the provincial level, who "became frightened and confused before the attack of the enemy" and fled, instead of carrying out "the instructions of the Central Committee" to organize partisans in the enemy-occupied territory.[13] Kim attributed the responsibility of the defeat to his subordinates, making them scapegoats and diverting the blame from himself. Those who were blamed were either demoted or lost their posts. Among them the most prominent was Mu-Jŏng, who received the severest criticism and the harshest punishment. Kim denounced him as follows:

> Mu-Jŏng . . . brought about heavy losses on our side as a result of not enforcing military order in the army and for his failure to organize battles correctly . . . he perpetrated such military excesses, in defiance of law, such as were committed by the feudal kings, who arbitrarily shot people without any legal procedure . . . Such deeds are liberalist and gangster-like deeds of cowards and defeatists who are not interested in organized party life whatsoever.[14]

Obviously Mu-Jŏng was singled out to be blamed for the military losses and the massacres committed by the communists during their retreat. Following the meeting, Mu-Jŏng lost his rank in the army, was charged with unwarranted manslaughter and insubordination, and was imprisoned, never to be seen or heard of again.[15] Mu-Jŏng, had he openly challenged Kim, might have found support among Chinese communist forces since he had been on intimate terms with their leaders. He was never given this opportunity.

The criticism and accusations of party and army leaders were followed by a denunciation of rank-and-file members of the party. Declaring that party discipline remained "weak," Kim said that "the war has shown clearly who is a genuine party member and who is a false one," and it "has exposed relentlessly the cowards and false members of the party." [16] Kim, in the name of the Central Committee, declared that "our party will purge itself of these kinds of elements and thus strengthen our ranks." [17] In response to this statement, party organs on various levels, following the Third Plenum, carried out purges of those who remained inactive by either hiding or through concealment of their identity during the short period of the enemy occupation of North Korea. To the dismay of the party leadership, however, it was said that in the course of the purge some 450,000 members out of the original 600,000 were expelled.

[88]

Those who lost party membership became discontented and antagonistic. To save the party from this grave situation, a conference of the Organization Department of the party was called on September 1, 1951. At the meeting Kim Il-sŏng instructed that the punitive measures against those who committed "some slight error" or who disposed of party identification cards should be rescinded. He also said that new members should be admitted into the party to replenish the membership.[18] However, local party officials were very cautious in readmitting those who had once been expelled, and, in many places, they continued to refuse readmittance. In addition, the instruction to admit new party members was not implemented smoothly.

Because of the predominantly agricultural nature of North Korean society, party membership had been mainly drawn from the peasant class. The preponderance of peasants became further pronounced during the war when many members of factory worker origin and other party activists were lost. According to a Japanese source, during the brief period of occupation of North Korea some 150,000 North Korean civilians, presumably all active communists, were either executed or forcibly carried away southwards by enemy troops.[19] In spite of this, local party officials refused to admit peasants on the grounds of their insufficient education and political preparation. As a result, the growth of the party was held back and it became "isolated from the masses." In order to rectify such "extreme leftist error" the Fourth Plenum of the Central Committee of the party was called November 1 to 4, 1951.[20] The occasion was also utilized by Kim Il-sŏng to eliminate another powerful communist leader, Hŏ Kai, making him a scapegoat for "defective organizational work."

Hŏ Kai was one of the Soviet-returnees who had arrived in North Korea in 1945 with the Soviet Army. Though summarily called Soviet-returnees, these communists were divided into two subgroups. One was the remnants of former communist partisans who had operated in Manchuria with Kim Il-sŏng. They were also known as the Kapsan faction, having operated in the area of the North Korean town of Kapsan in cooperation with local communists. The other subgroup was composed of Soviet Koreans who had not been active in the Korean independence movement prior to 1945. Hŏ Kai was the most influential man among those Soviet Koreans. Although during the period of the Soviet occupation of North Korea the two subgroups cooperated under the direction of the Soviet authorities, the relationship between the two was by no means congenial. Though Hŏ Kai himself helped put Kim Il-sŏng in power, Hŏ Kai used to assume a haughty attitude towards Kim Il-sŏng and his Manchurian partisans, and he boasted about being the "original Bolshevik." [21] Having seen the undependability of the majority of the party members during the period of enemy occupation of North Korea, Hŏ Kai, as head of the Organization Department, was unenthusiastic about the policy of rapid replenishment of party membership, and appeared defiant to Kim Il-sŏng. [22] However, by now, Kim had solidified his post, and circumstances were changing conveniently for the move against Hŏ Kai.

The Soviet Red Army, with whose support Hŏ Kai and other Soviet Koreans maintained their influence, had already withdrawn. In the "anxious moment," as later confessed by Kim Il-sŏng, [23] the Russian government expressed no more than moral support of North Korea and was not willing to commit its troops to save the North Korean regime. [24] Following the regime's bare avoidance of collapse, Malik, the Soviet delegate to the United Nations, on June 23, 1951, called for an armistice conference. The first meeting for the armistice took place on July 10 of that year in the town of Kaesŏng (the conference later moved to Panmunjŏm near Kaesŏng). By then the war had been stalemated for a few months along the 38th Parallel. The mere fact that the Soviet Union was prepared to talk in terms of an armistice must have made it clear to the North Koreans that their ally was ready to sacrifice the goal of Korean unification in the face of an escalation of the war. Under these circumstances, North Korean resentment toward the Soviet Union became widespread. [25] It was in this atmosphere that the Fourth Plenum of the Central Committee of the Korean Workers' Party was held. By then, Hŏ Kai, the head of the Organization Department of the party, had become a target of resentment among party members because of his arrogance. Taking advantage of the mood, Kim Il-sŏng now openly criticized "the error of closed-doorism" committed by Hŏ Kai, and attributed to the latter the entire responsibility for the slowness of party growth and for the discontent of those who had been expelled from the party. [26] Interestingly enough the Soviet Korean, Pak Ch'ang-ok, reportedly joined Kim Il-sŏng in denouncing Hŏ Kai. Pak was said to have blamed Hŏ Kai for the occasional ambushes carried out by members of the two non-communist parties on stragglers from the retreating North Korean armies. Hŏ Kai was also blamed for the failure of the rank-and-file party members to carry out orders during the occupation period.[27] After these accusations, Hŏ Kai was censured, which was followed by his pistol suicide.[28] In order to "expand party strength," the fourth plenum revised the old party rule regarding admittance of new members, lowering the required age and making it easier to apply for membership.[29]

Meanwhile, the party defined the act of Hŏ Kai as a symbol of "bureaucratism" and "exclusivism" and staged a mass movement ostensibly to combat such tendencies. In the process, a large number of members were admitted into the party who had allegedly fought "heroically" at their working places and had demonstrated "patriotism" when North Korea was invaded. As a result, the total number of the party members reached 1,000,000 at the end of 1952. In order to raise their political consciousness, the party required the new recruits to attend "study meetings," lectures, and "explanation works," all conducted by local party offices.[30]

Next the North Korean leaders moved to tighten control over local people's councils and to have local governmental officials maintain closer relations with the war-weary masses. To this end, on February 1, 1952, there was held the "Joint Conference of the Chairmen of Provincial, City, and County People's Councils and Party Leaders."

Production activities in North Korea were at a standstill. Almost all of the North Korean industrial complex had been destroyed, and many trained workers had been killed. Farming had been restricted to after dark because of the incessant air raids, and fishing had been stopped because of the enemy naval blockade. North Korea for some time had been dependent upon the aid of "friendly" countries for food, clothing, and shoes.[31] At the conference of February 1, 1952, Kim Il-sŏng acknowledged that there had been resentment and alienation among the masses ever since the outbreak of the war. According to Kim, however, this was due to the heavy taxes levied by local officials anxious to fulfill the quotas assigned to their districts. It was said, for example, that some farmers were forced to reap unripened grain in order to pay their tax in kind on time. In his effort to show that the local functionaries misunderstood the governmental orders and in hopes of making them responsible for all the excesses, Kim urged the congregation to rectify these kind of "bureaucratic styles and methods of work" and become "genuine workers for the people." [32] In short, Kim established himself as the spokesman of the war-weary people. Subsequently, on September 30th, the

[91]

Cabinet, prompted by the party and its Politburo, issued its order to exempt poor peasants from taxes and fees for usage of governmental irrigation facilities for the year 1952.[33]

All this time, the "struggle against bureaucratism" was vigorously carried out in the party and the people's councils at all levels. While this was going on, a Fifth Plenum of the Central Committee of the party was held on December 15–18, 1952. It was avowedly called to consolidate the rapidly expanding party. At the meeting, Kim Il-sŏng made a report entitled "The Organizational and Ideological Strengthening of the Party—the Basis of Our Victory." In the report Kim stressed the importance of "struggling" against "the remnants of sectarianism" in the party, members who had been "guilty of localism" by appointing their schoolmates, relatives, and hometown friends to posts in the party and people's councils. Kim urged the party to "fight resolutely" against such elements and admonished all those who were guilty of "anti-party activities" to confess their past deeds and give them up.[34] Following the Fifth Plenum there were held numerous "Thought Examination Meetings" in January to April of 1953, beginning at each local party cell and reaching up to the central party organization. Each member of a party unit was requested to submit himself or herself to "self-criticism," confessing "concretely and precisely" all his past misconduct such as "bureaucratism, flattery, useless obstinacy, and petit-bourgeois pride." Each member was also to criticize other members in order to struggle against "the enemies of the revolution" such as "irresponsibility and relaxation." Simultaneously, all party members were to study Kim's speech made at the Fifth Plenum, and they were to be on constant alert for spies and other "destructive elements" hidden in their localities.[35] These events were a prelude to a mass purge of members of the former South Korean Workers' Party, led by Pak Hŏn-yŏng, as well as the remaining prominent northern native communists.

The public came to realize the meaning of the events only on August 3, 1953, when posters appeared on the streets of P'yŏngyang, announcing the trial of 12 former leading members of the South Korean Workers' Party beginning that very day. It was said that at first people thought the posters were mistaken or were acts of anti-communists.[36] The trial was conducted, however, as announced, by a "special military tribunal" set up for that purpose, and it lasted four days. It was an "open" trial, and indictments were presented by the Prosecutor-General, Yi Song-un, who was a comrade-in-arms of Kim Il-sŏng in Manchuria. The names of the twelve indicted and the ranks they held in North Korea were:

1. Yi Sŭng-yŏp (born 1905): Secretary of Central committee of the Korean Workers' Party and Minister of Justice;
2. Cho Il-myŏng (born 1903): Deputy-Minister of the Department of Culture and Propaganda;
3. Im Hwa (born 1908): Deputy-Chairman of the Korean Society for Cultural Relations with the USSR;
4. Pak Sŭng-wŏn (born 1913): Deputy-Chief of the Liaison Department of the Central Committee of the Korean Workers' Party;
5. Yi Kang-kuk (born 1906): Director of the Import-Corporation attached to the Ministry of Foreign Trade;
6. Bae Ch'ŏl (born 1912): Chief of the Liaison Department of the Central Committee of the Korean Workers' Party;
7. Yun Sŭng-tal (born 1914): Deputy-Chief of the Liaison Department of the Central Committee of the Korean Workers' Party;
8. Yi Wŏn-cho (born 1906): Deputy-Chief of the Department of Agitation and Propaganda of the Central Committee of the Korean Workers' Party;
9. Cho Yong-pok (born 1905): Executive Official in the National Control (Inspection) Committee;
10. Pak Hyŏng-sik (born 1917): Executive Official in the Department of Internal Affairs, People's Council;
11. Maeng Chong-ho (born 1911): Unit Commander in the South Korean Partisan Detachment (consisting of South Koreans being trained in North Korea for operations in South Korea); and
12. Sŏl Chŏng-sik (born 1912): Official in the Political Administration Section, the Supreme Command of the North Korean People's

All the twelve men were of South Korean origin and had been active in the communist movement in South Korea under Pak Hŏn-yŏng until they were forced to migrate to North Korea and join the amalgamated Korean Workers' Party. In particular, Yi Sŭng-yŏp, Im Hwa, and Yi Kang-kuk were involved in communist activities in Korea as early as the Japanese occupation. All three were men of substantial learning. Yi Sŭng-yŏp was a graduate of the Keijō Imperial University (now Seoul National University), Yi Kang-kuk graduated from the University of Berlin, and Im Hwa was a poet of renown. Yi Wŏn-cho and Sŏl Chŏng-sik were also recognized literary figures. Significantly, Pak Hŏn-yŏng, the acknowledged leader of these twelve men, was not included among those who were tried. Pak's name did, however, appear in the documents of indictment against the twelve.

During the four-day period, all were charged with indentical "crimes," including "Plots to Overthrow the Democratic People's Republic of Korea, Anti-State Espionage and Terrorist Activities, and Anti-State Propaganda and Agitation." According to the charges, the twelve, led by Yi Sŭng-yŏp, 1) from the landing of the United States forces in South Korea in 1945 had acted as American spies and aided the "American imperialists" in bringing about the downfall of the "democratic forces" in the south; 2) had come to North Korea "on orders from American masters" and engaged in espionage, and had given the Americans secret military information and actively aided the Americans during the "Autumn Offensive" and during the U.N. occupation of North Korea in the autumn of 1951; 3) had plotted, on September 1, 1952, a *coup dètat* in North Korea by mobilizing the South Korean communist partisan units; and 4) planned to form a new government with Pak Hŏn-yŏng as Premier and Chu Nyŏng-ha and Chang Shi-u as Vice-Premiers in order to establish "capitalist domination in the country." [37]

It should be noted that Chu and Chang were native communists who had cooperated with Kim Il-sŏng in his early days in North Korea. But now, according to the indictment, they were involved in this anti-Kim Il-sŏng plot. According to a communist source, all of the twelve "confessed to the serious crimes they committed." [38] They were convicted by the court as charged, and all but two were sentenced to death on the fourth day of the trial. The two were Yun Sŭng-tal and Yi Wŏn-cho. Yun was sentenced to 15 years imprisonment and Yi received 12 years. It was on December 15, 1955, nearly two-and-a-half years after this trial that the alleged leader of the convicted twelve, Pak Hŏn-yŏng was brought to trial at a "secret military court." It lasted one day. Pak was accused of having been a Japanese spy from the late 1920's until 1945. According to the charge, he then came to North Korea on "orders" of the United States and worked to disrupt the "communist revolutionary movement" from the inside by "espionage, subversion, murder and terror." He was sentenced to death. [39]

However, the communist account of the "crimes" of Pak Hŏn-yŏng and the twelve men is unconvincing. Pak Hŏn-yŏng had been praised even by his nationalist enemies as a "splendid" or "genuine" communist revolutionary. The destructive activities carried out in South Korea, in which Pak and the twelve had played a leading role, makes it difficult for one to believe the charge that they were American spies. They fled South Korea and came to the north, not on "orders from their American masters," but because they were first wanted by the American authorities and then, later, by the South Korean government. The downfall of the "democratic forces" in South Korea itself was brought about by the American Military Government and the South Korean government. In South Korea, during the first year of the American occupation, communists were allowed to carry their activities openly, and it was easy for the authorities to trace them. Following the ban on communist activities by the American Military Governor, General Hodge, in September 1946, the communists continued their agitation, thus exposing themselves dangerously. During the three-month occupation of South Korea by North Korean troops, all hidden leftists openly emerged, making their identities known. When the North Korean troops were driven back, these South Korean leftists were either arrested by the South Korean authorities or fled to the north.[40] This marked the almost total destruction of leftist forces in South Korea.

The accusation that the twelve planned to overthrow the North Korean government by mobilizing the South Korean partisan units also appears untenable. According to South Korean sources, as of late 1952 there were up to 11 thousand South Korean partisans being trained in North Korea for guerrilla activities in the south. Yi Sŭng-yŏp was then the Minister of Justice in the North Korean cabinet and Secretary of the Central Committee of the Korean Workers' Party. The remainder of the accused were in charge of the South Korean partisan units mentioned above. Although these partisans consisted exclusively of South Koreans, their activities were under the direction and control of the Korean Workers' Party and the partisans were by no means in a position to move secretly in order to topple Kim Il-sŏng's North Korean government.[41] With the validity of the North Korean charges in doubt, it becomes necessary to seek the cause of the trials elsewhere.

While in South Korea, the twelve had been among the most trusted lieutenants of Pak Hŏn-yŏng, first in the Korean Communist Party, and then in the South Korean Workers' Party. As has already been noted, immediately after the liberation of Korea in 1945, Pak Hŏn-yŏng maintained an attitude of superiority toward Kim Il-sŏng in the north. Pak opposed the establishment of the North Korean Central (Communist) Bureau in October 1945 for fear that this would endanger his ambition for central leadership throughout Korea. In early

1946, Kim Il-sŏng advanced a proposal for a joint conference of the communist leaders to discuss an amalgamation of the North and South Korean Communist Parties. This proposal was rejected by Pak Hŏn-yŏng because he and his followers regarded their organization in Seoul as the central headquarters, and they did not see the need for the conference.[42] Even after his flight to North Korea in September 1946, Pak's attitude toward the North Korean communists apparently did not change.[43] It was only in June, 1949, that Pak was finally forced to amalgamate his South Korean Workers' Party with the North Korean Workers' Party, assuming a vice-chairmanship of the newly formed Korean Workers' Party headed by Kim Il-sŏng. By then, apparently Pak had to abandon the attitude of superiority he had once maintained towards Kim Il-sŏng. With this background, it is not difficult to imagine the secret maneuvering for power in the Korean Workers' Party between former members of the two different factions. It was complicated by the outbreak of the Korean War, the initiation of negotiation for armistice, and its subsequent conclusion.

When the Russian delegate to the United Nations proposed an armistice on June 23, 1951, North Korean leaders must have thought that Russia would not support their idea of unification by war. At the time the belligerents had been fighting positional battles roughly along the 38th Parallel, indicating that neither side was able or willing to conquer enemy territory. Already the United States, the major ally of South Korea, had made it clear that she would not carry the war again beyond the 38th Parallel. On April 11, 1951, the Commander of the United Nations forces, MacArthur, an advocate of complete victory throughout the Korean peninsula, was dismissed by President Truman.[44] The fact remained that North Korea, from the summer of 1951, was in no position to prosecute the war alone. Because of the intensity of enemy air raids, most of her industry had been destroyed during the first 18 months of the war, and she suffered a heavy loss of man power.[45] Thereafter, it was because of the presence of Chinese Communist "Volunteers" and Russian material aid that North Korea could continue fighting. It was under such circumstances that the talk for a cease-fire went on. By May, 1952, both sides had reached agreement on all issues except the disposition of communist prisoners of war. As a result, North Korean leaders were said to have been convinced that the fighting would shortly stop at the 38th Parallel.[46]

There was a further positive sign for eventual settlement of the war. It came from the communist side. On August 18, 1952, two weeks prior to the alleged day set for the uprising led by the twelve, a Chinese delegation, headed by Chou En-lai, Chinese Premier and Foreign Minister, arrived in Moscow for a series of meetings with top Soviet officials.[47] Western observers believed that Korea was the number one topic, and they even speculated that the leaders of the two countries would arrive at an agreement to terminate the Korean conflict.[48] Although the armistice talk stalled from October 1952 until March of next year, mainly over the question of prisoners of war, and although the fighting continued, Communist China was then believed to have little desire to prolong the military conflict longer.

Toward the end of 1952, Peking was maintaining over a million troops of her own in North Korea and her economy was strained. China had plunged into the Korean War scarcely one year after the proclamation of the People's Republic of China, following years of continuous civil and foreign wars. Confronted with a choice between continued internal economic strain with the possibility of a whole-scale war with the United States, the fledgling Peking regime apparently decided to choose a divided Korea and the guaranteed security of her own northern frontier. In March 1953, Peking proposed the resumption of full-scale armistice talks. The communists appeared "more anxious than they had been hitherto to reach an agreement," [49] virtually giving in on "almost every disputed issue" that had blocked the talks.[50] Eventually, the truce was signed on July 27, 1953.

From Pak Hŏn-yŏng's viewpoint, the conclusion of armistice agreement meant that he was finished as an important contender for power, since it meant the permanent loss of his political base in the south. In this frustrating situation, Pak and the twelve towards the end of 1952 were said to have advocated that unification be achieved by the continued use of force, calling the Armistice Agreement a policy of appeasement.[51] In retrospect, then, the Fifth Plenum and the subsequent "Thought Examination Meetings" were measures to tighten the party's control over the rank-and-file members as well as to create the right atmosphere to move against former members of the South Korean Workers' Party who would not accept the new party line of "peaceful unification." It was in such atmosphere that Pak Hŏn-yŏng and the twelve were arrested secretly in December,

1952.[52] Pak's post as Foreign Minister was filled by Nam Il, a Soviet Korean and Chief of the Armistice delegates at Panmunjom.[53]

In their final deadly move against the South Korean communists, however, Kim Il-sŏng and his associates had other considerations besides the seizure of power and differences over war policy. The North Koreans had kept the South Korean communists in the north for several years ultimately to utilize them in the south when all of Korea came under communism. But with an armistice imminent and the hope of the communist domination of the whole of Korea remote, the communists from the south lost their usefulness in the eyes of the North Korean leaders. Another consideration was to find a scapegoat for the failure in the war, although North Korea has never acknowledged this. Altogether, North Korea suffered a tremendous loss in human lives and materials. Implicit in the indictment were that North Korean troops were forced to retreat from South Korea, the north was invaded by enemy forces and finally failed in achieving her goal of unification because of the subversion of the twelve. In the end, the mass purge was intended to serve a variety of purposes for Kim Il-sŏng and his followers.

While the leaders of the South Korean Workers' Party were in confinement, the Armistice Agreement was finally signed on July 27, 1953. The next day Kim Il-sŏng announced over the radio his regime's acceptance of the agreement, saying that "the signing of the truce means . . . the first step toward achieving the peaceful settlement of the Korean question." [54] On August 5th, the third day of the trial of the twelve, the Sixth Plenum of the Central Committee of the Korean Workers' Party opened a five-day session. At the meeting, Kim Il-sŏng praised the Armistice Agreement as a positive first step toward "peaceful unification" and said that the Agreement indicated North Korea's "victory" in the war. Throughout his speech, Kim mentioned the existence of anti-party elements who were still working for the prolongation of the war, thus supporting unification by military forces. The correct line of the party, according to Kim, was to reconstruct and consolidate North Korea as a "solid democratic basis for peaceful unification" of Korea and to force the withdrawal of "American imperialism" by fomenting social revolution in the south.[55] Kim never publicly acknowledged failure in the war but implied that Pak Hŏn-yŏng and his followers were to blame for North Korea's lack of success in unification.[56]

During the five-day session of the Sixth Plenum it was formally announced that Pak Hŏn-yŏng, who was then in confinement, was expelled from the party. At the conference it was also declared that Chu Nyŏng-ha, who had been just recalled from his ambassadorship to Moscow, and Chang Shi-u, the Minister of Commerce, and other native veteran communists were expelled from the Central Committee as well as the party because of alleged "anti-party" and "anti-state" activities. As a result, any political influence exercised by the native communist leaders was eliminated. On the 15-member Presidium of the Central Committee that was reconstructed at the plenum were four former Korean communist guerrillas in Manchuria (Kim Il-sŏng, Kim Il, Kim Kwang-hyŏp, and Pak Kŭm-ch'ŏl), four Soviet Koreans (Pak Ch'ang-ok, Pak Yŏng-bin, Kim Sŭng-hwa, and Nam Il), two men from Yenan (Kim Tu-bong and Ch'oe Ch'ang-ik), and five native communists (Pak Chŏng-ae, Ch'oe Wŏn-t'aek, Chŏng Il-yong, Kim Hwang-il, and Kang Mun-sŏk). The five native communists owed their political eminence to their cooperation and collaboration with the ten foreign returnees, who dominated the new presidium. From among the 15 persons, a seven-member Politburo was elected. Members of the new Politburo were Kim Il-sŏng, Kim Tu-bong, Pak Chŏng-ae, Pak Ch'ang-ok, Kim Il, Pak Kŭm-ch'ŏl, and Pak Yŏng-bin. Only Kim Il-sŏng and Kim Tu-bong had served on the previous Politburo and the other five were new faces. Kim Il-sŏng was reelected the Chairman of the Central Committee of the party. The newly elected Vice-Chairmen were Pak Ch'ang-ok, Pak Chŏng-ae and Kim Il.[57]

Having excised the prominent native communists from the central party leadership, the North Korean communists moved to "uproot all the poisonous aftereffects" of the purge. To this end, immediately prior to and following the Seventh Plenum of the Party Central Committee held December 18–19, 1953, there were again held numerous "Thought Examination Meetings." Rank and file party members were urged once more to study Kim's speech delivered at the Fifth Plenum in December 1952 and to examine their party loyalty. In this process, masses of communists from South Korea were expelled or demoted from their posts in government and social organizations in North Korea.[58] Having eliminated the South Korean communist forces, the North Korean leaders finally, on December 15, 1955, "tried" Pak Hŏn-yŏng, who had been in solitary confinement, and sentenced him to death, thus ending the long-drawn-out struggle for power between the northern and southern communists.

For Kim Il-sŏng and his group, the Korean War time was crucial in establishing their position. It was during this period they facilitated the process of the monopolization of power by eliminating Mu-Jŏng, Hŏ Kai, and Pak Hŏn-yŏng. Though the country was left in ruins, the former guerrillas from Manchuria emerged from the war stronger than ever. The mass purges of the South Korean communists, however, had an important effect upon the subsequent molding of North Korean communism. During the post-liberation period in South Korea, communism had considerable appeal among intellectuals. Sizable segments of the liberal South Korean academic, literary, and artistic community had joined the communist movement, and they had played an important role in the entire South Korean leftist movement of the post-liberation period. Their destruction through the war and by purges deprived Korean communism of the chance to develop into an intellectually oriented, more liberal movement.

The liberalizing impact of intellectuals was tellingly felt in the developments within the Communist Party of Czechoslovakia between 1963 and the Soviet invasion of August, 1968. During this period the communist party in Czechoslovakia, urged by liberal members in the top hierarchy as well as by writers, artists, and scholars among its rank-and-file, veered toward less restrictive policies. This finally culminated in the "Prague Spring" of 1968 under Alexander Dubcek. Conversely, the Workers' Party of Albania (the Albanian communist party) under Enver Hoxha has been ruling the country in the Stalinist manner for nearly three decades without serious disruption. This is partly due to the party's early and systematic purges of veteran communists, mostly Western-educated, when it came to firm control of the country (1941–44). This policy was continued well into the late 1950's and early 1960's, and even today the party maintains tight control over what few intellectuals the country still possesses. Obviously, the presence or absence of a significant number of intellectuals in a cmmmunist party affects the quality and policy inclination of its leadership in opposite directions. Because of their belief in their critical role, the intellectuals would resist a tight Stalinist communist party structure since it would (among other things) smother the function of intellectuals. The strong presence of intellectuals in a party inevitably brings about decentralization of party authority and other forms of pluralism. Clearly, their party loyalty would appear dubious in the eyes of Stalinist communists such as Kim Il-sŏng, Enver Hoxha, and the Czechoslovakian communist leaders who monopolized the party posts following the Soviet invasion of August 1968.

8.

THE LAST PHASE
OF THE
INTRA-PARTY STRUGGLE

FOLLOWING THE ARMISTICE, THE NORTH KOREAN REGIME IM-
mediately addressed itself to the task of rebuilding the war-torn
economy. In a speech given by Kim on August 5, 1953 at the Sixth
Plenum of the Korean Workers' Party, the general line for the
post-war economic reconstruction was "the priority development
of heavy industry with the simultaneous development of light industry
and agriculture." [1] Subsequently, Kim's speech became the basis of
the First Three-Year Economic Plan (1954–56). [2] This industrial reconstruction was to be financed mainly by internal savings, [3] but
with some aid from the Soviet Union, Communist China, and other
Communist bloc nations as well. [4] Some three-fourths of the total
capital investment between 1954 and 1956 was allocated to heavy
industry; one-quarter of the total investment went to agriculture
and the production of consumer goods. [5] In agriculture, according
to Kim, collectivization was to be introduced into "certain areas
for experimental purposes" beginning in 1954. This was the beginning
of collective farms in a countryside that had been a land of predominantly individual farms. [6] Scarcely one year after the "experimental"
period, the regime decided to carry out the total collectivization
of private farms in North Korea after a new speech by Kim Il-sŏng
on agricultural policy made at a plenum of the Central Committee
held on November 3, 1954. [7] The speech was epoch-making since
Kim now formally expressed his determination to exterminate private
landownership and put all land into state-controlled collective farms.

Because of an intensive campaign carried out by the party, the number of farming families joining the collective farms increased steadily. In November 1954, 21.5 percent of all North Korean farming families were members of collective farms. By December of that same year, the number grew to 31.8 percent; by the end of 1955, to 49 percent; and to 65.6 percent in February 1956.[8] Thereafter, the regimentation of agricultural life continued. While industrial recovery and collectivization were proceeding rapidly, a new political slogan—"Building the Foundation for Socialism"—began to replace the slogan "Execution of Democratic Reforms." Although the "democratic reforms" themselves were implicitly socialistic, the North Korean communists had refrained from calling them so, lest it might frighten the people away.[9] The appearance of the new slogan, first put forth in April 1955, was an indication that the regime was determined to move further leftwards.

Amidst its effort for industrial recovery and socialization of agriculture, the party moved to tighten its control over the state-owned commercial enterprises that accounted for 71.9 percent of the total North Korean commercial activities as of late 1954.[10] In this connection, on April 4, 1955, Kim delivered a speech at a plenum of the Central Committee, in which he urged that a "confession movement" be started among the employees of the governmental commercial organs to "single out corrupt and wasteful elements and to punish them by law." [11] In response to this call, there were formed in May of 1955 numerous "Committees for the Struggle Against Corrupt and Wasteful Officials" throughout North Korea. The activities of the committees lasted for several months, during which period not only many employees in the government-owned trade organs but also numerous officials in other institutions "confessed" their past undesirable acts such as embezzlement of public funds, wastefulness, or bribery.[12] Those whose crimes were light were either expelled or demoted and sent to labor camps. Those whose crimes were grave were imprisoned, and some even were said to have received capital punishment from "people's courts." [13] By these acts the regime not only purged its various institutions of politically undesirable elements but also obtained an additional labor force, badly needed for the execution of the three-year economic plan. Simultaneously, the regime acted to reduce what remained of the private sector that accounted for 32.5 percent of North Korea's total commercial activities in 1953.[14] The reduction was brought about by tax and price

[102]

controls under the pretext of "limiting the development of capitalist elements." [15] It was said that the taxes imposed upon private tradesmen were "ridiculously" high, so that they had no choice but to leave their property in the hands of the government for the payment of taxes. [16] Under the mounting pressure, private business fell to 28 per cent at the end of 1954; and in late 1956, the share of private commerce further dwindled to 12.7 per cent, mostly consisting of the sale of surplus crops. [17] Those who were driven out of their trade had to either join the state-run stores or become laborers.

With the completion of the three-year economic plan less than eight months away, the Third Congress of the Korean Workers' Party convened from April 23 to 29, 1956. There, Chairman Kim, in his Report, declared the First Five-Year Economic Plan would be launched in 1957. [18] As in the three-year plan, the development of heavy industry was to play a leading role, with some 80 per cent of the total capital investment in industry to be allocated for this purpose. During the period of the five-year economic plan the socialist sector in every economic field was to be further expanded, and specifically the collectivization of agriculture was to be completed within the shortest possible time. [19] The Third Congress, in accordance with the new socialist themes, adopted a new party constitution. It had this to say about the character of the party:

[It] . . . is the revolutionary inheritor of the Korean people who fought against the Japanese and other colonists for national independence [and it *accepts Marxism-Leninism as its guiding principle.*

Regarding the party's programs the constitution enunciated that the Party would "pursue the smooth execution of *the construction of socialism . . . aiming ultimately at the realization of the construction of a communist society throughout the whole of Korea."* [20]

The basic tone of the three-year and the five-year economic plans by no means had the approval of all the party elite. On the contrary, it was decided by Kim Il-sŏng and his close associates, despite the opposition of Yenan and Soviet Koreans. Because of the stress on basic industry during the three-year plan, it was said that the production of consumer goods was almost at a standstill, producing far less than needed for the inhabitants who had been suffering an acute shortage of food and other necessities. [21] The hardship of the people was further increased by the regime's intensive labor procurement drive as well as by the crop failure caused by a typhoon in the autumn of 1954. [22] Although the three-year economic plan was quite

[103]

a success in reconstructing basic industry, the living condition of the people was "not made easier by it." [23] In spite of all this, the five-year economic plan was to proceed along the same general lines.

The heavy emphasis on basic industry became a cause of an intra-party dispute in 1953, when decisions were being made on the allocation of funds to each field of industry. The Yenan and Soviet Koreans opposed the party line set by Kim Il-sŏng and asked that more emphasis be put on the development of light industry and the agricultural sector. Following Kim's announcement of the five-year economic plan at the Third Party Congress, the opposition within the party circle was further increased.[24] Some of Kim's opponents were against the rapid collectivization on the ground that it would impede the future unification of the country since it might scare land-hungry peasants in South Korea away from communism.[25] Others contended that collectivization was impossible since North Korea was not producing any farm machinery at the time, and still others argued that the pace of collectivization was too fast. These latter pointed to the much slower process that had taken place in the Soviet Union in the late 1920's and in the 1930's.[26]

Arguing against the virtual expropriation of the capital of small private businessmen, the Yenan Koreans advocated the institution of more moderate methods of transformation of the private business sector into a socialistic sector. They suggested paying compensation to those merchants who voluntarily joined the cooperatives—a practice carried out in Communist China.[27] They proposed that small businessmen be given sufficient time to resettle themselves without drastic discomfort. The Yenan Koreans were said to have gained the upper hand for a brief time during the early months of 1956, when Yun Kong-hŭm, the Minister of Commerce, demoted or expelled some of his subordinates in his department who imposed excessive taxes on private businessmen.[28]

Adding their voice to the general clamor, some Soviet Koreans urged that North Korea do away with the militant anti-American slogans and relax the extreme tension that was permeating every corner of North Korean life.[29] They were encouraged by the new Kremlin leaders' tendency to relax on domestic policies and international affairs following the death of Stalin in March 1953.

Among Kim's opponents in the Yenan group were Ch'oe Ch'ang-ik and Yun Kong-hŭm (Minister of Commerce and a member of the Central Committee of the party) and among the Soviet Koreans were Pak Ch'ang-ok and Pak Yŏng-bin (a member of the Central Committee and the Director of the Organization and Guidance Department of the party).[30] Although the influence of the Soviet Koreans appeared to have diminished following the withdrawal of the Soviet occupation forces, their political strength remained substantial thanks to the new Kremlin leaders' support. On the other hand, the influence of the Yenan Koreans was said to have been substantially increased due to the stationing of the Chinese troops in North Korea during the war.[31] The Chinese continued to remain in North Korea, even after the Armistice Agreement was signed, though their number began gradually to decline.[32] In any case, beyond consideration of the external factors that contributed to the maintenance of the political strength of these opposition leaders, they were able to maintain their powerful positions by dint of their own merit. Their close cooperation with Kim Il-sŏng in 1953 had helped him to eliminate the former native communist leaders. It was said that the contribution made by Pak Ch'ang-ok was the greatest, and it was because of the service that he was made a vice-chairman of the party in August 1953. He was even considered to be No. 2 man in North Korea after the purge of Hŏ Kai.[33]

Kim's opponents were emboldened when Khrushchev revealed his startling policy changes at the 20th Congress of the Soviet Communist Party in February, 1956. Khrushchev's enunciation of the principles of collective leadership and peaceful coexistence with Western democracies was contrary to the practices of Kim Il-sŏng, who was keeping North Korea under tight control and in a tense atmosphere, very much in the Stalinist manner. Already the new Kremlin leaders had been exerting pressure on Kim to modify his postwar economic programs. Following the 20th Party Congress, the Soviet leaders pressed Kim to adopt the principle of collective leadership, which was tantamount to the abandonment of his near dictatorial position.[34] Under these circumstances, Kim moved to defend his position.

As early as April 4, 1955, at a plenum of the Central Committee of the Party Kim flatly stated that "today each person who came from the Soviet Union, China, or from South Korea must understand that he is one of the members of the Korean Workers' Party." [35] Thus Kim reminded his opponents in the party that their first loyalty was to the Korean Workers' Party, and presumably to him. He also implicitly warned the dissenters not to attempt to obstruct his economic plans whether in alliance with other potential dissenters within the party or with any foreign communist party. Two months later, Kim's domestic foes were obviously heartened by the thawing of the frozen relationship between Moscow and Yugoslavia following the Belgrade talks between the Kremlin leaders and Tito from May 27 to June 2. Prompted by such a development, Kim now openly slashed his opponents, urging that North Korea take an independent course in her national affairs in a speech delivered to the party workers for propaganda and agitation on December 28, 1955. The speech was entitled "On Eradicating Dogmatism and Formalism from Ideological Work and Firmly Establishing the Chuch 'e (Self-Image, Self-Independence or Self-Reliance)." [36]

The speech's opening portion was devoted to a review of past ideological problems of the party. Kim criticized the propagandists and agitators because they had fallen into "dogmatism and formalism" by mechnically imitating others without making an attempt to apply themselves "creatively to peculiar Korean conditions." As a result, the speaker continued, Korean characteristics had been neglected and a Korean "self-image" had not been established. [37] Recalling a past "futile" intra-party dispute over political methods to be employed within the North Korean People's Army, Kim declared:

> The important thing is to master revolutionary truth, Marxist-Leninist truth, and to apply it to the actual conditions of Korea. We cannot have an imperative principle of doing [everything] just as the Soviet Union does. Although certain people say that the Soviet way is best or that the Chinese way is best, have we not now reached the point we can construct our own way? [38]

Kim branded the Soviet Koreans and Yenan Koreans as "dogmatists and formalists." Proclaiming that "our revolution should be carried out by ourselves," Kim urged members of the audience to "construct our own way" and to "firmly establish a self-image." [39] Kim asked the party propagandists and agitators to begin the task by first studying Korean revolutionary history.

Concerning the "peculiar Korean conditions," Kim mentioned two controversial issues of the moment, which were the question of collectivization and the militant anti-Americanism. On both issues he denounced his opponents and rationalized his policies. According to Kim, the rapidity of the collectivization process was natural because:

> the Korean farmers had been trained politically and their revolutionary spirit had developed highly through their peasant movement during the Japanese time and then their participation in the democratic construction after the liberation. [40]

[106]

On the second issue, Kim answered Soviet Korean Pak Yŏng-bin's proposal that North Korea should deemphasize its strong anti-American slogans with the charge that this not only had "no common ground with revolutionary creativity," but it would paralyze the Korean people's "revolutionary awareness." [41] He explained that the situation in Korea and the Soviet Union differed because the southern half of Korea was "still being forcibly occupied by the Koreans' unforgivable enemy [Americans]" whereas no part of Russian territory was under foreign occupation in the late 1920's and early 1930's. Once more Kim branded his opponents in the party as adherents of dogmatism and formalism who merely followed foreign examples, especially those of the Soviet Union. Kim's rationalization of his policy on the swift collectivization of agricultural life, however, was groundless and self-contradictory.

Many Korean farmers had participated in the communist-instigated peasant movement during the Japanese occupation because they were primarily lured by the promise that they would become landowners once a new society was established. The Korean peasants' desire to possess land was so deep-rooted that the Korean communists raised only the banner, "Land to Tillers!" Never before had they advocated collectivization in which the peasants would turn into employees of the state. However, the threat of collectivization in a communist society had been utilized by the Japanese authorities as well as by Korean nationalists to discourage peasants from following communists. The popularity of the North Korean regime among the farmers in its early stage was largely a result of swift land reform whereby the peasants were made private landowners, although, to be sure, certain restrictions were imposed upon the exercise of their landownership. Recognizing the deep desire of the peasants to remain landowners, "some comrades" in the party, as acknowledged by Kim Il-sŏng, opposed even the thought of collectivization.[42]

The contradictory nature of Kim's statement was revealed in his assertion that rapid collectivization was "natural," because, at the Fourth Congress of the party in September 1961, Kim confessed that "socialist transformation in our country was accompanied by bitter class struggle in towns and villages." [43]

Thus the rather unsubstantiated argument for collectivization along with his denunciation of those who said that "the Soviet way is best" or "the Chinese way is best" was an effort on Kim's part to appeal to the patriotism of the North Koreans for support of his policies. Although the speech was not openly anti-Soviet in tone, Kim made clear his determination to continue his drastic policies, even at the risk of displeasing the Kremlin leadership. It is significant that Kim's emphasis on Korean characteristics which implied an independent road for North Korea preceded by two months Khrushchev's call for different roads to socialism at the 20th Congress of the CPSU. Referring back to his speech of December 28, 1955, Kim not only defended his post-war recovery programs, but also intimated that his opponents would be removed from their positions and the vacancies filled by his old comrades from the Manchurian days. According to Kim,

> because many comrades have neglected things Korean and Korean revolutionary history, they do not know how to respect revolutionaries [implying Kim's own followers]. As a result, many of these revolutionaries have been living in obscurity, without being awarded posts worthy of their merits.[44]

Among Kim's opponents whose influence had declined between 1954 and early 1956 were two Yenan Koreans, Pak Il-u and Ch'oe Ch'ang-ik, and two Soviet Koreans, Pak Ch'ang-ok and Kim Yŏl.[45] Pak Il-u had become Minister of Interior in September 1948, had served as a member of the Seven-Man Military Committee during the Korean War and had been a member of the Central Committee of the Party since August 1946. However, he was demoted from the ministership of the Interior to the ministership of Communications in March 1953, and subsequently he lost even that post in November 1955. The following month, at a plenum of the Central Committee, he was expelled from the party altogether because of his "factionalist and anti-party" activities.[46] Ch'oe Ch'ang-ik, a member of the Politburo of the party, a vice-premier and the Minister of Finance, was relieved of his ministership on November 18, 1954, after serving two years, the post being taken over by a relatively obscure native communist leader, Yi Chu-yŏn. There was no official reason given.[47] Pak Ch'ang-ok was relieved of his vice-chairmanship in the party in March 1954 and was made a vice-premier as well as the chairman of the State Planning Commission, which controlled the overall national economic plans.[48] However, Pak lost the chairmanship on the commission in January 1956, and in May of that year he became Minister of the Machine Building Industry. There were no official explanations given regarding his transfers and demotions. Kim Yŏl, following his return from the Soviet Union, had advanced steadily both in the party and the government. It should be remembered that at the Second Party Congress in March 1948 he joined Kim Il-sŏng in denouncing prominent native communists. Subsequently, in May of that year, Kim Yŏl was appointed a vice-minister of the State Inspection Department, in September was made a member of the presidium of the party, and in May of 1954 became a vice-minister of Department of Heavy Industry. Finally in February 1955, he became Chairman of the Hwanghae Provincial Party. This was the peak of his official career. Shortly afterwards he was demoted to an obscure managerial post of a local state-owned commercial enterprise. While occupying that post, Kim was sentenced to an eight-year prison term at a local "people's court" in September 1955, in the midst of the "confesssion movement," for rape and his alleged embezzlement of public funds. At a plenum of the Central Committee held in December 1955, he was finally expelled altogether from the party charged with having engaged in "factionalist and anti-party" activities.

It is not difficult to imagine that Kim Il-sŏng, who had been busily purging his opponents, perceived the threat to his political career in the series of ideological innovations, disclosed by Khrushchev at the 20th Congress of the Communist Party of the Soviet Union held in Moscow from February 14 to 25, 1956. Though Khrushchev's speech [49] was summarized and editorially endorsed in the North Korean party news organ, *Nodong Shinmun*, the paper was silent on the collective leadership principle. [50] It was not until April 2, 1956, when *Nodong Shinmun* translated *verbatim* a *Pravda* editorial of March 28 on "Why Is The Cult of the Individual Alien to the Spirit of Marxism-Leninism," [51] that the principle of de-stalinization became publicly known in North Korea. Two days after the appearance in Peking in the *Jen Min Jih Pao* on April 5, 1956 of an editorial "On Historical Experience Concerning The Dictatorship of the Proletariat," which was interpreted as an open refutation of the destalinization campaign by a Japanese observer,[52] *Nodong Shinmun* for the first time on April 7 editorialized on collective leadership:

> ... The collective principle in the guiding role of the party is of immense practical significance. Therefore the Central Committee of our Party, heedful of repeated emphasis of Comrade Kim Il-sŏng on the matter, has done its utmost to observe rigorously the Leninist principle of collec-

tive leadership in order to stimulate intra-party democracy, criticism, and self-criticism, and further to maintain close ties with masses.

Considering the events that were taking place inside the party, these remarks were, however, merely aimed at "staving off" the possible charge that Kim Il-sŏng was guilty of the Stalinist error.[53] It was during this potentially unsettling period for the North Korean regime that the Third Congress of the Korean Workers' Party opened its seven-day session in P'yŏngyang on April 23, 1956, attended by 914 representatives. Conspicuously enough, Kim Il-sŏng's portrait, which had been "a permanent fixture in public gatherings and places" in North Korea was lacking.[54]

At the Congress, Chairman Kim Il-sŏng reviewed the Korean communist movement during the Japanese time. He mentioned that the Korean Communist Party formed in 1925 was destroyed in 1928 because of "anti-Marxian factionalism within the party" and the brutal suppression of the Japanese authorities.[55] In the 1930's, there emerged "genuine communists" who engaged in armed struggle against the Japanese and who subsequently led "the masses" in their anti-Japanese movement. [56] Although Kim did not say explicitly, subsequent political developments made it obvious that he considered the "genuine communists" his guerrillas of the Manchurian days. According to Kim:

> The Korean people's anti-Japanese struggle for national independence, carried out under the leadership of these genuine communists, prepared the foundation for the future establishment of a Marxist-Leninist party in Korea, and it also became the shining tradition of our revolutionary movement.[57]

Kim now hinted that he and his Manchurian guerrillas alone were the communist revolutionaries during the Japanese occupation of Korea and, further, that he and his followers were the sole architects of the Korean communist revolutionary movement. Kim urged the gathering to engage in the task of "firmly establishing a self-image" by enlightening party members, school children and all the other North Koreans with "the noble revolutionary tradition." In order to accomplish this, Kim specifically mentioned the necessity of writing "our revolutionary history" by collecting hitherto neglected source materials.[58]

Kim's statements regarding his past partisan activities were the most self-aggrandizing thus far. They were also strongly suggestive that he and his close associates be accorded the highest honor in North Korea. His forceful assertion that Korea take an independent road was strengthened by the "different roads to socialism" policy suggested by Russian leaders at their 20th party congress, although the Soviets may not have intended their statement to be taken so literally. Yet, about the crucial issue of collective leadership which would have had such grave effect upon his political fortune, Kim Il-sŏng did not say a single word. He and his associates, however, paid lip service to the principle of collective leadership by including it in the party constitution adopted at the Third Congress. Article 25 of the constitution read that every party organ should carry out its activities "firmly based upon Lenin's principle of collective leadership." [59] Thus Kim was still obliged to comply at least outwardly with the principle of collective leadership.

On the last day of the seven-day meeting the 914 "party representatives" elected 71 regular and 45 candidate members of the Central Committee.[60] Among the former 67 Central Committee members selected at the Second Party Congress in March 1948, only 29 were reelected to the new 71-member Central Committee. The remainder, except Kim Ch'aek who had been killed in action during the Korean War, were all presumably victims of purges.[61] The new Central Committee elected 11 persons from among its own members to the newly-established Standing Committee of the party. This Standing Committee replaced the previous two separate organs, the Presidium and the Politburo, and it was to "guide" the Central Committee between the latter's plenums.[62] Of the eleven, five were former Korean guerrillas from Manchuria (Kim Il-sŏng, Ch'oe Yong-kŏn,[63] Kim Il, Pak Kŭm-ch'ŏl, and Kim Kwang-hyŏp), two pro-Kim Il-sŏng native leaders (Pak Chŏng-ae and Chŏng Il-yong), two Yenan Koreans (Kim Tu-bong and Ch'oe Ch'ang-ik), and the remaining two were Soviet Koreans (Rim Hae and Nam Il).[64] It should be noted that except Ch'oe Yong-kŏn who joined the party at the Third Party Congress for the first time, six of the seven members of the Kim Il-sŏng faction (the five former guerrillas from Manchuria and two pro-Kim native leaders) on the Standing Committee had been elected to the 15-member Presidium of the Central Committee at the time of the reorganization of the party high councils in August 1953. Their election to the Standing Committee at the Third Party Congress was apparently an indication that they were secure in their positions of growing political influence. The two Yenan Koreans, Kim and

Ch'oe, though awarded posts on the Standing Committee, were believed to have possessed no real political power. The two Soviet Koreans, Pak Ch'ang-ok and Pak Yŏng-bin, who had been elected to the seven-member Politburo in August 1953, failed to be reelected, a price of their opposition to Kim Il-sŏng. Instead, Nam Il, who had served on the previous 15-member presidium, and a new Soviet Korean, Rim Hae, were elected to the Standing Committee. The members of the Central Committee also elected the chairman and five vice-chairmen of the Central Committee. Kim Il-sŏng, naturally, was again elected the Chairman of the party. The five newly-elected Vice-Chairmen were Ch'oe Yong'kŏn, Pak Chŏng-ae, Pak Kŭm-ch'ŏl, Chŏng Il-yong, and Kim Ch'ang-man (Yenan Korean).[65] Except Pak Chŏng-ae, who became a vice-chairman in August 1953, all were newly elected to be vice-chairmen, all the five including Kim Ch'ang-man had been loyal to Kim Il-sŏng.

About a month after the Third Party Congress, Kim Il-sŏng went on a trip to the Soviet Union, Mongolia, and the East European communist countries, entrusting affairs at home to his faithful lieutenants.[66] During Kim's absence, secret maneuverings began among Yenan and Soviet Koreans to rally anti-Kim Il-sŏng forces. The leading Yenan Koreans in this move were Ch'oe Ch'ang-ik, Yun Kong-hŭm, Sŏ Hi (Chairman of the Trade Union Association and a member of the Central Committee of the party), and Yi Pil-kyu (a bureau chief of the Ministry of Construction and a member of the Central Committee of the party). Among the Soviet Koreans who were actively involved in this plot were Pak Ch'ang-ok and Kim Sŭng-hwa (Minister of Construction and a member of the Central Committee of the party). They were believed to have obtained the sympathy of the Soviet Ambassador in P'yŏngyang,[67] and the North Korean Ambassador to Moscow, Yi Sang-cho (Yenan Korean) was to negotiate for a concrete endorsement of the anti-Kim move from the Kremlin leaders.[68] All these men had come to the realization that the former guerrillas from Manchuria were intent ultimately on monopolizing power. They also knew that with the newly-elected party leadership at the Third Party Congress there would be no hope of changing the austere economic policies.

Meanwhile, a *Nodong Shinmun* editorial of July 16, 1956, entitled "Collective Leadership and Centralized Control," reacted to the growing dissatisfaction with Kim's position, or rather lack of position. The editorial contended that the collective leadership consisted of

[112]

two elements, intra-party democracy and centralized control, and inferred the latter to mean control from above, that is, dictatorial rule by Kim. While endorsing outright the CPSU's stand on the cult of the individual, the editorial equated it with "sectarianism that expresses itself in an intra-party struggle for hegemony." A commentator was later led to state that "from this novel interpretation it followed that any move to undermine Kim's authority was tantamount to an expression of [a] personality cult." [69] Shortly after Kim's return from his trip, *Nodong Shinmun* on August 1, 1956 again editorialized on the subject of collective leadership, stating that Kim, too, like the Kremlin leadership, was opposed to a personality cult. But the paper stressed that opposition to the cult of the individual should not become an obstacle in a fair evaluation of "the enormous contributions made by Stalin . . . to the success of the execution of socialist revolution . . . in Soviet Russia as well as to the international proletarian movement." Cautioning the potentially disruptive effect of the de-Stalinization campaign on the solidarity of the Communist camp, the *Nodong Shinmun* editorial warned that disunity existed in the wishful thinking of "the enemies of socialism" rather than in "the real Communist bloc affairs." The commentator previously mentioned was again led to remark that "in sum, while paying lip service to the CPSU decisions, the Korean Workers' Party showed no sign of translating them into action." [70] All this while, however, the anti-Kim forces persevered in their efforts to reverse the trend toward one-man rule and Kim's stringent economic policies.

A direct challenge to Kim Il-sŏng came at a plenum of the Central Committee of the party held for two days, August 30–31, 1956. At the plenum Kim was severely criticized by his opponents, who reportedly characterized Kim's policies as "anti-people." The attack was believed to have been spearheaded by six persons: Yun Konghŭm, Ch'oe Ch'ang-ik, Sŏ Hi, Pak Ch'ang-ok, Kim Sŭng-hwa and Yi Pil-kyu. [71] However, the revolt was subdued. Three opposition leaders (Yun Kong-hŭm, Sŏ Hi, and Yi Pil-kyu) were said to have fled to Manchuria across the Yalu River on the afternoon of the first day of the meeting, and the remaining three were arrested by Kim Il-sŏng's men. [72] On the second day of the plenary session the six, *in absentia*, were expelled from the party as "anti-party factionalists and destructive elements." All six were also duly "relieved" of their posts in the government. [73] As a result, the insurgency, instead of toppling the Kim Il-sŏng group, gave Kim an opportunity to strengthen himself further. The whole affair has been referred to by North Korean sources "the August Factionalist Incident," and they admitted it was a "crisis" in Kim's political life.

Kim now proceeded to crush the remnants of the opposition. A new blood bath that might have been of the same magnitude as that during the suppression of the Pak Hŏn-yŏng group was believed to have been averted, however, by the intercession of Peking and Moscow. The two governments dispatched P'eng Te-huai and Anastas I. Mikoyan, respectively to P'yŏngyang to urge, right the first time, moderation.[74] Subsequently, the opponents were released from prison and all the six were restored to party membership, but not to their official posts in the party and the government.[75] Kim Il-sŏng, however, would not tolerate the existence of his opponents even though their influence had reached a vanishing point. Consequently, the restoration of party membership turned out to be a temporary measure in order to placate Peking and Moscow.

Preparations for a mass purge of the "August Factionalists" were undertaken by Kim's cohorts immediately after the departure in early September of the two foreign emissaries. The first step toward that end was the reissuance of party identification cards among all members of the Party between late 1956 and the early months of 1957, during which period those who were suspected of having been sympathetic to the revolt of August were checked.[76] Following this, the Central Committee carried out the "Work of the Party's Concentrated Guidance" (Tang Jipjung Jido Sa'ŏp) for some ten months beginning in February 1957. Beginning with the province of P'yŏng'an Namdo, a little over a month was devoted to each of North Korea's nine provinces, during which time the Central Committee "concentrated" its "guidance" on party, government and other institutions. During the ten month period in each province there sprang up numerous "Activists' Meetings" of party members, where agents from the Central Committee denounced "the poisonousness of factionalism," and local followers of the anti-Kim movement in August 1956 were forced to "confess" their "factionalist and anti-revolutionary" activities in order to redeem themselves.[77] These measures were apparently aimed at isolating the leaders of the Yenan and Soviet factions from their local followers. The atmosphere in which the "Activists' Meetings" were held was reminiscent of that in which the "Thought Examination Meetings" were carried out in the spring of 1953, immediately prior to the mass purge of the communist leaders from South Korea.

In the meantime, the communist international scene began to change in favor of the hard line policy of Kim Il-sŏng. The general restiveness and discontent expressed with their leaders in the wake of the de-Stalinization movement finally culminated in the uprisings in Poland in June 1956, and in Hungary in October of the same year.[78] Confronted with such upheavals and their disruptive effects on the once solid world communist movement, the Kremlin leaders apparently began to think over the wisdom of their rather liberal policies. In Communist China the "Hundred Flowers" movement, begun in the spring of 1957 on the regime's own initiative in an attempt to loosen the rigid suppression of opposition opinion, came to an abrupt end within less than a year in the midst of vociferous complaints by intellectuals against their government.

Finally in December 1957 in Moscow the "Conference of 12 Communist and Workers' Parties of Socialist Countries" was held, attended by representatives of the 12 nations including those of North Korea, Communist China and the Soviet Union. The conference adopted a resolution calling for "intensification of the struggle against . . . revisionism and dogmatism and sectarianism" in the ranks of the Communist Parties.[79] According to the resolution, "the main danger" in the contemporary world communist movement was "revisionism" since it was an "international . . . manifestation of bourgeois ideology that demands the preservation or restoration of capitalism." The resolution, however, added that "dogmatism and sectarianism can also be the main danger at different stages of development in one party or another." Dogmatism lacks the "creative application of Marxist-Leninist theory in specific, changing conditions" and it "leads to the Party's isolation from the masses." Finally, it was stated in the resolution that "*each Communist Party determines what danger is the main danger to it at a given time.*" [80] The resolution, which was viewed by an observer as an expression of the intention on the part of world Communist leaders to return to Stalinism,[81] was tantamount to an open pledge from Moscow and Peking, especially from the former, that they would no longer interfere in the intra-party struggle of the Korean Workers' Party.

Presumably encouraged by the changing mood of the Communist world, Kim Il-sŏng finally carried out a mass purge of the "August

Factionalist" as well as all his other former opponents. The purge began in late October 1957 and lasted until early March of the next year, involving some 80 high-ranking officials in the party, the government, and the army as well as eminent persons in academic circles. The majority of the 80 removals were Yenan returnees,[82] among whom were Kim Tu-bong and Ch'oe Ch'ang-ik. At the time he was purged, Kim Tu-bong was merely a member of the Central Committee of the party, having been stripped of his other titles previously.[83] Ch'oe Ch'ang-ik's expulsion, the second one for him, resulted in the permanent loss of his party membership. Among Soviet Koreans, Pak Ch'ang-ok was expelled from the party for a second time, and Pak I-wan was "relieved" of his chairmanship of the State Construction Commission along with his membership on the Central Committee of the party. The vacated chairmanship on the Commission was filled by Kim Ung-sang, a former communist guerrilla from Manchuria.[84] At least twelve Soviet Koreans, all of whom had held at one time or another vice-ministerial posts or the equivalents and some of them even higher positions in the government, were purged because of their involvement in the anti-Kim insurgency of August 1956.[85] As a result, by 1960, all but a few Soviet Koreans had been removed from the scene in North Korea. Among the twelve at least nine subsequently returned to the Soviet Union, a return made possible following an agreement concluded between P'yŏngyang and Moscow on December 16, 1957, whereby persons having dual citizenship were compelled to choose one.[86] O Ki-sŏp, one of the most recalcitrant native communist leaders, was finally expelled from the party and dismissed from his governmental post in February, 1958, after a continued decline of his political influence. At the time of his final purge, O was the Minister of Food Purchase and Administration and also a member of the Central Committee.[87] As a result of the series of these purges, by the time the "First Conference of Party Representatives" [88] was held from March 3 to 6, 1958, the Korean Workers' Party had "completely rinsed itself of the ugly historical phenomenon of factionalism," [89] and Kim Il-sŏng had established himself firmly as the undisputed leader of North Korea.

Thereafter, all North Korean leaders became a single and solidly devoted group around Kim, irrespective of their previous factional allegiances. This factionalism, so characteristic of North Korean leadership, disappeared completely as a political feature, and the regime was well consolidated. Though this process necessitated the drastic elimination of Kim's rivals and thus had dreadful consequences for the losers, it performed a constructive function in that it helped establish an undisputed elite with sufficient authority to carry out far-reaching socio-political changes. As a result the one-time backward agrarian society was being transformed into an industrial society and material well-being of the North Koreans was markedly raised. This could not have been done had the country been beset by unresolvable factional struggle.

While the nationwide campaign was going on against "anti-revolutionary elements" and "anti-party factionalists," elections were held on August 27, 1957 to select representatives to the Supreme People's Assembly. According to North Korean sources, 99.92 per cent of the total eligible voters participated in the elections, and 99.92 per cent of the participants voted affirmatively for their candidates in 215 electoral districts.[90] In spite of the North Korean constitutional stipulation of a four-year term for the representatives (Article 36), this was the second election of its kind ever held in North Korea. The first elections were held in August 1948. As in the first elections, there was only one candidate for each electoral district and there were two boxes at each voting place, one for "Yes" and the other for "No." [91]

When the First Session of the Second Supreme People's Assembly opened on September 18, 1957,[92] its complexion was far different from that of the First Assembly. Whereas the First Assembly in 1948 had 572 members, the Second Assembly now had only 215. The decrease in the number of the representatives was due to the exclusion of most of the former representatives from South Korea in the second elections. Second, whereas in the First Assembly only 27 percent of the total representatives were members of the Korean Workers' Party, now 83 percent belonged to the same party. Third, whereas in 1948 only 55 percent of the total representatives were of worker and peasant origins, in 1957 their numbers increased to 84 percent. The average level of education among the members of the Second Assembly was lower than that of the members of the First Assembly.[93]

During its brief three-day meeting, the Assembly "entrusted" Kim Il-sŏng with the task of forming a new cabinet.[94] Out of the 36 members of the newly formed cabinet, 26 were members of the Central Committee of the Korean Workers' Party.[95] Among the holders of the 21 ministerial posts on the first cabinet formed in 1948, only eight were retained in the new cabinet.[96] The even distribution of the first cabinet posts among the various communist factions was no longer preserved, and the new cabinet was manned mostly by persons loyal to Kim Il-sŏng. During the selection of its officials, the Assembly elected Ch'oe Yong-kŏn to the chairmanship of its presidium.[97] The post had been held by Kim Tu-bong ever since the Supreme People's Assembly was first formed. Thus the new makeup of the various governing organs showed that by the latter half of 1957, North Korea was under a "proletarian dictatorship" spearheaded by Kim Il-sŏng and his cohorts.

Having exterminated the moderating influence of their opponents and having manned various institutions with their own reliable personnel, Kim Il-sŏng and his associates sped up the execution of their drastic domestic programs. In the commercial field, from October 1957 they began to carry out an open campaign for the total elimination of remaining private commerce in order to "eradicate the intermediary exploitation of the peasants by private merchants" and to "do away with the very cause of poverty among the peasants." [98] In agriculture, the movement for cooperatives (collectivization movements) was intensified from late 1957 to early 1958,[99] almost duplicating the commune movement in China.[100] By the end of August 1958, all the remaining private farmers had joined agricultural cooperatives (collective farms), and the entire North Korean countryside had been changed into "socialist villages." [101] By the end of the same year all the remaining private merchants had been "transformed into socialist workers," thus completely bringing a stop to private business transactions in North Korea.[102] Finally the fulfillment of the five-year economic plan itself was announced at the end of June 1959, two and a half years earlier than originally planned.[103] Following an 18-month interval, North Korea was to embark upon the First Seven-Year Economic Plan (1961–1967). Amidst all this, Communist China had withdrawn the last detachments of its "Volunteers" from North Korea by October 1958, thus completing its phased troop withdrawal.

The post-Korean War reconstruction period was the time in which the style of the present North Korean leadership was finally and definitely molded. Until the insurgency in the summer of 1956, Kim's position had been by no means beyond challenge, and divergence of opinions had been allowed among top echelon leaders. All this changed following the rout of Kim's foes. Kim's domestic adversaries had been encouraged by the change in policy of the post-Stalin Soviet regime. However, Kim asserted independence for North Korea, in spite of the opposition of the Kremlin leaders, upon whom North Korea was dependent for her postwar construction. He did this by his refusal of both the collective leadership principle and the moderate economic policies urged by Moscow. Such an assertion and practice were a necessity for Kim's political survival. The theme of an independent road and consequent nationalistic policy lines were utilized by Kim in order to appeal to North Koreans' patriotism and thus to execute his policies in the face of opposition from his domestic opponents and pressure from Moscow. At first asserted gingerly in 1955, these themes were emphasized by Kim in increasing degree; and, in the early 1960's, they appeared in more concrete form and also in a more defiant tone against the Soviet Union.

To some extent, Kim's success in the struggle seems to have been aided by the attitude of the Peking regime. Except for a brief intervention in the intra-party affairs in P'yŏngyang by P'eng Te-huai, there was no sign of opposition to Kim from Peking. On the contrary, Mao Tse-tung was much in the same situation as North Korea's Kim with regard to the new policies enunciated by the post-Stalinist Kremlin leaders. It was apparently because of the concurrence of interests between Mao and Kim that the Peking regime, which maintained its troops in North Korea until late 1958, remained aloof from the power struggle in P'yŏngyang, thus implicitly endorsing Kim's policies.

Chart of North Korean Communist Factionalism, 1949–1970
(Dwindling of space indicates decline of influence)

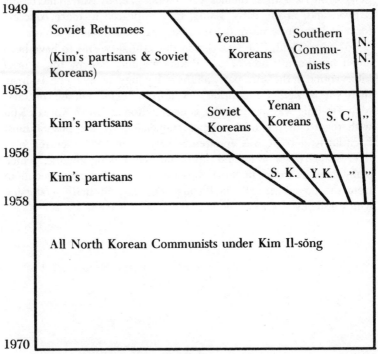

(N.N. means Northern Natives)

9.

THE EMERGENT NORTH KOREAN COMMUNIST LEADERSHIP

On September 11, 1961, the Fourth Congress of the Korean Workers' Party opened its eight-day session in P'yŏngyang, attended by 1,890 delegates representing 1,311,563 party members.[1] It was a "Congress of Victors"[2] since the meeting was completely dominated by former Korean communist guerrillas from Manchuria and their loyal followers. At the congress, Chairman Kim Il-sŏng, in his major report, duly declared that the party had succeeded in its effort to "exterminate factionalism" and had achieved "complete unity" among the rank and file members.[3] The pervasiveness of the power of Kim Il-sŏng and his former comrades-in-arms was well reflected in the new party leadership selected at the Fourth Congress, as well as in the new party constitution which the congress adopted.

The new Central Committee now was expanded to 85 members. Among the 71 members of the previous Central Committee, only 28 were reelected at the Fourth Party Congress. The remaining 43 names were dropped.[4] There were 57 new faces on the new Central Committee.[5] In order to understand the characteristics of the new Central Committee members, social and political backgrounds of 85 persons need to be studied.[6]

Out of the entire new Central Committee members, 57 were either Korean communist guerrillas from Manchuria or their underground agents who operated in the Korean-Manchurian border region. In this paper, all the 57 will continue to be called Korean communist guerrillas from Manchuria. Of these, 55 were born and raised either in Manchuria or in the northern-most four Korean provinces of pre-liberation days, and only one was of South Korean origin. Eight are known to have received a college education,[7] two attended middle school, and two did not go beyond primary school. Of the remainder, four are known to have been laborers and another two are said to have had no formal education. There was only one female among these 57 former partisans. Some 48 were either in the guerrilla units that were directly under Kim Il-sŏng's command or that operated in the southeastern part of Manchuria, the area where Kim Il-sŏng's partisan forces operated.

Next largest group on the 85-member Central Committee were those who may be called "newly emerging" native communists, who owed their political eminence to their subservient cooperation with the former Manchurian guerrillas. There were 13 of them. Five are known to have participated in the pre-1945 peasant movement, and three among the five had prison records.[8] Concerning pre-1945 educational backgrounds of the 13, two are known to be graduates of Japanese technical colleges, another two are graduates of normal schools (teacher-training schools of middle school level),[9] and five had been laborers. Two of the 13 were sent to the Soviet Union after 1945, where they studied for several years, indicating their youthfulness and rising status. There was no female among these newly emerging leaders, and all but two were of North Korean origin.

A third group on the Central Committee, numbering no more than eight, were old native leftists of the pre-liberation period. Of these veteran leftists, five were veteran communists. Of the eight, four are known to have received Japanese college educations, one received training in the Soviet Union, and another one was a renowned leftist writer. Out of the eight, three were from South Korea and four were northerners. Only one in this group was a woman.

Finally, there was one Soviet Korean, three persons of unconfirmed background, and three Yenan returnees, of whom two had been born in North Korea.

An analysis of the 85-member Central Committee reveals the following characteristics: first, it was dominated by former Korean communist guerrillas from Manchuria, most of whom had operated in southeastern Manchuria; second, virtually all of the 85 were born either in Manchuria or in North Korea; third, there were new native communist leaders, who had been emerging since 1945 and all of whom owed their position to their loyalty to the former Manchurian guerrillas; and finally, the Central Committee membership consisted almost exclusively of men.

At the Fourth Congress, 50 persons were elected to Central Committee candidate membership. Among them the identity of 39 is known, and a reading of their backgrounds gives a concrete picture of the characteristics of persons who were advancing in the ranks of North Korean power structure. Of the 39, 20 were Korean communist guerrillas from Manchuria, 18 were newly emerging native leaders, and one was a Yenan-returnee.

All of the 20 former partisans on the candidate membership fought in southeastern Manchuria, and thus it is safe to conclude that they were all either in guerrilla units led by Kim Il-sŏng or worked closely with him. Upon their return to North Korea, almost all of them began their career at the bottom of the power structure, typically either in the party or in the armed forces. Concerning their pre-liberation period education, one is definitely known to have received no formal education. Of the remaining 19, two engaged in farming, one was a laborer, and the rest probably had no formal schooling. There were three women among this group. Subsequently, for a few years after 1948, one member of the group attended a Soviet military academy, indicating that he was held in high regard.

Of the 18 newly emerging native communists on the candidate membership of the Central Committee, six are known to have had pre-liberation underground records. Regarding the pre-1945 schooling of the 18 persons, three are known to have studied at Japanese colleges, five received a middle school education, one did not go beyond primary school, and another one was a factory mechanic. There was also one laborer and a farmer. After the liberation, four in this group are known to have studied abroad.[10] The career beginnings of these native communists was distinctly different from those of the Manchuria-returnees on the candidate membership. 10 of these native communists started their post-liberation career in economic, academic, or cultural fields, and the remaining eight began in the party or governmental organs. Thus majority of these native leaders began their career in less crucial fields than the Manchurian guerrilla fighters who had started their career mostly either in the party or armed forces. There was no female in this group.

The only Yenan-returnee was a medical man, and he had been in health service. All the candidate members of the Central Committee whose identity is known were born and raised either in Manchuria or in Korea's northern provinces.

The 85-member Central Committee elected an 11-member Politburo, that was to replace the 11-member Standing Committee established at the Third Party Congress. The new Politburo was "the permanent and highest guiding party organ," and it was to "direct and guide" party affairs during the interval between plenums of the Central Committee.[11] The 11 persons who were elected to this all-powerful body were: Kim Il-sŏng, Ch'oe Yong-kŏn, Kim Il, Pak Kŭm-ch'ŏl, Kim Kwang-hyŏp, Pak Chŏng-ae, Chŏng Il-yong, Yi Chong-ok, Yi Hyo-sun, Nam Il, and Kim Ch'ang-man.

Chŏng Il-yong was a mechanic before 1945, Yi Chong-ok graduated from a college in Manchuria in 1940 and had connections with communist movement between 1940 and 1944, and Yi Hyo-sun was Kim Il-sŏng's comrade-in-arms. The Soviet Korean, Nam Il, was said to have been retained in the Politburo either because he had publicly confessed the mistake of his involvement in the anti-Kim revolt of the summer of 1956 or for the propaganda purpose of keeping this internationally-known figure in the regime.[12] As for the Yenan Korean, Kim Ch'ang-man, his political survival and promotion was largely due to his obsequiousness toward and collaboration with Kim Il-sŏng. For instance, it was a well known fact that Yenan Koreans maintained their military unit (a branch of the Korean Volunteer Corps) in Manchuria in pre-liberation days. But Kim Ch'ang-man, *in Kŭlloja*, categorically denied the existence of such an organization, saying that it was solely a "trick" of those who attempted to put the Korean Volunteer Corps on an "equal level" with Kim Il-sŏng's guerrilla troops, "the nucleus" of all Korean revolutionaries.[13]

It was from the eleven Politburo members that the members of the Central Committee were to choose the party's chairman and vice-chairmen. Kim Il-sŏng was again elected to the chairmanship, and Ch'oe Yong-kŏn, Kim Il, Pak Kŭm-ch'ŏl, Kim Ch'ang-man and Yi Hyo-sun became vice-chairmen. Thus the central party leadership was composed exclusively of individuals who had close personal connections with Kim Il-sŏng in the pre-liberation days or persons who showed unquestionable loyalty to him after the liberation.

Having firmly established their position, the new leadership at the Fourth Party Congress again redefined the character of the party.

According to the new definition, the Korean Workers' Party was now "the direct inheritor of the glorious armed anti-Japanese revolutionary tradition." [14] Now only Kim Il-sŏng and his Manchurian guerrillas were the precursors of the party and were to be taken as the only Korean revolutionaries who fought against Japan for the independence of Korea.

The reorganization of the party's high council in September, 1961, was followed by the reconstruction of the Supreme People's Assembly and the People's Council (the Cabinet) in October, 1962. In order to select new representatives for the Supreme People's Assembly, general elections were held on October 8, 1962. North Koreans claimed that 100 percent of all eligible voters participated in the elections, and all of them voted affirmatively for the single candidate standing in each of 383 electoral districts. [15] According to a South Korean source, the old black and white boxes were abolished and only one box was provided in each balloting place. Among the 383 representatives, 371 were members of the Korean Workers' Party, and only twelve were from other minor parties and social organizations. Thus the proportion of the members of the Korean Workers' Party in the composition of the representatives became far greater than in the two previous Supreme People's Assemblies. [16] Fifty-six percent of the newly elected representatives were of worker origin, and the remainder were classified as peasants, office workers and persons of other professions. Thus the proportion of workers in the Third Supreme People's Assembly was greater than in the previous two assemblies. The average educational background of the 383 representatives was lower than that in the two previous assemblies. [17]

The Third Supreme People's Assembly held its first meeting on October 22 and 23, 1962. During its two-day session the representatives "entrusted" Kim Il-sŏng with the task of forming the Third Cabinet. The new cabinet, consisting of 43 posts and headed by Premier Kim Il-sŏng, was formed exclusively by members of the Korean Workers' Party. Out of the eight vice-premiers, six were members of the 11-man Politburo elected at the Fourth Party Congress. [18] Also during the meeting Third Supreme People's Assembly elected its own new 23-man Presidium, of whom 16 were members of the Central Committee of the Korean Workers' Party. Ch'oe Yong-kŏn was again elected to the presidency of the presidium, and among the five vice-presidents were two members of the 11-man Politburo. [19]

[125]

The new North Korean leadership thus formed and consolidated in the early 1960's showed an increasingly independent stance. As early as in December 1955, Kim Il-sŏng, in the midst of pressure from Moscow, expressed his determination, though cautiously, to strike out on an independent road for North Korea by calling for the establishment of *Chuch'e* (self-image or self-reliance) among Koreans. On January 29, 1958, before a group of workers, Kim made a remarkably straight-forward statement, saying that "we have the right to speak and decide by ourselves." [20] Entering the 1960's, the idea of *Chuch'e* became more concrete, expressing itself in the form of political independence in the Communist bloc, a self-sufficient independent economy, and self-reliance in national defense. Now North Korea's assertion for Chuch'e became outspoken and militant.

In her pursuance of political independence, North Korea now took an openly anti-Moscow line. In his speech of November 27, 1961, at a plenum of the Central Committee of the party following his return from the 22nd CPSU Congress, Kim Il-sŏng for the first time explicitly rejected the collective leadership principle, to which he had previously paid at least lip service. Stating that at the 22nd Congress of the Communist Party of the Soviet Union "problems of Stalin's superstition" were discussed extensively, Kim continued:

> The name of Stalin is well known among communists and peoples of the entire world. However, the members of the Communist Party of the Soviet Union know him better than anyone else, and the question of how to evaluate Stalin's past acts in the Soviet Union is an intra-party problem of the CPSU. We maintain that no party [implying the CPSU] has the right to interfere in the internal affairs of a fraternal party [implying the Korean Workers' Party].[21]

Finally when the differences between Moscow and Peking became openly acrimonious following the Cuban missile crisis, the Sino-Indian boundary dispute, and Moscow's stepped-up wooing of "the Tito revisionist clique" in the fall of 1962, North Korea took sides with Peking, but without subordinating itself to the Chinese, even though it cost them Moscow's economic and military aid. This was followed by a series of virulent public denunciations of Soviet Union. The first of this kind appeared in October 1963 when the P'yŏngyang regime denounced the Kremlin leaders for their past deeds regarding North Korean domestic affairs. It complained that the CPSU under the pretext of opposing the personality cult of Kim Il-sŏng had attempted to interfere in the affairs of a fraternal nation in order to "overthrow" its leadership. It added that such an act would not be tolerated." [22] Again attacking the CPSU leadership by name in August 1964, the North Korean communists decisively rejected any kind of hierarchical authority pattern in the international communist movement:

> All fraternal parties are equal and independent. There may be a large party and a small party but not a higher party and a lower party, nor a guiding party and a guided party. No party can direct and control other parties from a central authority.[23]

Although *rapproachement* was achieved between P'yŏngyang and Moscow following Aleksei Kosygin's visit to P'yŏngyang in February 1965, immediately after the downfall of Khrushchev and the resumption of Soviet material aid, North Korea maintained its hardline ideological stance and continued its independent posture. As if to underscore its independence from both Moscow and Peking, North Korea, in the *Nodong Shinmun* editorial of August 12, 1966, entitled "Let Us Defend Our Independence," insisted that there were neither "superior" nor "inferior" communist parties and that each party should be the master within its own country. Similarly two months later, in his main report at "the Conference of Party Representatives," held from October 5 to 12, 1966, Kim made veiled criticism of Soviet "revisionism" as well as Chinese "Leftist opportunism." According to Kim, "Leftist" Peking refused to join Moscow in a communist-united front against the United States' "imperialist aggression" in Vietnam and did not take "concrete action," although Peking had "bragged" that it had been opposing "American imperialism." Declaring that North Korea was ready to dispatch its "volunteer soldiers" and fight side by side with Vietnamese "brethren" whenever North Vietnam requested, Kim asserted that the Korean Workers' Party would fight uncompromisingly against "Rightist and Leftist opportunism." [24] As a result of North Korea's continuous endeavor to pursue her independent course, North Koreans, according to Premier Kim's statement during his speech of December 16, 1967 made at the Fourth Supreme People's Assembly, had, by the mid-1960's, fully acquired "a position to enter the international arena on an equal footing with the people of big and small countries." [25]

In their attempt to build a self-sufficient and independent economy, the North Korean leadership has been making a great effort to get all the inhabitants to work with their maximum effort and to their utmost efficiency. The first well publicized movement of this kind was the "Ch'ŏllima Undong" ("the Flying Horse Movement"), named after a legendary horse that ran a thousand miles a day. With its inauguration in mid-June, 1958, every North Korean worker and farmer, including housewives, was asked to "run like the flying horse" to achieve the "victory of socialist construction and to pave way for the transition to communism." [26] Those who had done more than their share of work were awarded the honorary title of "Flying Horse Rider" and they became "labor heroes." There was a close parallel between North Korea's Flying Horse Movement and China's Great Leap Forward campaign with respect to timing, goals, atmosphere and scope. [27] The two campaigns were launched almost simultaneously. At the time, the commune movement in China was in full swing while the collectivization in North Korea was reaching its final stage. The goal of both Peking and P'yŏngyang was to modernize their respective nations in the shortest possible period. The peoples in both countries were called upon to overcome economic and cultural backwardness by exerting their utmost effort. They were to press ahead constantly to achieve greater and faster economic results. In order to achieve maximization of labor input, peoples from towns and cities, including office workers, were shifted to farms and factories, and there was a pervasive combat atmosphere fomented by the zeal of the people and their leaders to solve economic problems of their countries. Both the Flying Horse Movement and the Great Leap Forward campaign were actions of an entire society for economic development.

While the Flying Horse Movement was well underway, the "Ch'ŏng'san-ri Method" in the spring of 1960, and the "Daian System" in the winter of 1961 were introduced. The Ch'ŏng'san-ri. method was a result of Kim Il-sŏng's 15-day "on-the-spot-guidance" at collective farms in the spring of 1960 at the Ch'ŏng'san-ri village on the outskirts of P'yŏngyang, and it was to improve work methods on collective farms in North Korea. The Daian system, a "new system of industrial management" was born out of a 10-day fact-finding visit by Kim Il-sŏng to the Daian Electric Appliance Factory in December 1961. The Ch'ŏng'san-ri method directed leaders of agricultural cooperatives to "radically improve their old business-office-like methods of work," to visit farms frequently, and to invite suggestions from farmers and thus to maintain closer ties with agricultural workers. In the Daian work system, "the upper organs

[128]

help the lower organs, superiors help inferiors, the well-informed teach the less-informed, and all people give comradely cooperation." It is the "collectivist and communist principle of life, 'One For All, And All For One.' " [28] The Ch'ŏng'san-ri method and the Daian work system together were an imitation of China's "three unification movement" stressed during the Great Leap Forward campaign. It aimed at uniting party cadres, technicians, and the masses into single work teams. Both the Ch'ŏng'san-ri method and the Daian system were a "mass line" introduced to elicit mass support for the regime's efforts to increase economic production, and appeals were made more to the ideological and nationalist sentiments of the masses than to their materialist aspirations. The urging of officials at various levels of the necessity of making "on-the-spot-guidance" was an indication of the regime's immense concern for the maintenance of this mass line. Kim Il-sŏng himself was claimed to have made no less than 1,300 such tours between 1954 and 1961 to farms, factories, commercial enterprises, schools and other scientific and cultural institutions. Soviet economic and military aid had been suspended sometime before the end of 1962 and lasted until May 1965, it is believed.[29] This made the North Koreans further aware of the necessity of building a self-sufficient economy. North Korea's "mass line" and its consequent emphasis on ideology as the driving force in economic development also had its exact counterpart in China where it reached its highest point during the Great Leap Forward. The stress on the "mass line" was the result of the concern of leaders in both Peking and P'yŏngyang to reduce the gap between party cadres and the masses, and thus in preventing any chance of alienation, strengthening the foundation of their regimes. The emphasis on ideology as a motivating force seems to have stemmed from the belief of the leaders of the two countries that rapid economic progress without proper ideological control would breed revisionism and bourgeois ideas which, in their view, were then rampant in the Soviet Union, Yugoslavia, and other countries of Eastern Europe.

With regard to North Korea's economic growth, there is substantial evidence that she made a remarkable achievement from the post-Korean War period to the mid-1960's, although North Koreans' frequent claims of "over-production" or "completion earlier than planned" [30] were more propaganda and window-dressing than actual, and although the Seven Year Economic Plan (1961–1967) itself was not completed within the stated period and was extended until 1970.

Various observers of North Korean affairs have given both exalting and fairly favorable estimates of her economic accomplishments. For instance, President Mareira Keita of the Republic of Mali, after an inspection tour of North Korean factories in September 1961, expressed his admiration of North Korean economic achievements and promised that he would utilize North Korean methods to step up Mali's economic development.[31] Joan Robinson, the well-known British economist, following her visit to North Korea in October 1964, described the country as "a nation without poverty" and said that "all the economic miracles of the postwar world are put in the shade" considering the spectacular economic achievement of North Korea.[32] Even South Korean students have admitted that North Korea recovered her war-ravaged economy quickly and that in the post-Korean War decade she succeeded in developing from the old colonial agricultural and raw materials producing country to a diversified economic structure capable of producing all essential goods at home. They said that North Korea's industrial progress was "phenomenal," "a remarkable success," and "fairly impressive by Asian standards." [33] Based upon this evidence it can be safely concluded that North Korea's claim that she had been transformed into a "self-sufficient socialist industrial-agricultural society from the backward colonial agrarian society" [34] and that the basic problems of food, clothing, and housing had been "solved" [35] is by no means unfounded.

Along with the development of economic strength, the North Korean regime simultaneously paid attention to strengthening its military capability. In this field, as in the economy, the goal has been to achieve the capacity of self-reliance with its apparently ultimate aim being unification of the divided country under communism. Alarmed and disillusioned by the sudden ascension to power of militantly anti-communist army officers in Seoul following the *coup d'etat* there of May 16, 1961, she hurriedly signed mutual defense treaties with the Soviet Union on July 6, 1961 and a few days later on July 11 with the People's Republic of China. Thus North Korea's national security was guaranteed against potential military attack from South Korea. But the treaty with the Soviet Union did not change Moscow's then dwindling or possibly completely suspended military assistance to P'yŏngyang in spite of a North Korean military delegation's visit to Moscow in November 1962 for negotiations for military aid.[36]

Faced with the suddenly tense situation following the military's take-over of power in Seoul as well as their failure to obtain military assistance from Moscow, party leaders called a Fifth Plenum of the Central Committee from December 10, 1962 in order to discuss measures to further strengthen North Korea's national defense capability. During its five-day conference the plenum adopted a new "military line" for the party that set forth the following points: [37] 1) modernize the military equipment; 2) make a cadre out of every soldier by training him ideologically and in military technology; 3) arm the entire people, and let each worker hold "arm in one hand, and hammer and sickle in another hand"; and 4) turn the whole nation into an impenetrable fortress even if it constrains economic development.

The P'yŏngyang regime's increased concern for military affairs was also underscored by the creation of the Military Department in the Central Committee of the party between the adjournment of the plenum of December 1962 and the spring of the next year. The "military line" set in December 1962 was reaffirmed by the party's "Representatives' Conference" held from October 5 to 12, 1966.[38] At the same time the North Korean militia forces known as the Worker-Farmer Red Guards were augmented. Evolving from the original small forces formed in the spring of 1959, the Worker-Farmer Red Guards since 1963 have been increasing in number and their weaponry has been improving. Each unit of the Red Guards, organized at a working place, is armed with North Korean manufactured armored cars and automatic rifles. Comprising men and women of between 17 and 45 years of age, there are some 500,000 of them (as of 1967) out of the total North Korean population of 13 million. They are to act as an adjunct to the regular ground forces of some 350,000 men.[39]

Amidst the pursuance of the independent line policies, there were changes in top echelon personnel. At a Central Committee meeting of the party held June 25–26, 1964, Yi Chu-yŏn, a pre-liberation period native communist leader of North Korean origin, was elected to the Politburo, thus increasing its membership from 11 to 12. Also at the meeting, Kim Ch'ang-bong and Pak Sŏng-ch'ŏl, both of whom had been Kim Il-sŏng's comrades-in-arms in Manchuria, were selected to candidate membership of the Politburo.[40] Prior to participating in guerrilla activities in Manchuria in mid-1930's, Pak Sŏng-ch'ŏl attended college in Japan. Major reorganization of the elite personnel took place at the 14th Plenum of the Central Committee of the "fourth period" held on October 12, 1966, which was also the last day of the eight-day session of the party's "Representatives' Conference" that opened on October 5 in place of the Fifth Party Congress.[41]

First, the plenum decided to establish a six-man Standing Committee within the Politburo in order to "attend to daily problems of the party and the state." [42] The six were: Kim Il-sŏng (born in 1912), Ch'oe Yong-kŏn (born in 1900), Kim Il (born in 1912), Pak Kŭm-ch'ŏl (born in 1912), Yi Hyo-sun (born in 1896), and Kim Kwang-hyŏp (born in 1915). Thus this body, which might be called the "inner circle" of the North Korean elite consisted exclusively of former partisans from Manchuria. Among them, however, Pak Kŭm-ch'ŏl and Yi Hyo-sun took care of building underground apparatus in the 1930's along the Korean-Manchurian border area in coordination with Kim Il-sŏng's troops. All six men were born in the northern provinces of Korea, and at the time of this reorganization of October 1966 they were, except Ch'oe Yong-kŏn and Yi Hyo-sun, in their early 50's.[43] And their acknowledged leader Kim Il-sŏng, according to an account of a Japanese reporter who had met Kim in P'yŏngyang in the summer of 1963, looked much younger than his age and appeared very healthy.[44]

Second, the plenum added five new members to the Politburo, thus increasing its membership to 17 from the previous 12. The new five were Kim Ik-sŏn, Kim Ch'ang-bong, Pak Sŏng-ch'ŏl, Ch'oe Hyŏn, and Yi Yŏng-ho. The former three were elevated to full Politburo membership from candidate membership on this body. All five, perhaps except Kim Ik-sŏn who had graduated from a college in Soviet Russia before 1945 and was of South Korean origin, were born either in Manchuria or in the northern provinces of Korea. Again, excepting probably Kim Ik-sŏn, they had been Kim Il-sŏng's comrades-in-arms in Manchuria.

Third, the plenum chose nine new candidate members of the Politburo, increasing its total candidate membership to 12. The old three candidate members from the previous Fourth Party Congress were: Ha Ang-ch'ŏn (Yenan returnee), Han Sang-du (native communist of pre-1945 period), and Hyŏn Mu-kwang (a member of Kim Il-sŏng's guerrilla troops). The nine new candidate members were: Sŏk San, Hŏ Bong-hak, Ch'oe Kwang, O Jin-u, Im Ch'un-ch'u, Kim Tong-kyu, Kim Yong-ju, Pak Yong-guk,· and Chŏng Kyŏng-bok. All

[132]

except Pak Yong-guk, were former partisan fighters under Kim Il-sŏng. Pak Yong-guk is from a family whose elders had been members of underground apparatus that had been in operation along the Korean-Manchurian border in the 1930's in collaboration with Kim Il-sŏng's forces. Kim Tong-kyu is said to have graduated from a college in the Soviet Union following his entrance there in 1940. Kim Yŏng-ju is Kim Il-sŏng's younger brother. All the 12 candidate members, possibly except the Yenan returnee Ha Ang-ch'ŏn whose place of birth is unconfirmed, were born either in the northern provinces of Korea or in Manchuria.

Finally, the plenum abolished the chairmanship and the vice-chairmenship of the Central Committee. In their places Secretaryship-General and ten Secretariats were created, whose functions were to "organize daily affairs of the party and to execute its policies." [45] Kim Il-sŏng became the Secretary-General and all the remaining five members of the Standing Committee of the Politburo became Secretaries, each heading one Secretariat. The remaining five Secretariats were headed by Sŏk San, Hŏ Bong-hak, Kim Yong-ju, Pak Yong-guk, and Kim To-man. Kim To-man, of North Korean origin, had acted as an agent of the underground apparatus of Kim Il-sŏng's forces along the Korean-Manchurian border region.

As a result of this reshuffling, Korean communist guerrillas from Manchuria thoroughly entrenched themselves in the top echelon of the North Korean power hierarchy. Not only were they entrenched, but they attempted to impress their revolutionary deeds and thoughts upon the acts and minds of all North Korean inhabitants. Since the Fourth Party Congress, all the North Koreans have been openly admonished to educate themselves in communism. It has been urged that the study of communism should be conducted in accordance with "the revolutionary tradition" of the Korean communist partisans from Manchuria, who are "typical and exemplary communists" and whose "bloody and heroic struggle" have "deeply moved the whole working class." [46] Of these former partisans, it is Kim Il-sŏng who has been claimed by North Koreans to epitomize the revolutionary tradition and its glory, indicating that he is the indisputable leader of the former guerrillas and that he is the supreme leader in North Korea. Although the program to exalt his position began under the Soviet occupation, it has been intensified since the 1956 anti-Kim insurgency. It appears that the personality cult of Kim Il-sŏng has reached an unprecedented level, bordering on superstition or fanaticism, much the same as is accorded Mao Tse-tung of the People's Republic of China.[47] For North Koreans, Kim is their "beloved," "respected," and "sagacious" leader, and his words and thoughts have been studied and recited by them as the guiding principle in their daily activities. This personality cult of Kim serves the political purpose of keeping communists of new generations in undeviating and exclusive devotion to their supreme leader, thus insuring against possible factionalism, since in the process of the deification of Kim, all the achievements and contributions made by his once-prominent rivals have been erased. Inhabitants have become oblivious to these old communist revolutionaries. A foreigner, visiting P'yŏngyang in 1964, was led to speak of Kim euphemistically as "a messiah." Throughout North Korea, Kim's presence is everywhere evident; his portraits are displayed in all public places and meetings.

As noted in Chapter 2, Kim Il'sŏng began his partisan activities in Manchuria in 1932, the year after Japan's invasion of Manchuria. Until his flight to the Soviet Union in 1942, a fact which North Korea never admitted, Kim operated in the southeastern corner of Manchuria. This Manchurian region, adjacent to the northern provinces of Korea, had been a primary settling area for ever-swelling numbers of Korean immigrants, and, as of the latter part of the 1930's, nearly a million Koreans were living in this sector. They actually outnumbered the Chinese residents. The area had long been noted as a center of Korean anti-Japanese activities abroad. The overwhelming majority of those Koreans crossing the border into Manchuria were peasants, the down-trodden and neglected element of Korean society. They migrated to that foreign land in search of a better living because conditions continued to deteriorate at home under the Japanese colonists. Once in Manchuria, across the border, most of them resumed their old calling, the only job available for them, mostly under harsh Chinese landlords.[49] Living under stringent circumstances in a foreign hinterland, these Korean immigrants were naturally susceptible to communist and other political propaganda that promised them a better life and their return to a liberated homeland. It was among these Koreans eking out their existence in the countryside of Manchuria that Kim Il-sŏng recruited his troops and obtained support for his partisan activities,[50] much after the fashion of Mao Tse-tung who had been carrying on since 1927 the peasant-based communist revolution. And naturally Kim's troops and their supporting elements in rural areas of Manchuria led a life of tension, austerity, and simplicity. It was this kind of way of life

[134]

that contemporary North Koreans were urged to follow, and austerity was in evidence according to accounts of Japanese visitors to North Korea in the early 1960's.

Probably the most prominent feature of North Korean life was the almost equal standard of living between urban and rural population. The traditional discrepancies between affluent urbanites and poverty-stricken villagers had been eradicated by the regime's constant efforts to raise the farmers' living standard. The ordinary worker and farmer, unlike their counterparts of the pre-1945 period, were said to be living a decent life, provided with their basic necessities such as food, clothing, and living quarters.[51] Not only economic equality was achieved between the two sectors but also differences in clothing and even in manner between the urban dweller and the peasant disappeared. There was a uniformity with regard to the way of life of the North Koreans, and both men and women lived modestly without commodities beyond the immediate daily necessities, not to mention cosmetics or fashionable articles.[52] Thus the North Koreans were levelled into a common mass of subjects under what might be called a "plebiscitary dictatorship" [53] headed by Kim Il-sŏng. And even scholars and scientists were reported to have looked unlike "academic types" but could easily be mistaken for common laborers or farmers. All scientific research projects were set with national goals in mind to the exclusion of research for the satisfaction of individual curiousity. Academicians were said to have been conducting studies with the attitude of "struggle," and they were extremely patriotic. Their enmity towards Americans who were "occupying" South Korea was much stronger than expected, according to a report of Japanese visitors.[54] Furthermore, in spite of the constitutional guarantee of religious freedom, there were no Christian churches or Christian baptisms. No Buddhist temples were seen except in remote mountain areas. The dead were buried by relatives and friends without traditional rituals.[55] Any activity that did not contribute positively to or might conflict with the regime's effort of production and military preparedness and any social behavior that deviated from the official line were strictly forbidden. Thus by every sign North Korea under the dictatorship of former partisans from Manchurian hinterland was displaying the "profile of a garrison state." [56]

10.

CONCLUSION

THE NORTH KOREAN COMMUNIST FACTIONS FORMED IN THE POST-liberation period were based upon regions and localities in which these groups had originally organized themselves and operated. This factionalism resulted from the Japanese colonial rule that had forced Korean communists to flee the country in order to continue their revolutionary activities, and further from the division of the country between the north and south. The shared and common experiences within each geographical unit formed the basis of each faction. With the coming of Soviet troops to the northern half of Korea, all these separate and independent communist groups inevitably congregated under the Soviet umbrella to take part in the building of the communist state. This common objective led these factions to form an uneasy coalition, but while they cooperated for the achievement of their basic goal, intra-group (intra-party) struggles inevitably developed because of the aspiration of each faction to dominate or, at least, to preserve its position in the face of rival competition.

The first stage of the series of factional disputes occurred between 1945 to 1948. At the outset, a coalition of all three communist groups (the Soviet-returnees, Yenan Koreans, and northern native communist elite) was formed, motivated by each faction's commitment to communist ideology as well as the shared desire to eliminate the nationalists both at home (North Korea) and those in South Korea. At that time, it was generally believed that the country would be unified shortly and that there was a real possibility of confronting the South Korean nationalists not to mention those rightist groups still operating in the north. Because of this consideration, in the first year or so following the liberation, active cooperation of all communists was deemed a necessity, and thus power was somewhat equally, if temporarily, distributed among all the three communist factions.

As early as the spring of 1946, the only non-communist forces, the North Korean Democratic Party and the North Korean Youth Fraternal Party, had been, for all practical purposes, either decimated or emasculated, and there was little or no threat from them to the ascending communist forces. The decline of these non-communist elements was paralleled by the gradual elimination of individual members of the northern native communist faction. The dwindling influence of this faction grew out of the bi-factional struggle between the combined forces of the Soviet returnees and the Yenan group on the one hand, and the northern communists on the other hand, throughout 1946 and 1947. The alliance of all these Soviet and Yenan returnees could only be effected because of a common fear of their native opponents who had initially established a considerable power base at home. Correlatively with the decline of the latter group was the aggrandizement of power and enhancement of prestige of the former in the party and the government. The earlier precarious balance of power now swung in favor of the foreign returnees.

When the final assault of the Soviet-returnees and the Yenan faction was launched in March 1948, the northern native communists were so weakened that they could scarcely have withstood even an attack by the Soviet returnees alone. When the combined attack occurred, not only the threat from North Korean right wing groups had been removed, but also, and probably more significantly, any imminent confrontation with the South Korean rightists was remote since any hope that Korea might be unified through peaceful negotiations between the United States Military Government and the Soviet occupation authorities had already become a dim possibility. Apparently, under these circumstances, there was no more need to retain the northern native faction in the coalition. Furthermore, the Soviet returnees and the Yenan faction had felt by early 1948 that their positions had acquired legitimacy. In the previous years the coalition of all communists, particularly native communists with their considerable local following, was thought necessary for the public acceptance of the fledgling new communist regime. After the decline of the northern native communist elite, the coalition of the two factions ran North Korean affairs. The disintegration of the three-way coalition was, then, caused by the absence of external threat and the will of the ambitious returnees to increase their power and further consolidate their position at the expense of their native cohorts. This came about because two factions turned on another, because this move was given tacit support by the Soviet occupation authorities who remained in North Korea until December 1948, and because the returnees were increasingly able to reward those loyal members of the rank-and-file in the party and to chastize those who were opposing them by a distribution or deprivation of offices. Finally, the victors were able to control and manipulate propaganda.

The second stage of the factional dispute (1949–1953) also took the bi-factional form; this time, however, the South Korean communist group *versus* the joint forces of the Soviet Koreans and the Yenan Koreans. In spite of the bitter charges of American "spies" and related alleged political crimes directed against the South Korean communists, which were, in fact, fabrications to discredit them, the quarrel actually began over factional power disputes and over differences on the war. The policy difference over the war issue, which is believed to have existed between late 1952 and early 1953, arose from consideration of possible power dispositions in one way or the other depending upon continuation or cessation of the war. The disintegration of the coalition of the South Korean communist faction, the Soviet returnees, and the Yenan faction came about when its usefulness was believed to have ended with the coming of the truce in July 1953. Here again the absence of external threat (along with the need to find a scapegoat for the failure to win the war) prompted the disintegration of the three-way coalition and brought about the total destruction of the one wing. The direct external threat emanating from the forces of South Korea was waning with the approach of the truce, which once more hardened the demarcation line. The continuation of the North Korean regime was guaranteed by the Chinese communist "volunteers" who had poured into the Korean peninsula during the early winter of 1950, ostensibly to rescue the P'yŏngyang government. Significantly, it was during the Korean War that the Soviet influence in North Korea began to recede, due largely to the withdrawal of the Soviet armed forces, a process completed by December 1948. In addition, there was no direct commitment by the Kremlin leaders during the war to supply troops. The Chinese communist forces, upon whom North Korea depended for her survival, did not wield as absolute or as strong an influence as the

[138]

Soviet occupation authorities had done until just before the outbreak of the war. It is presumed that Kim Il-sŏng, who had worked with Chinese communists in Manchuria in the 1930's, and the Yenan faction that had closely collaborated with Chinese communists in Yenan until its return to North Korea, found it easier to cooperate with the Chinese communist "volunteers" during the Korean War than did the South Korean communists. The destruction of the South Korean communist group was an inevitable by-product of the dominance of the combined forces of the Soviet returnees and the Yenan faction built over the years against the weakened position of opponents who had left their home base in the south.

The third and final stage of the factional quarrel (1956–58) was preceded by factional realignment among the remaining groups in control of the North Korean regime. The Soviet returnees were split into two groups based upon the pre-liberation period geographical ties: one being composed of the former Korean communist partisans in Manchuria and another being composed of Soviet Koreans. This split was probably inevitable in view of the differences in their backgrounds of the pre-liberation period. This was discernable as early as the winter of 1951 when one of the leading Soviet Koreans (Hŏ Kai) was purged at a time when the resentment was mounting against the Soviet Union for its unwillingness to aid North Korea militarily. This process became apparent during the immediate post-Korean War period, when some Soviet Koreans, along with a few Yenan Koreans, were demoted and castigated. Their hatred of the growing power of the Korean communists from Manchuria under Kim Il-sŏng and their apprehension over their gradually dwindling influence led the Soviet Koreans into an alliance with the Yenan faction, of which at least two leading members had been purged as early as before 1951 (Han P'in and Mu-Jŏng). They challenged the communists under Kim Il-sŏng to stem the continuing and perilous trend. The policy differences in the post-war reconstruction, success or failure of the programs of one group against its opposition group—especially the issue of collective leadership principle—had direct effects upon the power of these two rival forces.

The failure of the Yenan faction and the Soviet Koreans could be attributable to several factors. Both groups were progressively weakened over the years through individual purges of their leaders as well as defections among their ranks. The defectors made their choice largely because of the personal advantages and promotion which were obtainable within Kim's increasingly powerful orbit. Kim's followers advanced rapidly following the Third Korean Workers' Party Congress held in April 1956. In this phase of the power struggle, Kim Il-sŏng's Manchurian background (his earlier connections with the Chinese communists) probably helped him maintain a cordial if not mutually enthusiastic relationship with the Chinese communist "volunteers." Of more critical importance was the issue of the collective leadership principle. The Chinese were unwilling to throw their weight behind Kim's opponents, who had clamored for collective leadership; and so they solicited the support of Moscow, with which Peking's relations were shortly to deteriorate beyond recovery. Both Kim Il-sŏng and Mao Tse-tung perceived a common danger to their positions in the implementation of collective leadership. This awareness on the part of Peking made that government, except momentarily at the initial phase, decide not to interfere in the North Korean power struggle, especially since it was apparent that the Yenan faction and the Soviet Koreans were losing anyway. Notably the outbreak of the "August Factionalist Incident" in the summer of 1956 and subsequent purgings of rebels also took place in the absence of an outside threat from non-communist sources, thanks to the cessation of the war. These purges were also conducted when the most arduous phase of the post-war reconstruction was over. It should be remembered that Communist China was still maintaining its "volunteers" in North Korea, though in declining numbers, until the end of 1958.

In summary, the quarrels among the North Korean communists took a bi-factional form, there being no third party to mediate and arbitrate the disputes. This might be a reason why the outcome of each dispute was so deadly. Each of the quarrels occurred when one group, either singly or in combined force, was stronger than its opponent and was willing to dispose of it. Each time, the dominant group acted when there was no external threat to the party. As long as non-communist forces threatened, all the existing communist forces faced the threat together. During these times, in the execution of other domestic programs, the dominant group was willing to maintain a coalition with its opponents.

In the road leading to his final victory, Kim showed himself a thoroughgoing Machiavellian. He displayed remarkable skill in balancing contending forces by mergers, making timely alliances with individuals or groups and changing such alliances when their usefulness was at an end. In the process, Kim successfully pursued two conflicting goals simultaneously. He gained the cooperation of various communist groups in order to initiate a new communist state and also to broaden popular support of the fledgling regime on the one hand, but he limited the participation of his rivals so they would not block the continued growth of his political strength and the implementation of his policies on the other. It was in his attempt to help solidify his newly acquired political footing that Kim even shared authority with the nationalists, although this was for only a brief period. Once that necessity was over and further participation by the nationalists became a liability, Kim did not hesitate to discard them. Again the early division of political power among the various communist factions was a necessary condition for obtaining cooperation from all of them in suppressing their common enemy, the nationalists. Here, too, Kim's rivals were eliminated one by one, as Kim and his cohorts strengthened their political position and gained experience in handling state affairs. It was only after some ten years of such manipulation and waiting that he and his close associates felt strong enough to move against all of their former allies, including the Soviet Koreans, who had been indispensable in every field of North Korean affairs and who, until then, had been used to eliminate more formidable figures. Kim was a master of timing and exploitation.

The disappearance of factionalism, though achieved through a series of dreadful methods, had an integrative effect since it enabled the regime to carry out various urgent socio-economic measures without serious domestic disruptions. If the regime had been beset by factionalism and the party plagued by internal dissension, no decisive action could have been taken in the face of the stupendous tasks of domestic construction in the immediate post-liberation period, crises in the Korean War, and then the enormous task of economic reconstruction in the post-Korean War period. The existence of factions could have become dysfunctional since it could have undermined the party structure, inhibiting its orderly growth and rendering North Korean policies too sectarian. This would have hampered the quick execution of the series of socio-economic and other programs by the regime. It would have been particularly so in view of the fact that the Korean Workers' Party was the sole governing party in North Korea and the nation depended upon the stability of the party for its existence. The intense growth of factionalism might have developed into sheer internecine competition, factional loyalty taking precedence over party loyalty, the preoccupation with the struggle causing less concern among the members of factions towards society as a whole and blinding them to the external threats which the regime had to deal with from its early years until the end of the Korean War. Had such severe factionalism spilt into the society, North Korea would have been plagued by continuous political instability and social unrest, all of which would have hampered its socio-economic growth. In this sense, Kim's stamping out of his opponents served a salubrious and integrative function since it brought about consolidation of the regime and political stability, enabling the regime to carry out a series of welfare measures and further promote economic development. Thus the emergence of strong-man rule in North Korea was a necessity for the nation's survival as a communist state. The positive aspects achieved under the totalitarian and dictatorial rule, however, were accomplished at considerable cost.

The condemnation of factionalism and the expulsion from the Korean Workers' Party of all communists suspected or convicted of joining opposite factions, and the outlawing of all the ideas and platforms at variance with official ideology stamped out any opportunity for creative dialogue within the party. In view of the wholesale suppression of all non-communist elements as well as the intolerance of any interest groups outside of the party, factions allowed to exist within the party might have provided channels for the meaningful exchange of information and ideas. This in turn would have stimulated politicization of the rank-and-file members in the party as well as the North Korean inhabitants as a whole since each faction would have endeavored to have its positions accepted by the party and the society as a whole. The suppression of factions, in this respect, was detrimental to the North Koreans' political growth, since it deprived the masses of the chance to make choices and of informal educational channels. The total destruction of the Korean Workers' Party during the first year of the Korean War might have been avoided, or at least not have been as disastrous as it actually was, had there been genuine political dialogue among the party members, provided that the factions and the rank-and-file members had been allowed to reach a level of real political awakening in the first place, which was not the case. In fact, such an awakening had been suppressed by the party's single-minded official indoctrination which, eventually, proved to be a failure. The immense formal indoctrination

[142]

of the party members that has been going on undeviatingly in conjunction with the promotion of the personality cult of Kim was the inevitable result of the absence of the factions, the "loyal opposition," which could have provided meaningful political discussion in an orderly and lively way. The uniformity of political and social behavior bordering on stagnancy, uniformly acknowledged by various recent foreign visitors to North Korea, might have been avoided by a tolerance of factionalism.

The all-out extermination of factionalism has eliminated many capable men from North Korean leadership. Not only has this brought about a deterioration in quality of those in high party offices but it has also resulted in a lack of resilience of the party, as was demonstrated during the Korean War. Should the party be faced again with a crisis on the scale of the Korean War, it might again collapse. It would seem, then, that the intense commitment of the present North Korean elite to the monopolization of power and to efficiency, to the exclusion of other values, which Jerome D. Frank would call the "blind commitment," [1] has proved dysfunctional for political progress of the North Korean society.

Unfortunately for the present North Korean regime, the destruction of the South Korean communist force has had a serious repercussion. The series of recent failures suffered by the regime in its attempt to establish guerrilla bases in South Korea and undermine the Seoul regime partly stems from the destruction of the South Korean communists. The destruction not only decimated the South Korean communist elite who could more effectively maintain contact with potential followers in the south, but it injected provincialism into the whole Korean communist movement. This provincialism seems to have the effect of deterring potential South Korean communist sympathizers from joining the communist activities in the south that are now directed exclusively and carried out by the north. This makes the communist goal of unification much more arduous, and might have been avoided had the regime kept the South Korean communist leaders in the fold. Although the purge of the South Korean elite was carried out under the rhetoric of patriotism, the P'yŏngyang regime is paying a heavy price for its action.

POSTSCRIPT[1]

Even after the reorganization of the central party organs in October, 1966, more reshuffling of party personnel occurred in P'yŏngyang. The turnover of party elite in the second half of the 1960's and up until the time of the Fifth Party Congress, held in November, 1970, were apparently the results of unsuccessful implementation of the "military line" set by the plenum of the Central Committee in December, 1962. The Central Committee plenum at that time, in line with the new "military line," decided upon reorganization and reorientation of the North Korean economy in order to put it on a wartime footing, and out of this plenum was born the policy of the "build-up of national defense and construction of economy in parallel." [2] Thereafter the party made continuous efforts to realize the policy in "real daily life," [3] and it was confirmed by the party's Representatives' Conference of October 5–12, 1966. Furthermore, the conference of October 1966 took "solid steps" [4] in simultaneously carrying on economic construction and defense preparations, and the national economic plan for implementation of such measures was set to begin in 1967.[5]

The "solid steps" taken, were, as subsequent events proved, all-out militant and violent guerrilla campaigns designed to "liberate" South Korea, preparations for which had been made since the December 1962 Central Committee plenum.

For instance, following the cease-fire in 1953, North Korea, having realized she could not conquer the Republic of Korea by force, made a series of proposals to the South for reunification by peaceful means but without foreign interference, an approach North Korea called "independent" and "peaceful unification." As the first prerequisite for the realization of this goal, the P'yŏngyang regime urged the withdrawal of the U.S. troops from South Korea. At the Fourth Party Congress held in September 1961, Kim Il-sŏng again urged "patriotic" South Koreans to create the right climate for "peaceful unification" and asked them to form a "Revolutionary Party" as the guiding organ. Kim, however, explicitly stated the party should strive to win "legal status." [6] As late as April 14, 1965, during his speech in Indonesia, Kim Il-sŏng, in spite of the policy of "fascist repression" in South Korea, expressed his hope of achieving "independent peaceful unification" by firmly building a "Revolutionary Party" in the south which would direct all South Korean "democratic forces" toward this end. [7]

However, by the time the Representatives' Conference was held October 5–12, 1966, North Korea had apparently recognized the futility of its efforts for "peaceful unification" [8] and chose instead to launch a series of guerrilla operations in the south as a result of the execution of the "dual line of economic construction in parallel with national defense." And at the October 1966 conference, Kim Il-sŏng urged South Korean "patriotic" forces to start "a positive struggle" for their "revolution for motherland liberation," using both "violent and non-violent" and "legal and illegal" methods. [9] This amounted to an open abandonment of "peaceful unification" in favor of a new militant policy toward the south. Subsequently, this resolution to "liberate" the south by force, not on the scale of the Korean War but by Vietnam-type warfare, was marked by an increasing number of armed North Korean infiltrators into South Korea. [10] Among them were commandos, thirty-one of whom—all officers— were involved in an unsuccessful attempt to raid the Presidential Palace in Seoul on January 21, 1968. [11] P'yŏngyang's determination to "liberate" the south was also expressed by its seizure of the U.S. Intelligence ship, *Pueblo*, on January 23, 1968, and the shooting down of a U.S. reconnaissance plane on April 15, 1969.

However, the cost for the execution of such a militant line was very heavy. The national economic plan for 1967, the first year for the implementation of the resolution of the party Representatives' Conference of October 1966, was a "tight" one, as was later admitted by Kim Il-sŏng [12], as the result of allocation of 30.2 percent of the total national expenditure of 1967 to military expenditure in contrast to approximately 5.6 percent annually during 1960 to 1966. For the year 1968, North Korea allocated 30.9 percent of their total budget to the military, an increase over 1967. Between 1967 and 1970, her annual defense expenditure constituted an average of 31.2 percent of the annual national expenditure.[13] As a result, the North Korean economy was overburdened, and the completion of the Seven-Year Economic Plan (1961–1967) had to be postponed for three years,[14] making it a *de facto* ten year plan.

In spite of the cost, North Korea failed to establish a covert "Marxist-Leninist Party" in the south as the "headquarters of revolution"[15] and simultaneously failed to maintain a guerrilla war. Reportedly the failure was attributed to several high-ranking party officials such as Pak Kŭm-ch'ŏl, Yi Hyŏ-sun, Kim To-man, and Ko Hyŏk, all former comrades of Kim Il-sŏng from his Manchurian days.[16] Specifically Yi Hyŏ-sun had been the Director of the Liaison Bureau of the party that had been supervising and directing all North Korean operations against the south since the adjournment of the Fourth Party Congress held in September 1961. The four persons were also believed to have serious misgivings about the "hawkish" line of the party against the south,[17] and they were all purged, most likely between March, 1967, and the 16th plenum of the Central Committee (the 4th period of the Party), convened June 28–July 3, 1967. The plenum was reportedly called to settle the aftermath of the purges[18] and to "realize continuously and thoroughly" the party line of "simultaneous carrying on of economic construction and national defense construction."[19]

Following the resolution of the plenum, North Korea continued to send armed infiltrators into the south in its efforts to build guerrilla bases. The biggest attempt was made by a North Korean raiding party consisting of 84 to 120 men in the autumn of 1968.[20] Though the raid was not a total failure, for it occupied some 40,000 South Korean soldiers and reservists for several months in the manhunt, virtually all of the men of the raiding party were either killed or captured[21] and thus were prevented from carrying out their mission to set up partisan bases. It is possible, that, as a result, three other high-ranking party officials were ousted between late 1968 and early 1969. This time, all were generals, unlike the four persons of predominantly civilian background purged between March and June, 1967.[22] The names of the three generals, all former comrades-in-arms of Kim Il-sŏng in Manchuria, and their ranks at the time of the

[146]

purge were Kim Ch'ang-bong (born 1919), Politburo member and Defense Minister; Ch'oe Kwang, candidate Politburo member and Army Chief of Staff; and Hŏ Bong-hak, candidate Politburo member and Director of the Liaison Bureau of the Party since December 1967.[23]

Kim Ch'ang-bong's position as Defense Minister was filled not later than December 1968 by General Ch'oe Hyŏn (born 1900), then a regular Politburo member. The post of Army Chief of Staff vacated by General Ch'oe Kwang was filled, not later than February 1969, by O Jin-u (born 1910), former comrade-in-arms of Kim Il-sŏng and then a candidate Politburo member. Prior to his succession to the office of the Army Chief of Staff, O had held the highest political office within the North Korean People's Army, the Directorship of the Politburo.[24]

As much as the two purges in the latter half of the 1960's were carried out in connection with the failure of P'yŏngyang's southern campaign, they could be construed as a means on the part of the purgers, especially Kim Il-sŏng, to guard their positions. Nevertheless, these two latest purges seem to differ from the previous ones (administered against the native communists, Yenan returnees, and Soviet Koreans) in that they were caused by frustration over policy failure whereas the earlier ones were primarily results of deadly power struggles among equally ambitious contenders. It was perhaps because of this that Pak Kŭm ch'ŏl and the other three reportedly disappeared "quietly" [25] from the public scene between March and June 1967, and the unfortunate generals lost their positions "without denunciations and without dramatics." [26]

In spite of the reshuffling of central party leaders, the basic characteristics of the North Korean leadership—namely, the absolutism of Kim Il-sŏng and the pervasive influence of his former partisans from Manchuria—remained the same. This was reflected in the reorganization of the central party organs at the Fifth Party Congress held November 2–13, 1970 in P'yŏngyang.[27] Judging from Kim's major speech delivered at the Fifth Congress, North Korea, during the period of a new Six-Year Plan (1971–1976), was to pursue essentially the same domestic and southern policies she had pursued for several years.[28]

In keeping with the established practice, the Fifth Congress elected a new Central Committee membership, this time totalling 172 (117 regular and 55 candidate members),[29] up from 135 elected at the

Fourth Party Congress of September 1961. Of these 172 persons, 119 (71 of the 117 regulars, and 48 of 55 candidates) were elected for the first time to the Central Committee, and they were all believed to be "ardent supporters" [30] of Kim Il-sŏng. The Central Committee in turn elected a new Politburo, the real center of political power in North Korea,[31] and a new Secretariat.

The new Politburo now consisted of eleven full members and four candidate members, down from its total twenty-nine membership (17 full and 12 candidate members) elected in October 1966. The eleven full members were, in the order of their positions: Kim Il-sŏng (born 1912), Ch'oe Yong-kŏn (born 1900), Kim Il (born 1912), Pak Sŏng-ch'ŏl (born 1912), Ch'oe Hyŏn (born 1900), Kim Yong-ju (born 1922), O Jin-u (born 1910), Kim Tong-kyu (born 1915), Sŏ Ch'ŏl (born 1907), Kim Jung-lin (born 1924), and Han Ik-su (born 1918). The first five (Kim Il-sŏng, Ch'oe Yong-kŏn, Kim Il, Pak Sŏng-ch'ŏl, Ch'oe Hyŏn) were on full Politburo membership at the time of the reorganization in October 1966, and all of them were Kim Il-sŏng's comrades-in-arms in Manchuria. The next three (Kim Yong-ju, O Jin-u, Kim Tong-kyu) were candidate members of the Politburo at the time of the reshuffling in October 1966, and all three are believed to be former partisans under Kim Il-sŏng during the 1930's. Of the last three, Sŏ Ch'ŏl participated in communist activities from 1933, most likely in Manchuria, Kim Jung-lin was a member of the underground political organization that cooperated with the partisans under Kim Il-sŏng along the Korean-Manchurian border,and Han Ik-su joined Kim Il-sŏng's guerrilla unit in Manchuria in 1936. It is clear, beyond doubt, that all the full members of the Politburo were former comrades of Kim Il-sŏng during his Manchurian days or were members of a guerrilla unit commanded by him.

The four candidate members elected to the Politburo were: Hyŏn Mu-kwang (born 1913), Chŏng Chun-t'aek (born 1902), Yang Hyŏng-sŏp, and Kim Man-kŭm (born 1905). Hyŏn Mu-kwang, the only candidate member on this newly elected body since the Fourth Party Congress, was a former guerrilla under Kim Il-sŏng in Manchuria. Of the remaining three, all were promoted to candidate membership quite some time after the October 1966 reorganization or for the first time at the Fifth Party Congress. Chŏng Chun-t'aek was a veteran native communist, Yang Hyŏng-sŏp graduated from a middle school in the southeastern part of Manchuria, and Kim

Man-kŭm is said to have joined a communist movement in Manchuria in 1945 following his graduation from a college in Japan.

The size of the Secretariat, whose duty is to organize the party's daily affairs and supervise the party's executive departments, was also trimmed to ten from eleven elected in October 1966. All ten were concurrently members of the Politburo (8 full and 2 candidate members) chosen at the Fifth Congress. Under the Secretary-General-elect Kim Il-sŏng, the nine secretaries were: Ch'oe Yong-kŏn, Kim Il, Kim Yong-ju, O Jin-u, Kim Tong-kyu, Kim Jung-lin, Han Ik-su, Hyŏn Mu-kwang, and Yang Hyŏng-sŏp. Once more, all the secretaries-elect were, with the possible exception of Yang Hyŏng-sŏp, former comrades of Kim Il-sŏng during his Manchurian days.

Thus as of the early 1970's, it is the former guerrillas from Manchuria or from the Korean-Manchurian border area who rule North Korea, and it is Kim Il-sŏng who stands above them. And in spite of the series of purges in the latter half of the 1960's, there has been no sign, even the slightest, that threatens the political stability of North Korea under Kim Il-sŏng. On the contrary, the reduced sizes of the Politburo and the Secretariat may have given him tighter control and more power than ever before.

NOTES

CHAPTER 1

[1] Ministry of Foreign Affairs, Republic of Korea, "Soryŏn nao'e in'nŭn Hangukin" ("Koreans in the Soviet Union"), *Oenu T'ongbo* (Seoul), No. 4 (September, 1954), pp. 88–100; Han Jae-duk, *Hanguk e Kongsan Chu'i wa Pukhan Yŏksa* (Korean Communism and North Korean History) (Seoul: Nae'oe Munhwasa, 1965), pp. 23–77; and George C. Guins, "The Korean Plans of Russian Imperialism," *The American Journal of Economics and Sociology*, VI, No. 1 (October, 1946), pp. 71–86.

[2] Gregory Henderson, *Korea, the Politics of the Vortex* (Cambridge, Massachusetts: Harvard University Press, 1968), pp. 312–14; and Kim San and Nym Wales, *Song of Ariran: The Life Story of a Korean Rebel* (New York: The John Day Company, 1941), pp. 51–54.

[3] "Korea—The Crossroads of Asia," *Amerasia*, IX, No. 17 (October 1945), pp. 271–79; "Korea Past and Present," *The World Today*, II, No. 4 (April, 1946), pp. 175–92; and "Divided Korea," *The Economist*, CL, No. 5341 (January 5, 1946), pp. 5–6.

[4] Chung In-t'aek, "The Korean Minority in Manchuria (1900–1937)" (unpublished Ph.D thesis) (Washington, D. C.: The American University, 1966), pp. 143–50. For instance, Zinoviev at the First Congress of the Toilers of the Far East held in January and February, 1922 made the following appeal to Korean delegation:

> The present Congress will have to tell all the Korean revolutionaries, regardless of their particular beliefs, sincerely and in a brotherly manner, that they must once and for all rid themselves and their people of any remnants of hope that the Korean national question can be solved in any way other than by a close union with the advanced revolutionary workers.

Communist International, *First Congress of the Toilers of the Far East* (Petrograd: Communist International, 1922), p. 31. See also Joseph V. Stalin, *Marxism and the National and Colonial Questions* (New York: International Publishers, 1935), pp. 74–192; Robert C. North, *Moscow and the Chinese Communists* (Stanford University Press, 1963), pp. 16, 60–61; Communist International, *The Second Congress of the Communist International* (Washington: Government Printing Office, 1920), p. 136; "Invitation to the Fourth World Congress of the Communist International," *Inprecorr*, II, No. 57 (July 17, 1922), p. 427; and Communist International, *Fourth Congress of* the *Communist International* (London: Communist Party of Great Britain, 1922), p. 292.

[5] Kim Kyu-sik, "The Asiatic Revolutionary Movement and Imperialism," *The Communist Review*, III, No. 3 (July, 1922), p. 147.

[6] When Yi Tong-hwi met Lenin in 1918 in Moscow, Lenin asked three elementary questions regarding communism and economic conditions of Korea. However, Yi failed to answer any of them. Kim San and Nym Wales, *op. cit.*, pp. 52–53; and Kim Jun-yŏp and Kim Ch'ang-sun, *Hanguk Kongsanchu i Undongsa*, Vol. I (*A History of the Korean Communist Movement, Vol. I*) (Seoul: Korea University Press, 1967), pp. 176–78.

[7] Yang Ho-min, *Pukhan e Ideologi wa Chŏngch'i* (Ideology and Politics in North Korea) (Seoul: Korean University Press, 1967), p. 11.

[8] Robert A. Scalapino and Chong-sik Lee, "The Origins of the Korean Communist Movement (I)," *Journal of Asian Studies*, XX, No. 1 (November, 1960), pp. 19–31; and Robert A. Scalapino and Chong-sik Lee, "The Origins of the Korean Communist Movement (II)," *Journal of Asian Studies*, XX, No. 2 (February, 1961), pp. 147–67.

[9] Kim Tŭk-hwang, *Hanguk Sasangsa* (*History of Korean Thought*) (Seoul: Namsan-dang, 1958), pp. 286–88.

[10] Glenn D. Paige, "Korea and the Comintern, 1919–1935," *Bulletin of the Korean Research Center*, No. 13 (December, 1960), pp. 1–25.

[11] Kim Jun-yŏp and Kim Ch'ang-sun, *Hanguk Kongsanchu'i Undongsa*, Vol. II (*A History of the Korean Communist Movement, Vol. II*) (Seoul: Korea University Press, 1968), pp. 57–149; Kim Chong-myŏng (ed.), *Chōsen Dokuritsu Undō, Kyōsan Undō-hen*, Vol. V (*A History of the Korean Independence Movement, The Communist Movement, Vol. V*) (Tokyo: Hara Shobō, 1967), pp. 391, 405–08; and Kim Sŭng-hak (ed.), *Hanguk Tongnip Undongsa* (*A History of the Korean Independence Movement*) (Seoul: Tongnip Munhwasa, 1966), pp. 246–47.

[12] *Tong-A-Ilbo* (Oriental Daily, leading newspaper in Seoul), June 4 and 9, 1925; and Itō Kenrō, "Chōsen Kyōsan-tō mebae no gore," ("The Embryonic Period of the Korean Communist Party"), *Kaizō*, XXXI No. 10 (October, 1950), pp. 107–11.

[13] Chi Chung-se (ed.), *Chosŏn Sasangbŏm Kŏmkŏ Shilhwa-rok* (*Collection of Stories of Arrests of Korean Political Criminals*) (Seoul: Shin-Kwang Ch'ulp'an-sa, 1946), pp. 24–47.

[14] *Tong-A-Ilbo*, November 17, 1926; and "Chōsen Shakai Undō Gaikan" ("General Outlook of the Korean Socialist Movement"), *Intanashonaru*, II, No. 2 (February, 1928), pp. 63–70.

[15] "The Factional Struggle among the Korean Communists," *Inprecorr*, XIV, No. 48 (September 14, 1934), pp. 1265–66.

[16] *Tong-A-Ilbo*, November 1 and 2, 1929.

[17] *Hanguk e issŏ sŏ ŭi Kongsanju'i* (*Communism in Korea*) (Seoul: The Office of Public Information 1968), pp. 26–7.

[18] Kim Sŭng-hak, *op. cit.*, p. 247.

[19] *Tong-A-Ilbo*, March 9, 10 and 17, 1934; *Ōsaka Asahi Shimbun*, July 3, 1932; "Yi Chae-yu T'alch'ul'ki" ("The Jailbreak of Yi Chae-yu"), *Shin Ch'ŏn-ji*, I, No. 3 (April, 1946), pp. 6–17; and *Shin Ch'ŏn-ji*, II, No. 4 (May 1946), pp. 54–63.

[20] Chi Chung-se (ed.), *op. cit.*, pp. 234–40.

[21] *Tong-A Ilbo*, February 17, and March 30, 1934; and "Chōsen Kyōsan tō Saiken Undō Jiken" ("The Korean Communist Party Reestablishment Movement Incident"), *Shisō Ihō*, No. 2 (March, 1935), pp. 31–33.

[22] Han, *Hanguk e Kongsan Chu'i wa Pukhan Yŏksa*, pp. 79–82.

[23] Chosŏn Kwahakja Tongmaeng (ed.), *Chosŏn Haebang-sa (An Emancipation History of Korea)* (Seoul: Mun-u Sŏkwan, 1946), pp. 112–16.

[24] Chōsen sōtokufu, Hōmukyoku, *Chōsen Dokuritshu Shisō Undō no Hensen (Changes in the Thoughts for the Korean Independence Movement)* (Keijō: Chōsen sōtoku-fu, 1931), pp. 192–99.

[25] "Resolution of the ECCI on the Korean Question, Adopted by the Polit-Secretariat of the ECCI on December 10, 1928," *Inprecorr*, IX, No. 8 (February 15, 1929), pp. 130–33; "Chōsen no Kakumeiteki RōdōKumiai Undō no Nimmu" ("The Duty of the Revolutionary Labor Movement in Korea"), *Intanashonaru*, IV, No. 17 (December, 1930), pp. 1–8; and "Chōsen ni okeru Shijisha ni atafuru Taiheiyō Rōdō Kumiai Shokikyoku no Kōkaijō" ("An Open Letter from the Pan Pacific Labor Union Secretariat to the Supporters of Union in Korea"), *Intanashonaru*, VI, No. 8 (June, 1932), pp. 62–74.

[26] Chosŏn Kwahakja Tongmaeng (ed.), *Chosŏn Haebang-sa*, pp. 113–15.

[27] *Tong-A Ilbo*, July 2 and 4, 1932; January 2, 3, 10 and 29, 1934; February 1, 3, 7, 28, 1934; and March 2, 6, 7, 1934; Kim Chong-bŏm and Kim Tong-un, *Haebang Chŏnu'ui Chosŏn Chinsang*, Vol. I (*The Actual Situation of Korea Before and After Emancipation*, Vol. I) (Seoul: Chosŏn Cŏngkyŏng Yŏngusa, 1945), pp. 54–61; and Chi Chung-se (ed.), *op. cit.*, pp. 261–300.

[28] Chosŏn Kwahakja Tongmaeng (ed.), *Chosŏn Haebang-sa*, pp. 106–07, 109, 111.

[29] Data in this section are derived from following sources: "Chŏngke Inmyŏng-rok" ("A Biographical Dictionary of Persons in Political Field"), in *Chosŏn Yŏng'am 1948* (Korean Annual 1948) (Seoul: Chosŏn T'ongshin-sa, 1948), pp. 457–73; "Chosŏn Haebang Undong T'usa kup Chŏngke Hwalyak e Inmul Yakyŏk" ("Short Biographies of Korean Revolutionaries and of Persons in Political Field"), in Kim Chong-bŏm and Kim Tong-un, *Haebang Chŏnhu'ŭi Chosŏn Chinsang*, Vol. II (*The Actual Situation of Korea Before and After Emancipation*, Vol. II) (Seoul: Chosŏn Chŏngkyŏng Yŏngusa, 1945), pp. 165–219; "Chōsen Kyōsan Undō Jiken Hanketsu" ("Trial Sentences of Korean Communists"), in Chōsen sōtokufu, Hōmukyoku, *op. cit.*, pp. 177–249; and scattered communist and non-communist material.

[30] *Chosŏn Yŏng'am 1948*, pp. 457–73.

[31] Among prominent nationalists in the pre-1945 period, Dr. Syngman Rhee was from an aristocratic family, Kim Sŏng-su (Vice President of South Korea, 1951–52) was one of the four richest men in Korea, and Cho Man-sik (see Chapter III of this manuscript) was a landowner. For more, see *Hyŏndae Han'guk Chŏng'ch'i-ka Kusipp-il-in-jip* (*Ninety-One Contemporary Korean Statesmen*) (Seoul: Shinjo-sa, 1957); and Han Ch'ŏl-yŏng, *Han'guk ŭi In'mul* (*Notable Persons in Korea*) (Seoul: Munhwa Ch'un-ch'u-sa, 1952).

[32] Li "B", "Renewed Wave of Japanese Terror in Korea," *Inprecorr*, XII, No. 39 (September 1, 1932) p. 820; "Save the Lives of the Korean Revolutionaries," *Inprecorr*, XIII, No. 57 (December 29, 1933), pp. 1305–306; "Shōwa Jūichinen do ni okeru Sennai Shisō Undō no Jōkyō" ("The Conditions of the Thought Movement in Korea During 1936"), *Shisō Ihō*, No. 10 (March, 1937), pp. 27–41; and "Chōsen ni okeru Kyōsan Shugi Undō no Kinkyō" ("Recent Conditions of the Communist Movement in Korea"), *Shisō Ihō*, No. 5 (December, 1935), pp. 43–6.

[33] "The Situation in Korea," *Inprecorr*, XIII, No. 55 (December 15, 1933), p. 1246.

[34] For backgrounds of Chinese communist leaders, see Robert C. North, *Kuomingtang and Chinese Communist Elites* (Stanford University Press, 1952); and Franklin W. Houn, "The Eighth Central Committee of the Chinese Communist Party: A Study of An Elite," *The American Political Science Review*, Vol. LI, No. 2 (June, 1957), pp. 392-404.

[35] V. I. Lenin, "What Is To Be Done?", in Lenin's *Selected Works*, Vol. II (London: Lawrence and Wishart LTD, 1963), pp. 138–39.

CHAPTER 2

[1] Foreign Ministry of Japan (ed.), *Chōsen Benran* (Summary Facts About Korea), Asian Series, No. 1 (Tokyo: Foreign Ministry of Japan, 1964), p. 95.

[2] O Yŏng-jin, *Hana-e Chŭng-ŏn* (Eyewitness: North Korea under the Soviet Occupation) (Seoul: Chungang Munhwa-sa, 1952), pp. 24–36, 116–17; and Han Jae-duk, *Kim Il-sŏng kwa Pukkoe ŭi Silsang* (Kim Il-sŏng and the Actual Situation of North Korea) (Seoul: Kongsankŏn Munje Yŏnguso, 1969), pp. 188–89, 236–37.

[3] Pak Tong-un, *Pukhan T'ongch'i Kikuron* (The Government Structure in North Korea) (Seoul: Korea University Press, 1964), p. 8.

[4] *Chosŏn Chung-ang Nyŏngam 1949* (*Korean Central Almanacs 1949*) (P'yŏngyang: Korean Central News Agency, 1949), pp. 52, 53.

[5] *Ibid.*, p. 53.

[6] For identity of this legendary figure, see Suh Dae-suk, *The Korean Communist Movement 1918–1948*(Princeton University Press, 1967), pp. 256–61.

[7] U. S. State Department, *North Korea: A Case Study in the Technique of Takeover* (Washington, D.C.: Government Printing Office, 1961), pp. 3, 13.

[8] *Chosŏn Chung-ang Nyŏngam 1949*, p. 63.

[9] Edward Grant Meade, *American Military Government in Korea* (London: Oxford University Press, 1951).

[10] Benjamin Min, "North Korea's Foreign Policy in the Post-War Decade, 1953–1963" (unpublished Ph.D thesis) (Amherst: University of Massachusetts, 1967), p. 123.

[11] The Research Institute for Internal and External Affairs, *North Korea under Communism: A Story of Suppression* (Seoul: The Research Institute for Internal and External Affairs, 1963), p. 8.

[12] Institute for Foreign Affairs (ed.), *Chōsen Yōran* (Survey of Korea) (Tokyo: Musashi Shobō, 1960), p. 150.

[13] R. E. Lauterbach, *Danger From the East* (New York: Harper & Row, 1947), p. 212.

[14] For information regarding Korean immigration into Soviet Russia, see Kim Jun-yŏp and Kim Ch'ang-sun, *Hanguk Kongsanchu'i Undongsa*, Vol. I, pp. 27–92; and Walter Kolarz, *The Peoples of the Soviet Far East* (London: George Philip and Son Limited, 1954), pp. 33–42.

[15] Tsuboe Senji, *Hokusen no Kaihō Jūnen* (Ten Years of Liberated North Korea) (Tokyo: Nikkan Rōdō Tsūshin-sha, 1956), p. 118.

[16] Kiwon Chung, "The North Korean People's Army and the Party," in Robert A. Scalapino (ed.), *North Korea Today* (New York: Frederick A. Praeger, 1963), p. 106.

[17] For information on Korean immigrants in Manchuria, see Yi Hun-gu, *Manju wa Chosŏn-in* (Korean Immigrants in Manchuria) (P'yŏngyang: Union Christian College Press, 1932); East-Asiatic Economic Investigation Bureau, *The Manchurian Year Book 1932–33* (Tokyo: East-Asiatic Economic Investigation Bureau, 1932), pp. 461–63; and Shen Mo, *Japan in Manchuria* (Manila: Grace Trading Co., Inc., 1960), pp. 269–82, 390–400.

[18] For a North Korean version of Kim Il-sŏng's background, see Pak Sang-hyŏk, *Chosŏn Minjokŭi Widaehan Chidoja* (The Great Leader of the Korean People) (Tokyo: Chosŏn Shinbosa, 1964); and Yi Na-yŏng, *Chosŏn Minjok Haebang T'ujaengsa* (A History of Korean People's Struggle for Liberation) (P'yŏngyang: Korean Workers' Party Press, 1958).

[19] Kim Chong-myŏng (ed.), *Chōsen Dokuritsu Undō, Kyōsan Undō-hen*, V. pp. 606–14; and Hatano Kennichi (ed.), *Chūgoku Kyōsantō-shi, 1936*, Vol. VI (History of the Chinese Communist Party, 1936, Vol. VI) (Tokyo: Jiji Tsūshin-sha, 1961), pp. 750–55.

[20] Tsuboe Senji, *Chōsen Minzok Dokuritsu Undō Hishi* (Hidden Story of the Struggle of Korean People for Emancipation) (Tokyo: Gennandō Shotten, 1966), pp. 128–29.

[21] *Tong-A Ilbo*, July 5 (extra edition), 6, 7, 1937. For a North Korean account of the attack, see Baik Bong, *Kim Il Sung: Biography*, Vol. I (Translated from Korean into English by the Committee for Translation of Kim Il Sung: Biography) (Tokyo: Miraisha, 1969), pp. 363–81.

²² Bang In-hu, *Pukhan "Chosŏn Nodongdang" ŭi Hyŏngsŏng kwa Palchŏn* (North Korean "Korean Workers' Party", Its Formation and Development) (Seoul: Korea University Press, 1967), pp. 77, 77f, 78.

²³ Joungwon A. Kim, "The Long March of North Korea's Kim," *The New York Times Magazine*, February 25, 1968, p. 33.

²⁴ *Facts About Korea* (P'yŏngyang: Foreign Language Publishing House, 1961), p. 33; and Han Im-hyŏk, *Kim Il-sŏng tongji e ŭihan Chosŏn Kongsandang Ch'angkŏn* (Establishment of Korean Communist Party by Comrade Kim Il-sŏng) (P'yŏngyang: Korean Workers' Party, 1961), pp. 21–22, 34.

²⁵ Han Jae-duk, *Kim Il-sŏng ŭl Kobal Handa* (I Sue Kim Il-sŏng) (Seoul: Nae'oe Munhwasa, 1965), pp. 111–16.

²⁶ Han Im-hyŏk, *op. cit.*, pp. 26, 52.

²⁷ For the communist movement in South Korea after the liberation, see Chapter 6.

²⁸ Kim Ch'ang-sun, *Pukhan Sip-o-Nyŏn-sa* (Fifteen Years of North Korean History) (Seoul: Chimunkak, 1961), p. 93.

²⁹ Kim Ch'ang-sun, *Pukhan Sip-o-Nyŏn-sa*, pp. 66–67; and *Jwa-ik Sakŏn Silrok*, Vol. I (Records of Leftist Incidents, Vol. I) (Seoul: Public Prosecutor's Office, 1965), p. 81.

³⁰ *Ibid.*, p. 83.

³¹ Tsuboe, *Chōsen Minzoku Dokuritsu Undō Hishi*, pp. 458–60.

³² Shannon McCune, *Korea: Land of Broken Calm* (Princeton: D. Van Nostrand Company, Inc., 1967), p. 124.

³³ Democratic People's Republic of Korea, Academy of Science, Center for Historical Studies, *Chosŏn T'ongsa*, Vol. III (Outline of History of Korea, Vol. III) (reprinted in Japan) (Tokyo: Hak-u Sobang, 1961), p. 16; and Han Im-hyŏk, *op. cit.*, p. 36.

³⁴ *Chosŏn T'ongsa*, Vol. III (1961), pp. 15–16; and Han Im-hyŏk, *op. cit.*, p. 52.

³⁵ *Chosŏn Nodongdang Ryŏksa Kyojae* (Textbook for a History of Korean Workers' Party) (P'yŏngyang: Korean Workers' Party, 1964), pp. 137–44.

³⁶ *Kim Il-sŏng Sŏnjip, Vol. I* (Selected Works of Kim Il-sŏng, Vol. I) (P'yŏngyang: Korean Workers' Party, 1963), p. 357; and Han Im-hyŏk, *op. cit.*, p. 55.

CHAPTER 3

¹ *Kim Il-sŏng Sŏnjip*, Vol. VI (*Selected Works of Kim Il-sŏng*, Vol. VI) (P'yŏngyang: Korean Workers' Party, 1960), p. 141.

² KYZ, "Sip'yŏng" (Comments on Current Events"), *Inmin* (People) (Seoul), II, No. 1 (January, 1946), p. 44.

³ John N. Washburn, "Russia Looks at Northern Korea," *Pacific Affairs*, XX, No. 2 (June, 1947), p. 153.

⁴ *Chosŏn Chung-ang Nyŏngam 1949*, p. 58.

⁵ Robert T. Oliver, *Korea: Forgotten Nation* (Washington, D.C.: Public

Affairs Press, 1944), pp. 122–28.

[6] Cornelius G. Osgood, *The Koreans and Their Culture* (New York: Ronald Press Company, 1951), p. 251.

[7] *Pukhan Kongsan Jipdan ui Hŭkp'i-so* (Story About the North Korean Leaders) (Seoul: Nae-oe Munje Yŏnguso, 1961), p. 58.

[8] It was said that in the beginning, Cho Man-sik, the leader of this Christian movement, was not enthusiastic about the formation of a party in the north, fearing that such an act would result in hardening the "temporary" 38th Parallel. But Kim Il-sŏng was said to have importuned Cho to go on and rally those North Koreans who were indignant about the "misdemeanors" of local communists. Kim reportedly added that he represented the Russian authorities and so he would be a liaison between the new party and the occupation authorities. *Daehan Minguk Chŏngdangsa* (A History of Korean Political Parties) (Seoul: Central Committee on Election Affairs, 1964), pp. 499–500.

[9] Yi Ki-ha, *Hanguk Chŏngdang Paltalsa* (History of the Development of Korean Political Parties) (Seoul: Uihoe Chŏngch'i'sa, 1961), pp. 154–55.

[10] Cho Yŏng-am, *Kodang Cho Man-sik* (Biography of Cho Man-sik) (Pusan: Chŏngch'i' Shinmun-sa, 1953), pp. 12–76.

[11] Yu Hŏn, *Pukhan Isip-nyŏn* (Twenty Years of North Korea) (Seoul: Taehan Bangkong Kyŏyukwŏn, 1966), p. 118; and Aleksander I. Gitovich and B. Bursov, *North of the 38th Parallel* (Translated from Russian by George Leonof) (Shanghai: Epoch Publishing Company, 1948), p. 114.

[12] *Jwa-ik Sakŏn Silrok*, Vol. I, pp. 71–78; and U. S. State Department, *North Korea*, pp. 67–84. *The New York Times* of October 27, 1945 reported: "Korean travellers consistently tell of systematic dismantling and removal northward from Korea of factory machinery and mining equipment." *New York Herald Tribune* on November 2, 1945 reported: "High Allied sources said today they have seen irrefutable proof that Russian troops are stripping northern Korea of valuable industrial machinery."

[13] Foreign Ministry of Japan, *Sengo ni okeru Chōsen no Seijijōsei* (Korean Politics in the Postwar Era) (Tokyo: Foreign Ministry of Japan, 1948), p. 81; Kim Sam-kyu, *Chōsen Gendai-shi* (Modern History of Korea) (Tokyo: Tsukuma Shobō, 1963), p. 52; and *Hanguk e issŏ sŏ ŭi Kongsanju'i*, pp. 91–96.

[14] Osgood, *The Koreans and Their Culture*, p. 322.

[15] Kim Chong-myŏng, *Chōsen Shinminshushugi Kakumei-shi* (A History of the New Democratic Revolution in Korea) (Tokyo: Gogatsu Shobō, 1953), p. 182.

[16] According to South Korean source, Kim Il-sŏng introduced these two persons to Cho Man-sik, pledging that they were "the most suitable men to carry out the work of the Democratic Party." In the beginning Cho did not suspect their real identity. *Daehan Minguk Chŏngdangsa*, p. 500.

[17] Gitovich and Bursov, *North of the 38th Parallel*, p. 114; and George

M. McCune, "Korea: The First Year of Liberation," *Pacific Affairs*, XX, No. 1 (March, 1947), pp. 3-17.

[18] U. S. State Department, *The Record on Korean Unification, 1943-1960*, State Department Publication No. 7084 (Washington, D. C.: Government Printing Office, 1961), p. 5.

[19] Democratic People's Republic of Korea, Academy of Science, Center for Historical Studies, *Chosŏn T'ongsa*, Vol. III (Outline of History of Korea, Vol. III) (P'yŏngyang: Nodong Shinmun Press, 1958), p. 458.

[20] Kang Dae-ho, "Mak-pu Sam-guk Oe'sang Hoe'i wa Chosŏn" ("The Moscow Three Foreign Ministers' Conference and Korea"), *Inmin* (People) (Seoul), II, No. 1 (January, 1946), p. 69; and Carl Berger, *The Korean Knot: A Military and Political History* (Philadelphia: University of Pennsylvania Press, 1957)p. 61. Berger in the same book (p. 61) mentions that the U. S. 24th Army Corps later obtained a document dated January 3, 1946, containing North Korean Communist "instructions to all levels and branches concerning the decisions on Korea made at Moscow."

[21] Chung Henry, *The Russians Came to Korea* (Seoul: The Korean Pacific Press, 1947), p. 83.

[22] Han, *Kim Il-sŏng ŭl Kobal Handa*, pp. 242-54.

[23] This is the term Kim Il-sŏng used in referring to Cho Man-sik during the time of the trusteeship turmoil. *Ibid.*, p. 252.

[24] Tsuboe, *Chōsen Minzoku Dokuritsu Undō Hishi*, p. 471; and *Jwa-ik Sakŏn Silrok*, I, p. 91.

[25] *Chosŏn T'ongsa*, Vol. III (P'yŏngyang, 1958), p. 458.

[26] Tsuboe, *Chōsen Minzoku Dokuritsu Undō Hishi*, p. 472; and *Jwa-ik Sakŏn Silrok*, I, pp. 91-92.

[27] *Kang Dae-ho op. cit.*, pp. 66-72; and *Chosŏn T'ongsa*, III (P'yŏngyang, 1958), pp. 459-61.

[28] During the 20-month period after the liberation some 400,000 North Koreans migrated to the south and about 300,000 Japanese were repatriated from North Korea. As a result, North Korean population declined by a twelfth. Ray Cromley, "North Korea Sovietized," *The Wall Street Journal*, May 5, 1947.

[29] Following the take-over of the central party apparatus of the Democratic Party by the communists, nationalists remained only in local party branches without being able to influence the political course of the north. During the Korean War these nationalists fought against North Korean stragglers, but they fled to the south in fear of communist retaliation. Thereafter, the Democratic Party membership decreased rapidly and all of its branch offices were abolished, leaving only the central party apparatus with nominal membership. Yu Hŏn, *Pukhan Isip-nyŏn*, pp. 118-19.

[30] Gitovich and Bursov, *North of the 38th Parallel*, p. 115.

[31] Kim Chong-myŏng, *Chōsen Shinminshushugi Kakumei-shi*, p. 183. The communist chairman of the Democratic Party, Ch'oe Yong-kŏn, returned

to his Korean Workers' Party in April, 1956 and assumed vice-chairmanship of the KWP. Currently, the Democratic Party is headed by Kang Yang-ok, former Christian minister and a relative of Kim Il-sŏng, and his party has no policies different from those of the Korean Workers' Party. Yu Hŏn, *op. cit.*, p. 119.

[32] Ishii Toshio, "Kyōso Sai Saigu ni okeru Tōgaku shisō no rekishiteki tenkai," ("The Historical Development of Tonghak Thought by Founder Ch'oe Che-u"). *Rekishigaku Kenkyū*, II, No. 1 (January, 1941), pp. 17–60.

[33] *Chōsen Benran*, p. 102.

[34] Kim Chong-bŏm & Kim Tong-un, *Haebang Chŏnhu'ŭi Chosŏn Chinsang, I*, pp. 128–30. At a nationwide congress of believers of the Teaching of the Way of Heaven held in Seoul on April 7, 1947, they made another declaration which read in part: "Our party is a public party whose principles are the precepts of the Teaching of the Way of Heaven and whose mission is to help the nation and pacify the people." Yi Ki-ha, *Hanguk Chŏngdang Paltalsa*, p. 157.

[35] United Nations, *Report of the United Nations for the Unification and Rehabilitation of Korea*, General Assembly, Officials Records: 6th Session, Supplement No. 12 (A/1881) (New York: 1951), p. 26.

[36] *Chosŏn Nodongdang Ryŏksa Kyojae*, p. 142.

[37] Philip Rudolph, *North Korea's Political and Economic Structure* (New York: Institute of Pacific Relations, 1959), p. 11.

[38] *Chosŏn Nodongdang Ryŏksa Kyojae*, p. 142. Members of the North Korean Youth Fraternal Party plotted an anti-communist uprising on March 1, 1948 to commemorate the Koreans' anti-Japanese uprising of March 1, 1919. In order to help implement the plan, the Youth Fraternal Party in Seoul dispatched its agents to North Korea. But the plot was detected because of the betrayal of some central officials of the North Korean Youth Fraternal Party, including the chairman Kim. Those who were involved in the plot were all arrested and imprisoned. Thereafter, the communists took oppressive measures against the North Korean Youth Fraternal Party. *Daehan Minguk Chŏngdangsa*, p. 504. During the Korean War, local members of the North Korean Youth Fraternal Party cooperated with the South Korean troops that occupied North Korea for a short while. Thereafter, all local offices of the North Korean Youth Fraternal Party were abolished. Currently, the party is allowed only to maintain its central office under Pak Shin-duk. The party, like the Democratic Party, has no party policies other than following the policies of the Korean Workers' Party. Kim, *Pukhan Sip-o-Nyŏn-sa*, pp. 164–65.

[39] *Chosŏn T'ongsa*, Vol. III (1958), pp. 492–93. The North Korean Democratic United Front changed its name on June 29, 1949 to the Democratic Front For the Unification of Motherland in order to include all leftist South Korean political parties and social organizations.

[40] For details of the decisions regarding the tasks of the Interim People's

Council, see *Kin Nichisei Senshū*, Vol. I (Selected Works of Kim Il-sŏng, Vol. I) (Tokyo: Japanese Communist Party, 1966), pp. 100-107. For an English version, see *Amerasia*, XI, No. 2 (February, 1947), pp. 55-56.

[41] For an understanding of traditional Korea, see, among others, Pak Munok, *Hanguk Chŏngbu-ron* (Korean Government) (Seoul: Pukyongsa, 1963), pp. 43, 243-45, 251-53; Song Chihak, *Chōsen Kyōiku-shi* (A History of Korean Education) (Tokyo: Kuroshiyo Shuppan, 1960), p. 168; Chŏn Sŏk-tan, *Chosŏn Kyŏngjesa* (A History of Korean Economy) (Seoul: Pakmun Ch'ulp'ansa, 1949), pp. 232, 295-96; Glenn D. Paige, *The Korean People's Democratic Republic* (Stanford: The Hoover Institution, 1966), p. 57; Park Dong-suh, *Hanguk Kwanryo Jedo ŭi Ryŏksadyok Dyŏnkae* (The Historical Development of the Bureaucracy in Korea) (Seoul: The Korean Research Center, 1961), p. 79; and Andrew J. Grajdazev, "Korea Divided," *Far Eastern Survey*, XIV, No. 20 (October 10, 1945), pp. 281-83.

[42] According to South Korean figures, at least 705,239 Japanese civilians left Korea in the immediate post-liberation period. The figures included Japanese from both the south and North Korea. *Kyŏngje Nyŏngam 1949*, Part II (Economic Yearbook 1949, Part II) (Seoul: Research Section, Bank of Korea, 1949), p. 158.

[43] B. Yarovoy, "Korea: Forgotten Nation," *New Times* (Moscow) (August 15, 1945), pp. 26-27.

[44] For a full Korean text on this decree, see *Chosŏn Chung'ang Nyŏngam 1949*, pp. 69-71. For an English translation of the full text, see Hankum Tralim, "Land Reform in North Korea," *Amerasia*, XI, No. 2 (February, 1947), pp. 55-61.

[45] *Chosŏn Chung'ang Nyŏngam 1949*, pp. 69-71.

[46] Rudolph, *North Korea's Political and Economic Structure*, p. 49.

[47] *Chosŏn Chung'ang Nyŏngam 1949* pp. 68-72.

[48] Edwin W. Pauley, *Report on Japanese Assets in Soviet-Occupied Korea to the President of the United States* (Washington: Government Printing Office, 1946), p. 3.

[49] Chong-sik Lee, "Land Reform, Collectivization and the Peasants in North Korea," in Scalapino (ed.), *North Korea Today*, p. 68; George M. McCune, *Korea Today* (Cambridge: Harvard University Press, 1950), p. 209; and Washburn, "Russia Looks at Northern Korea," p. 156.

[50] Max Beloff, *Soviet Policy in the Far East, 1944-1951* (London: Oxford University Press, 1953), p. 165.

[51] Pak, *Pukhan T'ongch'i Kikuron*, p. 158.

[52] Article III, Section 4 of the land reform decree stipulates regulations governing confiscation of lands belonging to all religious organizations. For the amount of land loss sustained by all religious groups, see United Nations, *Report of the United Nations for the Unification and Rehabilitation of Korea*, General Assembly, Official Records: 6th Session, Supplement No. 12 (A/1881) (New York: 1951), p. 61.

[53] For its text, see *Kim Il-sŏng Sŏnjip*, Vol. I (1963), pp. 54–57.

[54] For a full text of the labor law, see *Chosŏn Chung-ang Nyŏngam 1949*, pp. 74–77. For an English text, see Kim Doo-yong, "Labor Legislation in North Korea," *Amerasia*, XI, No. 5 (May, 1947), pp. 156–70.

[55] Lee Se-youl, "A Picture of North Korea's Industry," *Amerasia*, XI, No. 2 (February, 1947), pp. 61–62.

[56] N. Latsinnik, "Industrial Scenes in the Korean Republic," *New Times* (Moscow), No. 14 (March 30, 1949), pp. 26-30; V. Perlin, "Visit to North Korea," *New Times*, No. 2 (January 7, 1948), pp. 15–18; and Han Shi-yoon, "Factory Trade Unions," *New Korea* (P'yŏngyang), No. 6 (June, 1958), pp. 34–35.

[57] For a full text of the decree, see *Chosŏn Chung'ang Nyŏngam 1949*, pp. 77–78.

[58] Yoon T. Kuark, "North Korea's Industrial Development During the Post-War Period," Scalapino (ed.), *North Korea Today*, pp. 51-52.

[59] For a full text of the nationalization law, see *Chosŏn Chung'ang Nyŏngam 1949*, pp. 73–74.

[60] *Chosŏn T'ongsa*, III (1958), p. 473.

[61] Paige, *The Korean People's Democratic Republic*, p. 57.

[62] *Chosŏn Chung'ang Nyŏngam 1949*, pp. 79–80.

[63] Park Dong-suh, *op. cit.*, pp. 84–96; and KYZ, "Sip-yŏng," *Inmin*, II, No. 1 (January, 1946), pp. 43–44.

[64] U. S. State Department, *North Korea*, p. 87.

[65] More will be said about them in the subsequent chapters.

[66] U. S. State Department, *North Korea*, pp. 6, 8.

[67] *Chosŏn Chung'ang Nyŏngam 1949*, pp. 83–84.

[68] *Ibid.*

[69] Harold J. Noble, "North Korean Democracy: Russian Style," *The New Leader*, XXX, No. 22 (May 31, 1947) (Section 2), pp. 1–12.

[70] The North Korean Workers' Party will be discussed in Chapter 4.

[71] For details of the elections result, see V. Smolensky, "The Situation in Korea," *Pravda*, November 16, 1946, in the *Soviet Press Translations*, Vol. II, No. 5 (March 15, 1947) (Seattle: University of Washington), pp. 8–11; and P. Ivanov, "Elections in Northern Korea," *Izvestia*, November 16, 1946, in the *Soviet Press Translations*, Vol. I, No. 4 (December 14, 1946) (Seattle: University of Washington), pp. 18–22.

[72] *Pravda*, November 16, 1946.

CHAPTER 4

[1] Kim, "The Long March of North Korea's Kim," p. 33.

[2] For information about this man, see Pak T'ae-wŏn, *Yaksan kwa Uiyŏldan* (Yaksan and Uiyŏldan) (Seoul: Paekyang-sa, 1947). Yaksan is an alias of Kim Wŏn-bong.

[3] The original is in *Shisō Ihō*, No. 5, pp. 98–99. Transplanted from

Chong-sik Lee, *The Politics of Korean Nationalism* (Berkeley: University of California Press, 1963), p. 194.

[4] "Kaizi Futei Senjin no Jōkyō" ("Conditions of Recalcitrant Koreans Abroad"), *Tokkō Gaizi Geppō,* (April, 1938), pp. 95–97; (July, 1938), pp. 113–17; (August, 1938), pp. 88–92; (October, 1938), pp. 134–42; and "Zai shi Futei Senjin no Anyaku ni kansuru Jyōhō" ("Information Concerning the Secret Maneuvers of the Recalcitrant Koreans in China"), *Shisō Ihō,* No. 14 (March, 1938), pp. 218–31.

[5] For a full Japanese text of the declaration of the youth federation, see *Tokkō Geppō,* July, 1941, pp. 119–22.

[6] Tsuboe, *Chōsen Minzok Dokuritsu Undō Hishi,* p. 120.

[7] Minju Chui Minzok Chŏnsŏn (ed.), *Chosŏn Haebang Nyŏnbo 1946* (Korean Emancipation Annual 1946) (Seoul: Mun-u-in Sŏkwan, 1946), pp. 146–49.

[8] U. S. State Department, *North Korea,* p. 13.

[9] Sources of their biographical data are: "Tongnip Tong-maeng kŭp Ŭiyong-gun Yoin ŭi Yakyŏk" ("Short Biographies of the Important People of the Independence League and the Volunteer Corps"), *Shin Ch'ŏn-ji* (Seoul), I, No. 2 (March, 1946), pp. 242–44; "Kim Tu-bong Chusŏk ŭi T'ujaeng-sa" ("Record of the Struggle of Chairman Kim Tu-bong"), *Shin Ch'ŏn-ji,* I, No. 2 (March, 1946), pp. 205–07; "Chosŏn Ŭiyong-gun Ch'ong Saryŏng Mu-Jŏng Chang-gun Ildae-ki" ("Biography of Commanding General of the Korean Volunteer Corps, General Mu-Jŏng"), *Shin Ch'ŏn-ji,* I, No. 2 (March, 1946), pp. 238–41; Foreign Ministry of Japan (ed.), *Gendai Chūgoku Chōsen Jinmeikan* (Who's Who in Modern China and Korea) (Tokyo: Foreign Ministry of Japan, 1953); and a few other scattered materials.

According to a recent North Korean source, there had never been any "genuine" Korean communist organizations abroad except that under Kim Il-sŏng in Manchuria. Accordingly, the current North Korean regime summarily brands all documents that describe the activities of the Independence League in North China as "false." *Kŭlloja* (The Worker) (P'yŏngyang), No. 1 (January, 1960), pp. 10–21.

[10] *Chosŏn Haebang Nyŏnbo 1946,* p. 146.

[11] *Ibid.*

[12] Kim Ch'ang-sun, *Yŏksa ŭi Chŭng'in* (The Witness of History) (Seoul: Hanguk Asea Pangkong Yŏnmaeng, 1956), pp. 51–52.

[13] Kim, *Pukhan Sip-o-Nyŏn-sa,* p. 64.

[14] *Ibid.,* pp. 61–65; and Kim, "The Long March of North Korea's Kim," p. 33.

[15] Han, *Kim Il-sŏng ŭl Kobal Handa,* p. 225.

[16] Yang Ho-min, *Pukhan e Ideologi wa Chŏngeh'i,* p. 155.

[17] Tsuboe, *Chōsen Minzok Dokuritsu Undō Hishi,* p. 473.

[18] *Chosŏn Haebang Nyŏnbo 1946,* p. 147.

¹⁹ For a full Korean text of the platform of the New People's Party, see *Chosŏn Haebang Nyŏnbo 1946*, pp. 146–49.

²⁰ For the policies of the North Korean Communist Party, see Chapter 3.

²¹ U. S. State Department, *North Korea*, p. 115.

²² According to North Korean source, prior to the land reform about 20 per cent of total North Korean farming families had their own lands and were considered as landowners. *Chosŏn Chung'ang Nyŏngam 1949*, p. 72. Among them ten per cent had more than five chungbo and 90 per cent had holdings of five chungbo or less. Rudolph, *North Korea's Political and Economic Structure*, p. 46. Since each family was given less than 1.5 chungbo, it is assumed that a sizable segment of the former landowning class was disaffected.

²³ *Chosŏn Nodongdang Ryŏksa Kyojae*, pp. 132–35; *Kim Il-sŏng Sŏnjip*, Vol. I (P'yŏngyang, 1963), p. 17; and *Chosŏn Haebang Nyŏnbo 1946*, p. 147.

²⁴ Baik Bong, *Kim Il Sung: Biography*, Vol. II (Tokyo: Miraisha, 1970), 141; and Lee Ch'ŏl-chu, "Pukke Chosŏn Nodongdang" ("The North Korean Communist Party"), *Shin Tong-a* (Seoul), May 1, 1965, p. 267.

²⁵ Tsuboe, *Chōsen Minzoku Dokuritsu Undō Hishi*, p. 471.

²⁶ Baik Bong, *Kim Il Sung: Biography*, II, p. 141.

²⁷ *Ibid.*, p. 144; and *Kin Nichisei Senshū*, Vol. I (Tokyo, 1966), p. 172.

²⁸ Kim, *Chōsen Shinminshushugi Kakumei-shi*, p. 188; and Baik Bong, *Kim Il Sung: Biography*, II, p. 144.

²⁹ Kim, *Pukhan Sip-o-Nyŏn-sa*, p. 100.

³⁰ *Kim Il-sŏng Sŏnjip*, Vol. I (1963), pp. 178–79, 190.

³¹ *Ibid.*, pp. 177–78. On September 26, 1946, Kim Il-sŏng gave more detailed explanation for the necessity of establishing the North Korean Workers' Party (*Ibid.*, pp. 202–03):

> A party is the *avant-garde* of a class, defending and fighting for its interests. The Communist Party protects the interests of the proletariat. The New People's Party protects the interests of the peasantry and the working intelligentsia. Despite the fact that the Communist and New People's Parties thus represent the interests of their respective classes, they have carried out a common task from the day of their establishment—namely, the articulation of the common interests of the workers, peasants and intelligentsia. These interests have been the basis for the struggle for democracy and also serve as the basis for the merger of the Communist and New People's Parties.

³² *Ibid.*, p. 187.

³³ *Ibid.*, pp. 180–82. As the goal of the North Korean Workers' Party Kim set forth the following tasks: the consolidation of the land reform; the nationalization of all Japanese industrial plants; the adoption of the eight-hour working day and a system of social security; introduction of a new tax system; the placing of all power in the people's councils; universal suffrage; guaranteeing all citizens the freedom of speech, assembly, demon-

stration and organization; giving all citizens the right to education and the introduction of a system of public education; the introduction of a system of obligatory military service; and the establishment of friendly relations with all "peace-loving nations."

[34] For the complete text of Kim Tu-bong's speech, see *Chosŏn Haebang Nyŏnbo 1946*, p. 457.

[35] It was said that the communists deliberately yielded the chairmanship to the leader of the Yenan Koreans in order to appease the insecure feeling on the part of the delegates of the New People's Party, who were uncertain of the meaning of the merger and secretly suspected that the call for unity was only a scheme to allow the Soviet-returnees to absorb the forces of the New People's Party. Kim, *Pukhan Sip-o-Nyŏn-sa*, pp. 99–101.

[36] F. I. Shabshina, "Korea: After the Second World War," in A. M. Dyakov *et al.*, *Crisis of the Colonial System: National Liberation Struggle of the Peoples of East Asia* (Bombay: People's Publishing House, Ltd., 1951), p. 175; and Rudolph, *North Korea's Political and Economic Structure*, p. 27.

[37] Bang In-hu, *Pukhan "Chosŏn Nodongnang"* (etc.), pp. 101–02. The ten departments and their heads were:

Organization Department	Hŏ Kai (Soviet Korean)
Training "	Mu-Jŏng (Yenan Korean)
Agitation and	
Propaganda "	Kim Ch'ang-man (Yenan-Korean)
Labour "	Name Unknown (Soviet Korean)
Agriculture "	Name Unknown (Yenan Korean)
Culture "	Han Sŏl-ya (Native Communist)
Women's "	Pak Chŏng-ae (Woman, Native Communist)
Youth "	Name Unknown (Soviet-returnee)
General Affairs "	Chang Ji-min (Yenan Korean)
Finance "	Kim Kyo-yŏng (Native Communist)

[38] According to communist sources, at the time of the formation of the North Korean Workers' Party the total party membership was 366,000, thus making it the largest political party in North Korea. Out of the total party members, 14.7 per cent were of labor origin; 35 per cent were of poor peasant origin; and 50.3 per cent were office workers and men of other social backgrounds. Kim Chong-myŏng, *Chōsen Shinminshushugi Kakumei-shi*, p. 189; and *Kin Nichisei Senshū*, Vol. I (Tokyo, 1966), pp. 120–21.

CHAPTER 5

[1] *Chosŏn Chung'ang Nyŏngam 1950*, p. 201.

[2] *Chosŏn Chung'ang Nyŏngam 1949*, p. 84. The People's Assembly was replaced by the Supreme People's Assembly following the election of August 25, 1948. For more, see Chapter 6.

[3] Shabshina, "Korea: After the Second World War," in Dyakov *et al.* (eds.), *Crisis of the Colonial System*, p. 176.

[4] *Chosŏn Chung'ang Nyŏngam, 1950*, p. 201.

[5] *Chosŏn Chung'ang Nyŏngam 1949*, p. 85.

[6] *Ibid.*

[7] *Ibid.*

[8] Cho Soon-sung, *Korea in World Politics, 1940–1950* (Berkeley: University of California Press, 1967), p. 128.

[9] Shabshina, "Korea: After the Second World War," in Dyakov *et al.* (eds.), *Crisis of the Colonial System*, p. 176.

[10] Pak, *Pukhan T'ongch'i Kikuron*, p. 9. See also Pak Tong-un, "The Character of the Constitution of Communist North Korea and Its Establishment Process," *Journal of Asiatic Studies*, VI, No. 2 (December, 1963), pp. 25–28.

[11] It was reported that North Korea in early 1948 had some 350,000 troops. *Nippon Keizai Shimbun* (Japan Economy Newspaper), March 2, 1948.

[12] The People's Economic Plan For 1947, the first one-year economic plan, was proposed by Kim Il-sŏng on February 19, 1947 at the Congress of People's Councils, and the proposal was endorsed by the Congress. For a full text of Kim's proposal, see *Kim Il-sŏng Sŏnjip*, Vol. I (1963), pp. 294–314.

[13] The One-Year People's Economic Plan For 1948 was proposed by Kim Il-sŏng on February 6, 1948 at the Fourth Congress of the North Korean People's Assembly, and the Assembly approved the proposal. For a full text of Kim's proposal, see *Kim Il-sŏng Sŏnjip*, Vol. II (P-yŏngyang: Korean Workers' Party, 1964), pp. 45–72.

[14] *Chung Kongŏp Palchŏn ŭl wihan uridang'e Chŏngch'aek* (Policy of Our Party for the Development of Heavy Industry) (P'yŏngyang: Korean Workers' Party, 1961), pp. 5–12.

[15] Yi Shin-hyong, *Kyŏngje Sangsik* (Economic Fundamentals) (P'yŏngyang: Korean Workers' Party, 1960), p. 90; and Maruo Itaru and Mura Tsuneo, *Bunretsu Kokka ni okeru Keizai Hatten no Futatsuno Ryūkei* (Two Patterns of Economic Development in the Divided Nations) (Tokyo: Kokusai Mondai Kenkyū-sho, 1962), pp. 49–52.

[16] For the decline of the private sector and the growth of the state sector between 1946 and 1948, see *Facts About Korea* (1961), p. 96.

[17] Pak Ch'ŏl, *Puk Chosŏn Nosŏn Pip'an* (Criticism of the North Korean Course) (Seoul: Shinjo-sa, 1961), pp. 52–9.

[18] U. N., *Report of the United Nations Commission for the Unification and Rehabilitation of Korea* (New York, 1951), p. 28.

[19] Wilbur Schram and John W. Riley (Jr.), "Communication in the Sovietized State, as Demonstrated in Korea," *American Sociological Review*, XVI, No. 6 (December, 1951), pp. 757–66; and Wilbert B. Dubin, "The Political

Evolution of the P'yŏngyang Government," *Pacific Affairs*, XXIII, No. 4 (December, 1950), pp. 388–89.

[20] In order to infuse dynamism into the Korean society, the North Korean communists made efforts for the industrialization of North Korea and they were successful in their efforts. Between 1946 and 1949 the agricultural production itself increased. However, its share of total North Korean production decreased because of a more rapid increase in industrial production. *Facts About Korea* (1961), p. 101. North Korea rehabilitated most of her destroyed industrial plants by the end of 1947 and then pushed ahead to increase her industrial production. *Chung Kongŏp Palchŏn ŭl wihan uridang'e Chŏngch'aek*, p. 12.

[21] *Kim Il-sŏng Sŏnjip*, Vol. I (1963), p. 348.

[22] *Ibid.*, p. 362.

[23] *Ibid.*, pp. 364–65.

[24] Kim, *Yŏksa ŭi Chŭng'in*, pp. 204–06; and Tsuboe, *Chōsen Minzoku Dokuritsu Undō Hishi*, pp. 459–60.

[25] Han, *Kim Il-sŏng ŭl Kobal Handa*, p. 219.

[26] Lee Dong-jun, *Hwansangkwa Hyŏnsil: naŭi Kongsanju'i Kwan* (Fantasy and Fact: My Observations of Communism) (Seoul: Tongbang T'ongsinsa, 1961), p. 270; and Tsuboe, *Chōsen Minzoku Dokuritsu Undō Hishi*, pp. 497–98.

[27] *Kin Nichisei Senshū*, Vol. I (Tokyo, 1966), p. 120.

[28] *Ibid.*, p. 121.

[29] Bang In-hu, *op. cit.*, pp. 106–08.

[30] *Kim Il-sŏng Sŏnjip*, Vol. I (1963), p. 347.

[31] *Kin Nichisei Senshū*, Vol. I (Tokyo, 1966), p. 120.

[32] *Ibid.*, p. 121

[33] U. S. State Department, *North Korea*, p. 14.

[34] Pak Ch'ang-ok, "Puk Chosŏn Nodongdang Kyuyak Haesŏk" ("Interpretation of the Regulations of the North Korean Workers' Party"), *Kŭlloja* (P'yŏngyang), No. 5 (May, 1947), pp. 43–50, cited in Bang In-hu, *op. cit.*, pp. 103–05.

[35] *Kin Nichisei Senshū*, Vol. I (1966), p. 131.

[36] *Ibid.*, pp. 118–19.

[37] According to article 9 of the North Korean Workers' Party regulations adopted at the First Party Congress held in August 1946, party congress was supposed to be held once a year. Thus, the Second Party Congress opened about half a year later than the party rule stipulated. Yi Ki-ha, *op. cit.*, p. 152.

[38] Cho Soon-sung, "United States Policy Toward the Unification of Korea: 1943-50" (unpublished Ph.D thesis) (Ann Arbor: University of Michigan, 1960); and Baik Bong, *Kim Il Sung: Biography*, II, pp. 188–89, 240.

[39] *Chosŏn Nodongdang Ryŏksa Kyojae*, p. 215.

[40] *Puk Chosŏn Nodongdang Che I'ch'a Chŏndang Taehoe Hoe'irok* (Docu-

ments of the Second Congress of the North Korean Workers' Party) (P'yŏn-gyang: North Korean Workers' Party, 1948), p. 2, cited in Bang In-hu, *op. cit.*, p. 111.

[41] *Kin Nichisei Senshū*, I (1966), pp. 77–114; and Baik Bong, *Kim Il Sung: Biography*, II, pp. 189–92.

[42] *Kim Il-sŏng Sŏnjip*, Vol. II (P'yŏngyang: Korean Workers' Party, 1953), pp. 84–85, cited in Bang In-hu, *op. cit.*, p. 111.

[43] Yu Hŏn, *Pukhan Isip-nyŏn*, p. 76.

[44] Kim, *Pukhan Sip-o-Nyŏn-sa*, p. 107.

[45] Baik Bong, *Kim Il Sung: Biography*, II, p. 194.

[46] Chu Nyŏng-ha held the vice-chairmanship of the party only until September 1948. He was apparently allowed to keep that post by Kim Il-sŏng in order to check O Ki-sŏp. Both Chu and O were from Ham-kyŏng Namdo province.

[47] U. S. Joint Publications Research Service, *Translations on North Korea No. 42* (Biographical Data on Prominent North Koreans), JPRS 40950 (Washington: Government Printing Office, 1968), pp. 13, 48.

[48] *Puk Chosŏn Nodongdang Che I'ch'a Chŏndang Taehoe Hoe-irok*, pp. 128–29, cited in Bang In-hu, *op. cit.*, p. 112. At the Conference of Communist Representatives and Enthusiasts held in October 1945 O Ki-sŏp asserted that "since the first stage of revolution which was the democratic revolution has been accomplished with the arrival of the Soviet Army," communists "now have to strive for the establishment of socialism." O Ki-sŏp and his comrades subsequently made futile attempts, in opposition to the Soviet-returnees, to set up workers' and peasants's soviets in their localities. Such "leftist" tendencies of native communists touched off the widespread anti-communist uprisings in North Korea throughout late 1945 and early 1946.

[49] Kim, *Pukhan Sip-o-Nyŏn-sa*, pp. 107–11.

[50] *Puk Chosŏn Nodongdang Che I'ch'a Chŏndang Taehoe Hoe'irok*, p. 138, cited in Bang In-hu, *op. cit.*, p. 113.

[51] Kim, *Yŏksa ŭi Chŭng'in*, pp. 152–68.

[52] Han, *Kim Il-sŏng ŭl Kobal Handa*, p. 227. Although there are fairly detailed descriptions available about Han Pin's activities of pre-1945 period in Kasumigaseki Kai (ed.), *Gendai Chōsen Jinmei Jiten* (Who's Who in Modern Korea) (Tokyo: Kaikō Jihō-sha, 1960), (in p. 255) as well as in Kasumigaseki Kai (ed.), *Gendai Chōsen Jinmei Jiten* (Tokyo: Sekai Jānaru-sha, 1962) (in p. 337), both books are silent on him after his return to North Korea indicating his early political eclipse in the north.

[53] *Kim Il-sŏng Sŏnjip*, Vol. II (1953), pp. 131–32, cited in Bang In-hu, *op. cit.*, p. 114.

[54] *Kim Il-sŏng Sŏnjip*, Vol. II (1953), pp. 129–30, cited in Bang In-hu, *op. cit.*, pp. 114–15. According to Kim Il-sŏng, O Ki-sŏp pledged his support

when the party in January 1946 decided to change the name of the existing Communist Youth Association into the Democratic Youth Association in order to prevent the desertion of young people to other non-communist political parties. Yet O Ki-sŏp did not keep his promise by giving "another story" on the change of the name during his tour of the countryside.

55 For the fate of the PKI, see Sheldon W. Simon, *The Broken Triangle: Peking, Djakarta, and the PKI* (Baltimore: The John Hopkins Press, 1969).

56 According to the recruitment regulations decided at the First Party Congress (at the time of the amalgamation of the Communist Party and the New People's Party in August 1946), "all males and females who are over 20 years of age" could become party members if they submitted their applications supported by recommendations of two party members. *Kŭlloja*, No. 5 (May, 1947), p. 50, cited in Bang In-hu, *op. cit.*, p. 117. However, according to the new regulations revised at the Second Party Congress, the two sponsors had to have been party members for more than one year and they had to have known the candidate for more than one year through party work. Also the sponsors had to take full responsibility for the behaviour of their protegés. Kō-an Chyōsachyō (ed.), *Hokusen no Kaihō Undōshi* (A History of the North Korean Liberation Movement) (Tokyo: Kō-an Chyōsachyō, 1957), pp. 285–86.

57 Bang In-hu, *op. cit.*, p. 118.

58 *Chosŏn Nodongdang Ryŏksa Kyojae*, p. 219.

59 *Puk Chosŏn Nodongdang Che I'ch'a Chŏndang Taehoe Hoe-irok*, p. 230, cited in Bang In-hu, *op. cit.*, p. 119.

60 For communist underground activities of Chang Sun-myŏng between 1930 and 1933, see *Tong-A Ilbo*, March 8, 1934. Party devotion and diligence were rewarded with economic and social benefits, such as preferential treatment in government, industry, trade unions, the armed forces and elsewhere, and privileged access to special factories and ministerial shops where scarce items might be purchased at favorable prices. Thus it would be natural for ordinary party members to desert disgraced leaders. Dubin, "The Political Evolution of the P'yŏngyang Government," p. 387f.

61 Kim, *Pukhan Sip-o-Nyŏn-sa*, p. 112.

62 *Puk Chosŏn Nodongdang Che I'ch'a Chŏndang Taehoe Hoe'irok*, p. 231, cited in Bang In-hu, *op. cit.*, pp. 119–20.

63 *Puk Han Koeroe Shilchŏng, Chŏngch'ipyon* (Real Situation of North Korean Political Affairs) (Seoul: date of publication and name of publisher are not given), p. 59. This document is classified as "top secret" and it is assumed to be a South Korean governmental document.

64 *Gendai Chūgoku Chōsen Jinmeikan* (1953); Sekai Seikei Chōsa-kai (ed.), *Kankoku, Kita Chōsen Jinmei Jiten* (Who's Who in South and North Korea) (Tokyo: Sekai Seikei Chōsa-kai, 1966); *Daehan Minguk Chongdangsa*, p. 478; and JPRS, *Translations on North Korea No. 42*. The 15-man Pre-

sidium became a 17-man Presidium in September 1948 by adding Kim Yŏl (Soviet Korean) and Pak Yŏng-sŏn (origin unconfirmed).

[65] Yu Ho-il, *Gendai Chōsen no Rekishi* (History of Modern Korea) (Tokyo: San Ichi Shobō, 1953), p. 71.

[66] Lee, Ch'ŏl-chu, "Pukke Chosŏn Nodongdang," p. 269; and Pak Tong-un *Pukhan T'ongch'i Kikuron*, pp. 128-29.

CHAPTER 6

[1] Chang Pok-sŏng, *Chosŏn Kongsandanng P'ajaensa* (The History of the Factional Struggle in the Korean Communist Party) (Seoul: Taeryuk Ch'ulp'ansa, 1949), pp. 49-52; and Kim Chong-bŏm and Kim Tong-un, *Haebang Chŏnhu'ui Chosŏn Chinsang*, II, p. 66.

[2] Chang Pok-sŏng, *op. cit.*, pp. 52-53; and Han Im-hyŏk, *Kim Il-sŏng tongji* (etc.), pp. 24-25.

[3] Kim Chong-bŏm and Kim Tong-un, II, *op. cit.*, pp. 62-66.

[4] United States, Commander-in-Chief, United States Army Forces, Pacific, *Summation of the United States Army Military Government Activities* (Hereafter will be cited as Summation), No. 7 (April, 1946), p. 15.

[5] David J. Dallin, *Soviet Russia and the Far East* (New Haven: Yale University Press, 1948), p. 295.

[6] *Chosŏn Haebang Nyŏnbo 1946*, pp. 146-49; and Chang Pok-sŏng, *op. cit.*, pp. 64-68.

[7] *Summation*, No. 8 (May, 1946), p. 5; and Yi Ki-ha, *op. cit.*, pp. 52-53.

[8] *Summation*, No. 9 (June, 1946), p. 16; *Summation*, No. 11 (August, 1946), p. 101; *Summation*, No. 13 (October, 1946), p. 16; and Han T'ae-su, *Hanguk Chŏngdangsa* (A History of Political Parties in Korea) (Seoul: Shin T'ae-yang-sa, 1961), pp. 33-54.

[9] *Seoul Shinmun* (Seoul Daily), November 30, 1945.

[10] Yi Kang-kuk, "Rhee Pak-sa wa Chung'ang Hyŏp'i-hoe" ("Dr. Rhee and Central Consultative Association"), *Inmin* (People) (Seoul), II, No. 1 (January, 1946), pp. 11-15; and *Jwa-ik Sakŏn Silrok*, I, pp. 26-41.

[11] Chōsen Jijyō Kenkyū-sho (ed.), *Hokui Sanjū Hachidosen* (The 38th Parallel) (Tokyo: Chōsen Jijyō Kenkyū-sho, 1946), pp. 10-13; and Meade, *American Military Government in Korea*, pp. 55-63.

[12] Kang Dae-ho, "Mak-pu Sam-guk Oe-sang Hoe'i wa Chosŏn," pp. 66-71; *Jwa-ik Sakŏn Silrok*, I, p. 105; and Malcolm D. Kennedy, *A Short History of Communism in Asia* (New York: Frederick A. Praeger, 1957), p. 349.

[13] *Chosŏn Chung'ang Nyŏngam 1949*, p. 722; and *Chosŏn Haebang Nyŏnbo 1946*, pp. 128-33.

[14] *Summation*, No. 8 (May, 1946), pp. 16-22; and Hayashi Takehiko, *Kankoku Gendaishi* (Modern History of Korea) (Tokyo: Shiseidō, 1967), pp. 42-47.

[15] O Che-do, *Pulgun Gunsang, che il Jip* (The Red Multitude, The First Series) (Pusan: Namkwang Munhwa-sa, 1951), pp. 1-144; *New York Times*,

May 11, 1946; *Summation*, No. 11 (August, 1946), p. 23; *Summation*, No. 15 (December, 1946), p. 24; and *Jwa-ik Sakŏn Silrok*, I, pp. 187–91.

16 Dallin, *Soviet Russia and the Far East*, pp. 295–96; and *Summation*, No. 9 (June, 1946), p. 18.

17 *Summation*, No. 9 (June, 1946), p. 19; *Summation*, No. 10 (July, 1946), pp. 60–61; and *Summation*, No. 11 (August, 1946), p. 23.

18 *Summation*, No. 12 (September, 1946), pp. 17, 76; and Hayashi Take-hiko, *op. cit.*, p. 52.

19 *Summation*, No. 12 (September, 1946), p. 15; and *Summation*, No. 16 (January, 1947), p. 15.

20 Hayashi Takehiko, *op. cit.*, p. 52; and *Jwa-ik Sakŏn Silrok*, I, pp. 191–92.

21 *Ibid.*, pp. 233–45; *Summation*, No. 12 (September, 1946), pp. 12–14; *Chosŏn Chung'ang Nyŏngam 1949*, p. 226; and Dallin, *Soviet Russia and the Far East*, pp. 296–97.

22 *Summation*, No. 13 (October 1946), pp. 23–26; *Summation*, No. 15 (December, 1946), p. 24; *Summation*, No. 18 (March, 1947), p. 18; Tsuboe Senji, *Nansen no Kaihō Jūnen* (Ten Years of Liberated South Korea) (Tokyo: Rōdō Tsūshinsha, 1956), pp. 90–91; and *Jwa-ik Sakŏn Silrok*, I, pp. 246–78.

23 *Ibid.*, pp. 222–25.

24 Baik Bong, *Kim Il Sung: Biography*, II, pp. 141–46, 149.

25 *Ibid.*, pp. 148, 151–52; *Summation*, No. 11 (August, 1946), p. 15; and Chang Pok-sŏng, *op. cit.*, pp. 64–65.

26 Bae Sŏng-yong, *Chaju Chosŏn e Jihang* (Direction of the Independent Korea) (Seoul: Kwang-munsa, 1949), pp. 22–30; and Baik Bong, *Kim Il Sung: Biography*, II, p. 152.

27 Chang Pok-sŏng, *op. cit.*, pp. 61–67; and Yi Ki-ha, *op. cit.*, pp. 138–41.

28 *Summation*, No. 13 (October, 1946), p. 19; Tsuboe, *Nansen no Kaihō Jūnen*, pp. 87–89; and Baik Bong, *Kim Il Sung: Biography*, II, pp. 153–54.

29 For a full text of the program of the South Korean Workers' Party, see *Daehan Minguk Chŏngdangsa*, p. 92.

30 Baik Bong, *Kim Il Sung: Biography*, II, p. 153; and Chang Pok-sŏng, *op. cit.*, pp. 68–69.

31 *Summation*, No. 14 (November, 1946), pp. 18–19; *Summation*, No. 15 (December, 1946), p. 18; and *Summation*, No. 16 (January, 1947), pp. 15–16.

32 The three-point program of the Working People's Party was:

1. The establishment of a democratic nation by amassing the strength of all Koreans. 2. The complete emancipation of the whole nation by establishing a planned economy. 3. The establishment of a progressive national culture and contribution to a world culture. *Chŏngdang e Kiku Kinŭngkwa Chŏngkang Chŏngch'aek Tanghŏn* (Structures, Functions, Platforms, Programs, and Constitutions of Various Political Parties) (Seoul: Central Committee on Election Affairs, 1965), p. 118.

33 *Summation*, No. 19 (April, 1947), pp. 19–20; and Han T'ae-su, *Hanguk Chŏngdangsa*, pp. 55–56.

[34] Yi Ki-ha, *op. cit.*, p. 147.

[35] Tsuboe, *Nansen no Kaihō Jūnen*, pp. 99–101; and Yu Ho-il, *Gendai Chōsen no Rekishi*, pp. 83–85.

[36] Yi Ki-ha, *op. cit.*, p. 147.

[37] Yu Ho-il, *op. cit.*, pp. 88–91; and Glenn D. Paige, "Korea," in Cyril E. Black & Thomas P. Thornton (eds.), *Communism and Revolution* (Princeton: Princeton University Press, 1964), pp. 223–27.

[38] Kō-an Chyōsachyō (ed.), *Hokusen no Kaihō Undōshi*, pp. 190–92; and Yun Ki-jŏng, *Hanguk Kongsan chu'i Undong Pip'an* (Critique of the Korean Communist Movement) (Seoul: T'ongil Ch'unch'u-sa, 1959), pp. 194, 195.

[39] Yun Ki-jŏng, *Hanguk Kongsan chu'i Undong Pip'an* pp. 177, 194, 196; *Jwa-ik Sakŏn Silrok*, I, p. 429; Paige, "Korea," pp. 223–27; Matsumoto Hirokazu, *Gekkidō suru Kankoku* (Turbulent Korea) (Tokyo: Iwanami Shotten, 1963), pp. 23–25; and Tsuboe, *Nansen no Kaihō Jūnen*, pp. 140–50. On May 10, 1950, North Korea suddenly proposed to the South Korean government to exchange Kim Sam-yong and Yi Chu-ha for Cho Man-sik who had been held in custody in the north since early 1946. While negotiations were going on, the Korean War broke out and Kim Sam-yong and Yi Chu-ha were executed by a firing squadron of the South Korean Army on May 28, 1950.

[40] Kim O-sŏng, *Jidoja-ron* (Discussion on Leadership) (Seoul: Chosŏn Chŏngp'ansa, 1946), pp. 119–32.

[41] For a full text of the declaration of the Korean Communist Party of September 14, 1945, see *Daehan Minguk Chŏngdangsa*, pp. 465–66.

[42] *Jwa-ik Sakŏn Silrok*, I, p. 25.

[43] Kim Chong-bŏm and Kim Tong-un, *Haebang Chŏnhu'ŭi Chosŏn Chinsang*, Vol. II, p. 66.

[44] U. S. State Department, *North Korea*, p. 14; and Han Im-hyŏk, *Kim Il-sŏng tongji e ŭihan Chosŏn Kongsandang Ch'angkŏn*, pp. 26, 32.

[45] Bang In-hu, *op. cit.*, p. 49; and *Jwa-ik Sakŏn Silrok*, I, pp. 426–30.

[46] Rin Eiju *et al.*, *Chōsen Sensōshi* (History of the Korean War) (Tokyo: Koria Hyōronsha, 1967), pp. 70–71; and Kō-an Chyōsachyō (ed.), *Hokusen no Kaihō Undōshi*, p. 192.

[47] Rin Eiju, *et al.*, *op. cit.*, p. 69 (italics mine)

[48] Pak, *Pukhan T'ongch'i Kikuron*, pp. 23–27; Ch'oe Sang-dŏk, *Pukhan Goeroe Jiptan Chŏngch'e* (The Nature of North Korean Puppet Regime) (Seoul: Office of the Public Information, South Korea, 1949), p. 16; and Baik Bong, *Kim Il Sung: Biography*, II, p. 256.

[49] R. Smith, "Hokusen no akai Hoshi," ("Red Star in North Korea"), *Kaizō*, XXXIV, No. 9 (July, 1953), p. 187.

[50] Rin Eiju *et al.*, *op. cit.*, p. 70; Baik Bong, *Kim Il Sung: Biography*, II, p. 255; and Kō-an Chyōsachyō (ed.), *Hokusen no Kaihō Undōshi*, p. 193.

[51] U. S. State Department, *North Korea*, p. 17.

[52] Rin Eiju *et al., op. cit.,* p. 71.

[53] Kim Tu-bong was made chairman of the Presidium of the Supreme People's Assembly in September 1948. The Supreme People's Assembly was considered by observers of North Korean politics as a "national sanatorium of retired politicians" in North Korea. Smith, *Hokusen no akai Hoshi,* p. 186.

[54] The Politburo of the Korean Workers' Party at the time of the 1949 merger consisted of the following nine members:

Kim Il-sŏng	(North Korean Workers' Party or NKWP)
Pak Hŏn-yŏng	(South Korean Workers' Party or SKWP)
Kim Ch'aek	(NKWP)
Pak Il-u	(NKWP)
Hŏ Kai	(NKWP)
Yi Sŭng-yŏp	(SKWP)
Kim Tu-bong	(NKWP)
Kim Sam-yong	(SKWP, Kim remained in the south, was arrested and executed by the South Korean Army in May 1950)
Hŏ Hŏn	(SKWP)

It was believed that the five members of the North Korean Workers' Party did wield actual authority in the Politburo and that the four from the south were not influential. U. S. State Department, *North Korea,* pp. 21–22.

CHAPTER 7

[1] "The Struggle of the Korean People for a United, Independent Democratic Korea," *Bolshevik,* No. 11 (June 15, 1949), in *Soviet Press Translations* (Seattle: Far Eastern Institute at University of Washington), IV, No. 18 (October 15, 1949), pp. 549–57.

[2] This phase of North Korean military buildup was reportedly guided by a 40-man Russian Special Military Advisory Corps. The Russian military advisory corps arrived in North Korea in late December 1948 in order to replace the Soviet occupation forces that had been training the North Korean Army. Kyril Kalinov, "An ex-Soviet Officer Tells: How Russia Built the North Korean Army," *The Reporter,* III, No. 7 (September 26, 1950), pp. 4–8.

[3] *North Korean Radio Broadcast,* June 26, 1950, cited in *Kin Nichisei Senshū* (1966), I, pp. 137–45.

[4] *Chosŏn Chung'ang Nyŏngam 1951–52,* p. 82.

[5] *North Korean Radio Broadcast,* July 8, 1950, cited in *Kin Nichisei Senshū* (1966), I, pp. 147–58.

[6] Wilfred G. Burchett, *Again Korea* (New York: International Publishers, 1968), p. 131.

[7] *New York Times,* June 28, 1950.

[8] *North Korean Radio Broadcast,* October 11, 1950, cited in Kim Sam-kyu, *Chōsen Gendai-shi,* p. 80.

[9] *Kin Nichisei Senshū* (Selected Works of Kim Il-sŏng), Vol. IV, Part II (Tokyo: Japanese Communist Party, 1964), p. 110.

[10] Allen S. Whiting, *China Crosses the Yalu* (New York: The Macmillan Company, 1960), pp. 116–50; and Rin Eiju *et al.*, pp. 131–32.

[11] Kō-an Chyōsachyō (ed.), *Hokusen no Kaihō Undōshi*, p. 223; Pak Tong-un, *Pukhan T'ongch'i Kikuron*, p. 206; and *Hanguk e issŏ sŏ ŭi Kongsanju'i*, pp. 277, 381.

[12] Kim Il-sŏng, "The Present Situation and Our Immediate Tasks—Report by Comrade Kim Il-sŏng made at the 3rd Regular Meeting of the Central Committee of the Korean Workers' Party," in *The Great Liberation War of the Korean People for Freedom and Independence* (P'yŏngyang: Ministry of Culture and Propaganda, 1951), p. 103.

[13] *Ibid.*, pp. 110–18.

[14] *Ibid.*, p. 118.

[15] *Hanguk e issŏ sŏ ŭi Kongsanju'i*, pp. 360–61.

[16] Kim Il-sŏng, "The Present Situation and Our Immediate Tasks," p. 144.

[17] *Ibid.*; and Kō-an Chyōsachyō (ed.), *Hokusen no Kaihō Undōshi*, p. 217.

[18] *Kin Nichisei Senshū*, Vol. IV, Part II (1964), p. 110; Bang In-hu, *op. cit.*, p. 147; and Baik Bong, *Kim Il Sung: Biography*, II, p. 370. Since at the time of the Second Congress of the North Korean Workers' Party in March 1948 there were some 750,000 members and following the amalgamation of the South and North Korean Workers' Parties the party members must have reached beyond 750,000, it is presumed that over 150,000 members either died in the war or were captured by enemy troops.

[19] Tera-o Korō, *Sanjū Hachidosen-no Kita* (North of the 38th Parallel) (Tokyo: Shin Nippon Shuppan-sha, 1959), p. 24.

[20] *Chosŏn Chung'ang Nyŏngam, 1958*, p. 175; Kō-an Chyōsachyō (ed.), *Hokusen no Kaihō Undōshi*, p. 227; Baik Bong, *Kim Il Sung: Biography*, II, pp. 369–70; and Tera-o Korō, *Sanjū Hachidosen-no Kita*, p. 24.

[21] Kim, "The Long March of North Korea's Kim," p. 107.

[22] Rin Eiju *et al.*, *op. cit.*, pp. 131–40; and Baik Bong, *Kim Il Sung, Biography*, II, p. 369.

[23] Kim Il-sŏng, "Great October Socialist Revolution and National Liberation Struggle of Korean People," *For a Lasting Peace, For a People's Democracy*, No. 44 (156) (November 2, 1951), p. 4.

[24] Min, "North Korea's Foreign Policy in the Post-War Decade, 1953–1963," unpublished Ph.D thesis, pp. 133–34.

[25] Kim, "The Long March of North Korea's Kim," p. 107.

[26] Kim Il-sŏng, "Regarding the Improvement of the Organizational Activities of the Party—The Concluding Words of the Fourth Plenum of the Central Committee of the Korean Workers' Party, November 2, 1951," in *Kin Nichisei Senshū*, Vol. I (Tokyo: 1966), pp. 170–75; and Baik Bong, *Kim Il Sung: Biography*, II, p. 370.

27 *Hanguk e issŏ sŏ ŭi Kongsanju'i*, p. 363.

28 Yun Ki-jŏng, *Pukhan Hŭkmak* (Inside Story of North Korea) (Seoul: T'ongil Ch'unch'u-sa, 1962), pp. 51–52.

29 Kō-an Chyōsachyō (ed.), *Hokusen no Kaihō Undōshi*, pp. 285–87. According to the old rule adopted at the Second Party Congress in March 1948 (see Chapter 5), a person over 20 years of age could apply for membership if his or her application was supported by two sponsors who had been party members for more than one year and who had known the candidate for more than one year. At the Fourth Plenum the required age was lowered from 20 to 18, and it was decided that two sponsors did not have to be acquainted with the applicant for more than a year.

30 *Chosŏn Nodongdang Ryŏksa Kyojae*, pp. 283–84; *Nodong Shinmun*, January 16, 17, 20, 1952; February 1, 6, 20, 1952; March 6, 23, 1952; and May 29, 1952.

31 *Chosŏn T'ongsa*, III (1961), p. 285; Tera-o Korō, *Sanjū Hachidosen-no Kita*, pp. 19–20; and Kō-an Chyōsachyō (ed.), *Hokusen no Kaihō Undōshi*, pp. 221–22, 230.

32 *Nodong Shinmun*, February 19, 1952; and Baik Bong, *Kim Il Sung: Biography*, II, p. 373. Lower officials at local levels were not only eager to supply their quotas on time but they also made false reports on their products by inflating the actual quantity in order to outdo other officials. Thus reported a Japanese who visited the North Korean countryside in the early 1960's. *Chōsen Kenkyū Geppō* (Monthly Bulletin of Korean Studies, issued by Nippon Chōsen Kenkyū'sho in Tokyo), No. 16 (April 25, 1963), p. 13.

33 *Nodong Shinmun*, October 5, and 27, 1952; and Kō-an Chyōsachyō (ed.), *Hokusen no Kaihō Undōshi*, p. 230.

34 Bang In-hu, *op. cit.*, pp. 156–58; and Baik Bong, *Kim Il Sung: Biography*, II, pp. 387–92.

35 *Nodong Shinmun*, February 13, 14; March 30, 31; and April 2, 1953.

36 Lee Ch'ŏl-chu, "Im Hwa e taehan Kisojang" ("Indictment Against Im Hwa"), *Sasangke* (Seoul), June, 1964, pp. 269–75; and *Hanguk e issŏ sŏ ŭi Kongsanju'i*, p. 421.

37 For a text of the verdict, see Ch'oe Sŏk, *Hanguk T'ongil Munje e taehan Mosaek* (Search for the Unification of Korea) (Seoul: Shin Munhwa-sa, 1967), Appendix, pp. 20–27; and Kō-an Chyōsachyō (ed.), *Hokusen no Kaihō Undōshi*, pp. 234–35.

38 *Pravda*, August 8, 1953, in *Current Digest of the Soviet Press*, Vol. V, No. 32 (September 19, 1953), pp. 18–19. For an account of the trial scene, see Lee Ch'ŏl-chu, "Puk'e Shi'in kwa Unmyŏng," ("The Fate of A Poet in the North"), *Sasangke* (Seoul), July, 1964, pp. 252–59.

39 *New York Times*, December 19, 1955; and *Hanguk e issŏ sŏ ŭi Kongsanju'i*, p. 357.

40 John W. Riley (Jr.) and Wilbur Schramm, *The Red Takes a City: The*

Communist Occupation of Seoul with Eyewitness Accounts (New Brunswick, N. J.: Rutgers University Press, 1951), pp. 31–201; Yun Ki-jŏng, *Hanguk Kongsan chu'i Undong Pip'an*, pp. 197-98; and *Hanguk e issŏ sŏ ŭi Kongsanju'i*, pp. 277-79.

[41] Lee Ch'ŏl-chu, "Pak Hŏn-yŏng kwa Yukyoktae" ("Pak Hŏn-yŏng and Partisans"), *Sasangke* (Seoul), May, 1964, pp. 238–39; and *Hanguk e issŏ sŏ ŭi Kongsanju'i*, p. 354.

[42] *Kin Nichisei Senshū*, Vol. IV, Part II (1964), pp. 248–52.

[43] *Ibid.*, p. 251. According to Kim Il-sŏng's speech made on April 23, 1956, at the Third Congress of the Korean Workers' Party.

. . . the Pak group [prior to the merger of the South and North Korean Workers' Party in 1949] carried out fivefold and tenfold movements to show that the South Korean Workers' Party was numerically superior to the North Korean Workers' Party.

[44] John W. Spanier, *The Truman-MacArthur Controversy and the Korean War* (New York: W. W. Norton and Company, Inc., 1965), pp. 84–187; and Rutherford M. Poats, *Decision in Korea* (New York: The McBride Company, 1954), pp. 151–72.

[45] *Chosŏn T'ongsa*, III (1961), p. 285; Tera-o Korō, *Sanjū Hachidosen-no Kita*, pp. 19–20; and Rin Eiju *et. al.*, p. 150.

[46] Lee Ch'ŏl-chu, "Pak Hŏn-yŏng kwa Yukyoktae," p. 239.

[47] *Pravda*, August 18, 1952, in *Current Digest of the Soviet Press*, IV, No. 33 (September 27, 1952), pp. 16–17.

[48] *New York Times*, August 19, 20, 21, 1952.

[49] Leland M. Goodrich, *Korea: A Study of United States Policy in the United Nations* (New York: Council on Foreign Relations, 1956), pp. 194–95.

[50] Mark W. Clark, *From the Danube to the Yalu* (New York: Harper & Brothers, 1954), p. 258.

[51] Kim Sam-kyu, *Konnichi no Chōsen* (Korea Today) Tokyo: Kawade Shobō, 1956), pp. 91–103.

[52] *Hanguk e issŏ sŏ ŭi Kongsanju'i*, p. 355; and Baik Bong, *Kim Il Sung: Biography*, II, pp. 392–93. In his message dated December 17, 1952 and addressed to Lester B. Pearson, President of the General Assembly of the United Nations, Foreign Minister Pak Hŏn-yŏng protested the "inhuman" actions such as "bombardments, bombings and germ warfare" being carried out by the United Nations forces in Korea against the North Korean population. *Nodong Shinmun*, December 18, 1952. This was the last North Korean official statement in which Pak Hŏn-yŏng's name appeared in the capacity of Foreign Minister.

[53] *New York Times*, January 29, 1953; and August 15, 1953.

[54] For a full text of Kim Il-sŏng's radio speech of July 28, 1953, see Kim Il-sŏng, "To the Entire People on the Occasion of the Signing of the Armistice, July 28, 1953," in *All For the Post-War Rehabilitation and*

Development of the National Economy (P'yongyang: The New Korea Press, 1954), pp. 5–24. See also *Nodong Shinmun,* July 28, 1953.

[55] For Kim Il-sŏng's full text of speech delivered at the Sixth Plenum, see "All for the Post-War Rehabilitation and Development of the National Economy," in *All for the Post-War Rehabilitation and Development of the National Economy,* pp. 25–55.

[56] On April 23, 1956, Kim Il-sŏng at the Third Congress of the Korean Workers' Party again stated:

> While in the south, the Pak Hŏn-yŏng clique admitted many impure and undesirable elements into the party and organized wanton riots with the purpose of exposing the party apparatus to the enemy, enabling the enemy to kill many patriots and alienating the party from the masses . . . At the time of the amalgamation [of the South and North Korean Workers' Parties] we did not know the true colors of the Pak clique since we had not had enough time to examine their activities . . . *Had it not been for the damnable and criminal activities of the sectarians, our party would not have been destroyed and Korea must have been unified already.*

Kim Il-sŏng Sŏnjip, Vol. IV (1960), pp. 534–41. (italics mine)

[57] "Tō Kanbu no Chuihŏ to Shin Yakuin no Kaobure" ("Exile of the Party Leaders and the Faces of the New Officials"), *Soren Geppō,* No. 193 (August, 1953), pp. 870–73, and Tsuboe, *Hokusen no Kaihō Jūnen,* pp. 123–24. Of the nine members of the previous Politburo elected in 1949 immediately after the merger of the South and North Korean Workers' Parties (refer to Chapter VI), Kim Ch'aek died at the front line during the Korean War and Hŏ Hŏn died of old age. Pak Il-u's failure to be reelected at the Sixth Plenum is yet to be explained.

[58] Baik Bong, *Kim Il-Sŏng: Biography,* II, pp. 442–43; and *Hanguk e issŏ sŏ ŭi Kongsanju'i,* p. 258.

CHAPTER 8

[1] For a text of Kim's speech of August 5, 1953, see *Nodong Shinmun,* September 28, 1954 or *Kim Il-sŏng Sŏnjip,* Vol. IV (1960), pp. 1–56. See also *Atarashī Chōsen* (New Korea, monthly periodical from P'yŏngyang), *Supplement,* April, 1958, pp. 3–15.

[2] On April 20, 1954 while the economic recovery program was in execution, Premier Kim Il-sŏng submitted the First Three-Year Economic Plan to the Seventh Congress of the Supreme People's Assembly, where it was duly approved. Suh Nam-won, "North Korean Economic Policy, 1945–1960," *Studies on Communist Affairs,* I, No. 1 (September, 1964), p. 73. (Written in Korean, but titles were given in English.)

[3] Cho Ch'ae-son, *Chosŏn Minjujui Inmin Konghwaguk Sahoe Kyŏngje Jedo* (The Socio-Economic System in the Democratic People's Republic of Korea) (P'yŏngyang: Korean Workers' Party, 1958), p. 36.

⁴ For details of the foreign economic assistance from 1954 to the early 1960's and its proportion to the North Korean annual national budget, see *The Japan Annual of International Affairs*, No. 1 (1960), p. 150; *Far Eastern Economic Review 1962*, p. 149; *Minju Chosŏn* (Democratic Korea), April 24, 1963; and Kim Sam-kyu, *Chōsen no Shinjitsu* (The Truth About Korea) (Tokyo: Shiseidō, 1960), p. 74.

⁵ *Kŭlloja*, No. 19 (November, 1962), p. 14; and Cho Ch'ae-son, *op. cit.*, pp. 35–36.

⁶ At the time of the land reform of March 1946, the North Korean regime withheld a portion of land which had formerly belonged to the Japanese government and public organizations. It constituted less than two percent of the total arable land in North Korea. From its very early days the regime turned these lands into state farms, hiring farmers and paying them wages. Rudolph, *North Korea's Political and Economic Structure*, pp. 48, 54.

⁷ For a full text of Kim's speech, see *Nodong Shinmun*, November 4, 1954; and *Kim Il-sŏng Sŏnjip*, Vol. IV (1960), pp. 168–95. See also Cho Ch'ae-son, *op. cit.*, pp. 36–40.

⁸ *Kin Nichisei Senshū*, Vol. I (Tokyo, 1966), pp. 245–53; *Kin Nichisei Senshū*, Vol. IV, Part II (Tokyo, 1964), p. 124; and Cho Ch'ae-son, *op. cit.*, p. 54.

⁹ For the belated proclamation of the socialist theme, Kim Il-sŏng on April 4, 1955 explained at a plenum of the Central Committee of the party:

Our party proposed political and economic tasks that fit each definite period . . . in our country . . . If we had yelled about building socialism in the period of construction directly after liberation, who would have accepted it? The people wound not have come over to our side. If we ask why, it was because the Japanese imperialists had spread the evil propaganda that socialism meant sleeping under the same quilt and eating out of the same pot. If we had not taken account of this at the time and had raised socialist slogans, we would have frightened the people, and they would not have joined us.

Kin Nichisei Senshū, Vol. I (Tokyo, 1966), p. 335.

¹⁰ *Pukhan Yoram* (Concise Facts About North Korea) (Seoul: The Office of Public Information, Republic of Korea, 1962), p. 194.

¹¹ *Kim Il-sŏng Sŏnjip*, Vol. IV (1960), p. 276.

¹² *Nodong Shinmun*, August 31, 1955.

¹³ Cho Seong-jik, "Process of Extermination of Private Business in North Korea," *Studies on Communist Affairs*, I, No. 1 (September, 1964), p. 168. (Though written in Korean, titles were given in English)

¹⁴ *Pukhan Yoram* (1962), p. 194.

¹⁵ *Kyōno Chōsen* (Korea Today), (P'yŏngyang) *Supplement*, 1959, No. 28 (1), p. 5. See also *Atayashī Chōsen* (New Korea), *Supplement*, July 1958, (1), pp. 11–20.

[16] Cho Seong-jik, *op. cit.*, p. 183.

[17] *Pukhan Yoram* (1962), p. 194; and Philip Rudolph, "North Korea and the Path to Socialism," *Pacific Affairs*, XXXII, No. 2 (June, 1959), pp. 134–35.

[18] For a full text of Kim's report, see *Kim Il-sŏng Sŏnjip*, Vol. IV (1960), pp. 433–571. See also *Kin Nichisei Senshū*, Vol. IV, Part II (Tokyo, 1964), pp. 157–285.

[19] *Kim Il-sŏng Sŏnjip*, Vol. IV, pp. 475–76; *Kin Michisei Senshū* Vol. IV, Part II (Tokyo, 1964), pp. 196–97; *Chosŏn Chung'ang Nyŏngam 1964*, p. 194; and Cho Ch'ae-son, *op. cit.*, pp. 35–36. See also *Atarashī Chōsen*, Supplement, April 1958 (no number given), pp. 16–38; July 1958 (2), pp. 14–39; and *Kyōno Chōsen*, Supplement, 1959, No. 28 (1) (no month given), pp. 2–26. The first five-year economic plan was submitted by Premier Kim Il-sŏng on June 9, 1958 to the Supreme People's Assembly, where it was approved as proposed.

[20] *Chosŏn Nodongdang Kyuyak Haesŏl* (Interpretation of the Korean Workers' Party Regulations) (Adopted at the Third Congress of the Party on April 28, 1956) (Tokyo: Hak-u Sobang, 1960), pp. 1–2. (italics mine)

[21] Cho Seong-jik, *op. cit.*, p. 161; Choi Kwang-suk, "Ideological Education in North Korea; Its Forms and Contents," *Studies on Communist Affairs*, I, No. 2 (November, 1965), p. 49 (Though written in Korean, titles were given in English); and *Kyōno Chōsen*, Supplement, 1959, No. 28 (1), p. 4.

[22] *Nodong Shinmun*, March 7, 1955.

[23] Cho Soon-sung, "Politics of North Korea's Unification Policies," *World Politics*, XIX, No. 2 (January, 1967), p. 227.

[24] *Nodong Shinmun*, December 13, 1960; *Kim Il-sŏng Sŏnjip*, Vol. V (1960), pp. 145–47; and *Kim Il-sŏng Sŏnjip*, Vol. VI (P'yŏngyang: Korean Workers' Party, 1960), p. 517.

[25] *Kin Nichisei Senshū*, Vol. II (Tokyo: Japanese Communist Party, 1966), p. 162; and *Kyōno Chōsen*, Supplement, 1959, No. 28 (1), p. 9.

[26] *Nodong Shinmun*, September 12, 1961. In the Soviet Union the collectivization movement began some ten years after the October Revolution, absorbing four percent of her total farming population. By the end of 1932, some three-fifths of all private landholding were collectivized, and it was only in 1938, after many ups and downs, that 99 percent of all Russian farming families had joined collective farms. Clearly, the process in Soviet Russia was slower than in North Korea. See Pierre Sorlin, *The Soviet People and Their Society* (New York: Frederick A. Praeger, Publishers, 1968), pp. 143–60, 153–57, 207–08; George von Rauch, *A History of Soviet Russia* (New York: Frederick A. Praeger, Publishers, 1967), pp. 177–86; and Isaac Deutscher, *Stalin, A Political Biography* (New York: Oxford University Press, 1967), p. 331.

[27] The Peking regime in its early days confiscated and nationalized property owned only by "monopolistic capitalists" and "counter-revolutionaries," and they left alone small-scale enterprises and business transactions of "national capitalists" for several years. It was in 1953 that the Peking regime started to nationalize the remaining private enterprises, beginning with the larger ones, and, by the end of 1956, all private businesses were eliminated. However, the former owners of these enterprises were given five percent interest on capital assets of their confiscated enterprises annually until 1962 regardless of the profit or loss of their business activities. In 1962, the Peking government announced that the payment of five percent interest would be extended for another three years. See Wu Yuan-li, *The Economy of Communist China* (New York: Frederick A. Praeger, 1965), pp. 9–10, 74–78; and Edgar Snow, *The Other Side of the River, Red China Today* (New York: Random House, 1961), pp. 195–96.

[28] Cho Seong-jik, *op. cit.*, pp. 171–72. Later in February, 1959, after the purge of Kim Tu-bong and other Yenan Koreans, Kim Il-sŏng stated:

"As everyone knows, our Workers' Party was created by merging the Communist Party and the New People's Party. The New People's Party was a petit-bourgeois party, which can not be viewed as completely approving communism."

Kim Il-sŏng Sŏnjip, Vol. VI (1960), p. 266.
"The appropriate condition" for the merger of the two parties in 1946, according to a recent North Korean publication, was created by the coincidence of the platform of the New People's Party with minimum objectives of the Communist Party. *Chosŏn Nodongdang i kŏrŏ on Yŏngkwangsurŏun Kil* (The Glorious Past of the Korean Workers' Party) (Tokyo: Chosŏn Ch'ŏngnyŏnsa, 1965), pp. 102–05.

[29] It was the Soviet Korean Pak Yŏng-bin who first advocated the relaxation of tension after his trip to the Soviet Union sometime between March 1953 and December 1955. *Kim Il-sŏng Sŏnjip*, Vol. IV (1960), p. 333.

[30] The official titles of these opposition leaders were only those held by these men from approximately from late 1954 to August 1956.

[31] Han Jae-duk, "Problems of Kim Il-sŏng's 'Self-Dependence' and 'Self-Reliance'," *Studies on Communist Affairs*, I, No. 1 (September, 1964), p. 46. (Written in Korean but titles were given in English)

[32] After the cease-fire, Chinese troops began to withdraw from North Korea. However, it was in October, 1958 that the last Chinese contingents, consisting of some 70,000, withdrew, thus completing the phased withdrawl of Chinese troops from North Korea. *Atarashī Chōsen, Supplement*, 1958, No. 26 (1) (no month given), pp. 2–6.

[33] Ilpyong J. Kim, "North Korea's Fourth Party Congress," *Pacific Affairs*, XXXV, No. 1 (Spring, 1962), pp. 38–39; and Han, "Problems of Kim Il-sŏng's 'Self-Dependence' and 'Self-Reliance'," p. 46.

[34] It was through the threat of reduction or total cutback of the economic and technical aid provided by the Soviet Union for some ten years after the Korean War that the Kremlin leaders exerted pressure on Kim Il-sŏng. Recalling this Soviet pressure, a North Korean source later stated:

> Some people [implying Soviet leadership], taking advantage of their aid, attempted to interfere with the internal affairs of a fraternal party . . . to impose their will unilaterally. Utilization of aid for political interference . . . is a big power exclusivism."

Nodong Shinmun, October 28, 1963.

[35] *Kin Nichisei Senshū*, Vol. I (Tokyo, 1966), p. 346.

[36] For a full text of Kim's speech of December 28, 1955, see *Kim Il-sŏng Sŏnjip*, Vol. IV (1960), pp. 325–55. A Japanese observer believes that the immediate cause of this speech was the improved relationship between Moscow and Belgrade following the Belgrade talks of summer 1955, and that the speech was intended by Kim not only to denounce his domestic foes but also Khrushchev's foreign policy. *Chōsen Kenkyū*, No. 37 (February/March, 1965), pp. 17–18.

[37] *Kim Il-sŏng Sŏnjip*, Vol. IV (1960), pp. 325–30. We know that the Yenan Koreans, by insisting on application of "the Chinese way", attempted to modify the radical process of the extermination of private business. Otherwise, strangely enough, the Yenan Koreans opposed Kim Il-sŏng's collectivization plan which was strikingly similar to the Chinese commune movement in substance and timing. In his speech of December 28, 1955, Kim did not explain what the "Chinese way" was as advocated by his opponents, although he specifically mentioned the "Soviet way" in one instance as will be seen shortly in this chapter. Thus Kim's speech should be construed as his defense of his policies against the Soviet Union.

[38] *Ibid.*, pp. 335–37.

[39] *Ibid.*, p. 332.

[40] *Ibid.*, p. 333.

[41] *Ibid.*

[42] *Kin Nichisei Senshū*, Vol. II (Tokyo, 1966), p. 162.

[43] *Nodong Shinmun*, September 12, 1961.

[44] *Kim Il-sŏng Sŏnjip*, Vol. IV (1960), p. 331.

[45] Information on the posts held by these men, their demotion and loss of positions is based on: *Translations on North Korea No. 42; Kankoku, Kita Chōsen Jinmei Jiten* (1966); and *Gendai Chōsen Jinmei Jiten* (1962). Additional footnotes are supplementary.

[46] *Taejung Chŏngch'i Yong'ŏ Sajŏn* (Everybody's Dictionary of Political Terms) (P'yŏngyang: Korean Workers' Party, 1964), p. 345. On April 4, 1955, at a plenum of the Central Committee of the party Kim said:

> "Pak Il-u has been thinking and acting as if he were the representative of the Yenan Koreans. Complaining that our party has not appointed enough Yenan Koreans to party posts, Pak has been gathering around him persons whose class consciousness is weak and who have ulterior motives."

Kim Il-sŏng Sŏnjip, Vol. IV (1960), p. 267.

[47] *Nodong Shinmun*, November 21, 1952; and November 21, 1954.

[48] Yu Hŏn, *Pukhan Isip-nyŏn*, p. 269.

[49] A full text of Khrushchev's speech appeared in *Pravda* on February 15, 1956, in *The Current Digest of the Soviet Press*, VIII, No. 4 (March 7, 1956), pp. 3–15, 29; VIII, No. 5 (March 14, 1956), pp. 3–15; and VIII, No. 6 (March 21, 1956), pp. 3–9.

[50] *Nodong Shinmun*, February 16, 17, and 18, 1956.

[51] *The Current Digest of the Soviet Press*, VIII, No. 9 (April 11, 1956), p. 3.

[52] *Chōsen Kenkyū*, No. 37 (February/March, 1965), p. 18.

[53] B. C. Koh, "North Korea and the Sino-Soviet Schism," *The Western Political Quarterly*, XXII, No. 4 (December, 1969), p. 943.

[54] *Ibid.*

[55] *Kim Il-sŏng Sŏnjip*, Vol. IV (1960), p. 524.

[56] *Ibid.*

[57] *Ibid.*, pp. 524–25.

[58] *Ibid.*, p. 557.

[59] *Chosŏn Nodongdang Kyuyak Haesŏl* (1960), p. 9.

[60] *Nodong Shinmun*, April 30, 1956.

[61] For a list of the 67 Central Committee members elected at the Second Party Congress in March 1948, see *Pukhan Ch'ongkam 1945–1968* (A Summary of Complete Facts About North Korea 1945–1968) (Seoul: Kongsan Munje Yŏnguso, 1968), p. 117.

[62] *Chosŏn Nodongdang Kyuyak Haesŏl* (1960), pp. 10–11.

[63] The communist Ch'oe Yong-kŏn, who had been the chairman of the Democratic Party, joined the Korean Workers' Party for the first time at the time of the Third Congress. The vacated chairmanship of the Democratic Party was taken over by Kang Yang-ok, a pro-communist former Christian minister.

[64] *Nodong Shinmun*, April 30, 1956.

[65] For a complete list of central party officials elected at the Third Party Congress, see *Nodong Shinmun*, April 30, 1956. Kim Ch'ang-man, though a vice-chairman, was not elected to the Standing Committee at the Third Party Congress.

[66] *Nodong Shinmun*, July 16, 1956.

[67] Chong-sik Lee and Ki-wan Oh, "The Russian Faction in North Korea," *Asian Survey*, VIII, No. 4 (April, 1968), p. 287.

[68] *Pukhan Ch'ongkam 1945–1968*, p. 178; Cho, "Politics of North Korea's Unification Policies," pp. 227–28; and Lee Dong-jun, *Hwansankwa Hyŏnsil*, pp. 195–97.

[69] Koh, "North Korea and the Sino-Soviet Schism," p. 944. Five months later an article in *Kŭlloja*, while praising "the adherence to the principle of collective leadership . . . by the Central Committee headed by Comrade Kim Il-sŏng," denounced Kim's opponents as "hero worshippers." Hŏ Il-hun,

"Jippch'ejŏk Jido Wŏnch'ikŭi Jŏnghwakhan Kwanch'ŏl ŭl wihan myŏtkaji Munje" ("Various Problems in the Correct Fulfillment of the Principle of Collective Leadership"), *Kŭlloja*, No. 12 (December, 1956), pp. 92–102.

[70] Koh, "North Korea and the Sino-Soviet Schism," p. 944.

[71] Lee Dong-jun, *op. cit.*, pp. 197–98; Cho Seong-jik, "The Process of Abolishing Private Business in North Korea," pp. 171–72; and Kim, "North Korea's Fourth Party Congress," p. 39.

[72] Kim Sam-kyu, *Chōsen Gendai-shi*, p. 177; *Kin Nichisei Senshū*, Vol. II (Tokyo, 1966), p. 252; and Lee Ch'ŏl-chu, "Pukke Chosŏn Nodongdang," p. 284.

[73] *Nodong Shinmun*, September 5, 1956; and readings from *Translations on North Korea No. 42*, and *Gendai Chōsen Jinmei Jiten* (1962).

[74] Kim, *Pukhan Sip-o-Nyŏn-sa*, p. 157.

[75] Cho, "The Politics of North Korea's Unification Policies," p. 228. The three men who had escaped to Communist China did not return to North Korea even after their party membership was restored.

[76] *Nodong Shinmun*, March 11, 1957; *Kim Il-sŏng Sŏnjip*, Vol. V (1960), p. 240; and Bang In-hu, *op. cit.*, p. 228.

[77] *Nodong Shinmun*, May 13, 31, and September 28, 1957; *Kim Ilsŏng Sŏnjip*, Vol. V (1960), p. 240; and *Taejung Chŏngch'i Yong'ŏ Sajŏn* (1964), p. 374.

[78] The anti-Kim revolt of August 1956 was to some extent stimulated by the restiveness of the Eastern Europeans and the uprising in Poland. Terming them as "the revisionist trend" in his report at the plenum of the Central Committee on December 5, 1957, Kim Il-ŏng stated:

> As is known, in our country revisionism has been unable to exert a big influence. We should not forget, however, that the revisionist trends which raised their heads internationally may exert certain influence upon and evoke sympathy in a small number of unsound elements and petty bourgeois, wavering elements also in our country. The slogans and actions which the sectarian elements, exposed and criticized at the August 1956 Plenum, put up for achieving their dirty aims show this. They denied all the results attained by the party in the past, rejected the party's leadership and advocated unprincipled 'democracy' and 'freedom', opposing the party's democratic centralism, blared about the 'usefullness of sects' and even committed such intolerable, anti-class acts as conniving with hostile elements or becoming their cat's paw.

New Korea (English periodical issued in P'yŏngyang), December 1957, *Supplement*, pp. 12–13.

[79] For a full text of the resolution, see *Pravda*, November 22, 1957, in *Current Digest of the Soviet Press*, IX, No. 47 (January 1, 1958), pp. 3–7.

[80] italics mine.

[81] H. Gordon Skilling, *Communism, National and International: Eastern Europe After Stalin* (Toronto, University of Toronto Press, 1964), p. 12.

[82] *Pukhan Ch'ongkam 1945–1968*, p. 178.

[83] *Translations on North Korea No. 42*, p. 46. With regard Kim Tu-bong, Kim Il-sŏng stated on March 6, 1958 at the "First Conference of Party Representatives":

Although Kim Tu-bong worked with us for ten years, he has always dreamed different dreams from us, and has confided to Han Pin and Ch'oe Ch'ang-ik instead of doing so to us. In spite of the fact that Han Pin was a destructive element in our party and was most hated by our party, Kim Tu-bong thought of him as his dearest friend and took Han Pin's opinions more seriously than those of our party. Whenever he spent a night at Han Pin's, he schemed against the party. Kim Tu-bong's crimes were grave. While serving as the President of the Presidium of the Supreme People's Assembly, he corrupted many innocent people in the Supreme People's Assembly as well as many youths in the country.

Kim Il-sŏng Sŏnjip, Vol. V (1960), pp. 385–86, 388.

[84] *Nodong Shinmun*, January 3, 1958; *Kim Il-sŏnjip*, Vol. V (1960), p. 392; and *Translations on North Korea No. 42*, pp. 7, 19. The Soviet Korean Kim Sŭng-hwa who had spoken against Kim Il-sŏng group in August 1956 was not expelled from the party at this time. His expulsion occurred in August 1958, and, subsequently, he returned to the Soviet Union. *Translations on North Korea No. 42*, p. 9.

[85]Lee and Oh, "The Russian Faction in North Korea," pp. 275-84.

[86] For a text of the agreement between North Korea and the Soviet Union, see "Convention between the Union of Soviet Socialist Republics and the Democratic People's Republic of Korea regulating the Citizenship of Persons Having Dual Citizenship, Signed at P'yŏngyang, on December 16, 1957," in United Nations, *Supplement to the Volume on Laws Concerning Nationality, 1954* (ST/LEG/SER/B/9) (New York, 1959), pp. 100–01.

[87] *Translations on North Korea No. 42*, p. 26. Regarding O Ki-sŏp, Kim Il-sŏng on March 6, 1958 at the "First Conference of the Party Representatives" said:

Although O Ki-sŏp worked with us for ten years . . . he has always harboured different dreams from us . . . Although O carried out factionalist activities, he engaged in them covertly like a stealthy cat. However, his acts were finally detected by the party.

Kim Il-sŏng Sŏnjip, Vol. V (1960), pp. 386, 392.

Later, on March 23, 1959, at a plenum of the Hamkyŏng Pukto Provincial Party, Kim Il-sŏng again denounced O's bygone acts:

. . . localism and favoring family members in the selection of party officials are direct causes for producing factionalism. . . . Yet, O Ki-sŏp, in the past, took men from his province with him whenever he was transferred to another province. Such a conduct was exactly the same as those Chinese warlords like Chang Tso-lin and Wu P'ei-fu did.

Kim Il-sŏng Sŏnjip, Vol. VI (1960), p. 327.

[88] According to the party regulations adopted at the Third Party Congress, the "representatives" of the party were to be selected by party congress among members of the Central Committee. Their number was

not to exceed one-fifth of the total Central Committee membership. The "Conference of Party Representatives" was to be convened to discuss "party policies of a tactically urgent nature," and its decisions were to be approved automatically by the Central Committee. All party members were obliged to carry out its decisions. Also the "Conference of Party Representatives" had a right to recall those members of the Central Committee who "failed to perform their duties" and to select new members to the Central Committee. *Chosŏn Nodongdang Kyuyak Haesŏl* (1960), p. 12.

[89] *Nodong Shinmun*, March 6, 1958; and *Taejung Chŏngch'i Yong'ŏ Sajŏn* (1964), pp. 349–50.

[90] *Nodong Shinmun*, June 28, August 28, and August 30, 1957; and *New Korea* (P'yŏngyang), August 1957, No. 8, p. 50.

[91] Pak, *Pukhan T'ongch'i Kikuron*, p. 46.

[92] *Nodong Shinmun*, September 19, 1957.

[93] Pak, *Pukhan T'ongch'i Kikuron*, pp. 46–48; and *Chosŏn Chung'ang Nyŏngam 1958*, p. 175.

[94] *Nodong Shinmun*, September 20, and 21, 1957.

[95] *Nodong Shinmun*, April 30, 1956; September 21, 1957; and *Korea* (English periodical from P'yŏngyang), October, 1957, No. 10, p. 3. *Nodong Shinum*, September 21, 1957 contains a list of names of the second cabinet members.

[96] For a list of names of the 21 ministers of the first cabinet formed in 1948, see Kim, *Pukhan Sip-o-Nyŏn-sa*, pp. 232–33.

[97] *Nodong Shinmun*, September 21, 1957.

[98] *Nodong Shinmun*, October 1, 3, and November 19, 1957; and *Kim Il-sŏng Sŏnjip*, Vol. V (1960), pp. 378–79.

[99] *Nodong Shinmun*, December 16, 22, 1957; and January 3, 16, 1958.

[100] *Chōsen Kenkyū*, No. 32 (August, 1964), p. 30.

[101] *Nodong Shinmun*, September 3, 1958; *New Korea*, March 1958, No. 3, p. 11; and *Kim Il-sŏng Sŏnjip*, Vol. V (1960), pp. 376, 379.

[102] *Pukhan Ch'ongkam 1945–1968*, pp. 359–60; and *Kim Il-sŏng Sŏnjip*, Vol. V (1960), p. 19.

[103] *Nodong Shinmun*, July 16, 1959.

CHAPTER 9

[1] *Nodong Shinmun*, September 12, 1961.

[2] Baik Bong, *Kim Il Sung: Biography*, Vol. III (Tokyo: Miraisha, 1970), p. 225.

[3] For a full Korean text of Kim's speech, see *Nodong Shinmun*, September 12, 1961. The text of Kim's speech is also available in *Chosŏn Nodongdang che Sach'a Taehoe Munhŏnjip* (The Documents of the Fourth Korean Workers' Party Congress) (P'yŏngyang: Kŭlloja-sa, 1961) as well as in Kim Il-sŏng, *Chosŏn Nodongdang che Sach'a Taehoe esŏ'han Chung'ang Wiwŏnhoe Saŏp Poko* (Report on the Work of the Central Committee

at the Fourth Korean Workers' Party Congress) (P'yŏngyang: Korean Workers' Party, 1961).

[4] Among the discarded members were 15 Yenan Koreans, 12 Soviet Koreans, and 16 native communist leaders.

[5] Among the 57 were 12 candidate members, one from the Auditing Committee, and another from the Inspection Committee of the previous Congress.

[6] For a list of the party officials elected at the Fourth Congress, see *Nodong Shinmun*, September 19, 1961. For backgrounds of these officials, see "Puk'koe Inmyongrok," in *Pukhan Ch'ongkam 1945-1968*, pp. 1019-1057; and *Translations on North Korea, No. 42.*

[7] Of the eight who received college education, three studied in the Soviet Union, two in China, and two in Japan, and one at some undetermined location.

[8] Of the remainder of the 13, one is from a family whose elders collaborated with Kim Il-sŏng in pre-liberation days in establishing underground bases near the Korean-Manchurian border area.

[9] The two normal school graduates had taught at primary schools until 1945.

[10] Three studied in Soviet Russia and one in East Germany.

[11] *Chosŏn Nodongdang Kyuyak Haesŏl* (1963) (Interpretation of Korean Workers' Party Regulations Adopted at the Fourth Party Congress) (Tokyo: Hak-u Sobang, 1963), pp. 185-86.

[12] Lee and Oh, "The Russian Faction in North Korea," p. 278.

[13] Kim Ch'ang-man, "Chosŏn Nodongdang Yŏksa Yŏngu e cheki doenŭn myŏtkaji Munje" ("Several Problems Arising from Research in the History of the Korean Workers' Party"), *Kŭlloja*, No. 1 (January, 1960), p. 17.

[14] *Chosŏn Nodongdang Kyuyak Haesŏl* (1963), p. 16.

[15] *Nodong Shinmun*, October 8, 9, and 10, 1962.

[16] *Pukhan Ch'ongkam 1945-1968*, p. 125.

[17] Pak, *Pukhan T'ongch'i Kikuron*, p. 47.

[18] *Nodong Shinmun*, October 23 and 24, 1962. At this point the North Koreans dropped the term People's Council and adopted the term Cabinet. The six vice-premiers were: Kim Il (First Vice Premier), Kim Kwang-hyŏp, Kim Ch'ang-man, Chŏng Il-yong, Nam Il, and Yi Chong-ok.

[19] *Nodong Shinmun*, October 24, 1962. The two vice-presidents were Pak Chŏng-ae and Pak Kŭm-ch'ŏl. These two persons along with Ch'oe Yong-kŏn did not hold posts on the Third Cabinet. On November 25, 1967, elections were held to select 457 representatives to the Fourth Supreme People's Assembly. According to North Korean sources, 100 percent of all eligible voters participated in the elections and all of them cast their ballots affirmatively for the 457 candidates. The newly elected representatives met on December 16, 1967 and they "unaminously approved"

the list of Fourth Cabinet members submitted by Kim Il-sŏng. At the meeting the representatives again elected Ch'oe Yong-kŏn to the Presidency of the Presidium of the Fourth Supreme People's Assembly. For the names of the 457 representatives, see *Nodong Shinmun*, November 27, 1967. For the names of the Fourth Cabinet and those of the officials of the Fourth Supreme People's Assembly, see *Nodong Shinmun*, December 17, 1967.

[20] *Kim Il-sŏng Sŏnjip*, Vol. V (1960), p. 284.

[21] *Nodong Shinmun*, November 28, 1961.

[22] *Nodong Shinmun*, October 28, 1963; and *North Korean Radio Broadcast*, October 28, 1963, in *Daily Report*, October 30, 1963.

[23] *North Korean Radio Broadcast*, August 30, 1964, in *Daily Report*, August 31, 1964. For a similar independent theme, see also *North Korean Radio Broadcast*, January 29, 1963, in *Daily Report*, January 30, 1963.

[24] For a text of Kim Il-sŏng's speech of October 5, 1966 made at "the Conference of Party Representatives," see *Nodong Shinmun*, October 6, 1966. The text of the speech is also available in *Kim Il-sŏng Jŏjak Sŏnjip*, Vol. IV (Selected Works of Kim-Il-sŏng, Vol. IV) (P'yŏngyang: Korean Workers' Party, 1968), pp. 317–403.

[25] *North Korean Radio Broadcast*, December 17, 1967, in *Daily Report*, December 21, 1967.

[26] *Nodong Shinmun*, June 13, 14, and December 3, 1958.

[27] For details of the Great Leap Forward, see Franz Schurmann, *Ideology and Organization in Communist China* (Berkeley: University of California Press, 1966), pp. 74–128, 216–397, 465–67.

[28] *Chōsen Kenkyū (Geppō)*, No. 16 (April 25, 1963), pp. 12–19; and Baik Bong, *Kim Il-sung: Biography*, III, pp. 179–99, 200–22.

[29] *Tōitsu Chōsen Nenkan, 1967–68* (One-Korea Yearbook, 1967–68) (Tokyo: Tōitsu Chōsen Shimbunsha, 1967), p. 470.

[30] For North Korean statistics on North Korea's economic achievements for a decade after the Korean War, see, among others, *Nodong Shinmun*, July 16, 1959; *Chosŏn Chung'ang Nyŏngam 1958*, p. 177; *1961*, p. 321; *1962*, pp. 357–58; *1963*, pp. 230–31; *1964*, pp. 197–99; and *1965*, pp. 136, 149–50, 161–62.

[31] *North Korean Radio Broadcast*, September 27, 1961, in *Daily Report*, September 29, 1961.

[32] Joan Robinson, "Korean Miracle," *Monthly Review*, XIX, No. 9 (January, 1965), pp. 541–42.

[33] Yoon T. Kuark, "North Korea's Industrial Development During the Post-War Period," Scalapino (ed.), *North Korea Today*, p. 63; Cho, "Politics of North Korea's Unification Policies," *op. cit.*, p. 229; and Koh B. C., "North Korea: Profile of a Garrison State," *Problems of Communism*, XVIII, No. 1 (January, 1969), p. 23.

[34] Cited in speech of Pak Kŭm-ch'ŏl, the head of the North Korean

congratulatory delegation, made on February 17, 1961 at the Fourth Congress of the Albanian Labor Party. *Nodong Shinmun*, February 20, 1961; and *North Korean Radio Broadcast*, February 19, 1961, in *Daily Report*, February 20, 1961.

[35] Cited in the speech by Kim Il-sŏng to Fourth Supreme People's Assembly on December 16, 1967 presenting DPRK Government Political Program. *North Korean Radio Broadcast*, December 17, 1967, in *Daily Report, Supplement*, December 21, 1967, p. 3.

[36] *Tōitsu Chōsen Nenkan, 1967–68*, p. 356.

[37] *Chōsen Kenkyū*, No. 37 (February/March, 1965), p. 19; and *Chosŏn Chung'ang Nyŏngam 1963*, pp. 184–85.

[38] *Tōitsu Chōsen Nenkan, 1967–68*, p. 355; and *Nodong Shinmun*, October 13, 1966.

[39] *Tōitsu Chōsen Nenkan, 1967–68*, p. 356.

[40] *Nodong Shinmun*, June 28, 1964.

[41] For details of the "Representatives' Conference," see *Nodong Shinmun*, October 6–13, 1966.

[42] *Nodong Shinmun*, October 13, 1966.

[43] Information concerning personnel changes here and in the remainder of this chapter are based, unless otherwise footnoted, upon: *Nodong Shinmun*, October 13, 1966; "Puk'koe Inmyŏngrok," *Pukhan Ch'ongkam 1945–1968*, pp. 1019–1057; and *Kankoku, Kita Chōsen Jinmei Jiten* (1966).

[44] *Chōsen Kenkyū* (Geppō), No. 24 (December 25, 1963), p. 2.

[45] *Nodong Shinmun*, October 13, 1966.

[46] *Nodong Shinmun*, September 12, 1961, and October 22, 1964.

[47] See, among others, *Hang'il Palch'isan Ch'amkajadŭl'e Hoesangki*, Vol. I–X (Memoirs of the Anti-Japanese Partisans, Vol. I–X) (P'yŏngyang: Korean Workers' Party, 1960–1968); *Nodong Shinmun*, October 12, 1967, and January 7, 1969; and Baik Bong, *Kim Il Sung: Biography*, Vol. I, II, III.

[48] Robinson, "Korean Miracle," p. 584.

[49] Chung In-taek, "The Korean Minority in Manchuria (1900–1937)" (unpublished Ph.D. thesis), pp. 37–47; 85–87, 173–77; and *Chōsen Kenkyū* (Geppō), No. 36 (January, 1965), p. 3.

[50] *Ibid.*

[51] Shii Motoyuki, "Flying Horseman," *Atlas*, Vol. XVII (June, 1969), p. 48; *Chōsen Kenkyū* (Geppō), No. 21 (September 25, 1963), pp. 17–18; and No. 35 (December, 1964), pp. 12–13.

[52] Shii Motoyuki, "Flying Horseman," pp. 48–49; and *Chōsen Kenkyū*, No. 35 (December, 1964), p. 12.

[53] Hans H. Gerth, "The Nazi Party: Its Leadership and Composition," in Robert K. Merton *et al.* (eds.) *Reader in Bureaucracy* (New York: The Free Press, 1952), p. 109.

[54] *Chōsen Kenkyū* (Geppō), No. 21 (September 25, 1963), pp. 1–21.

[55] *Chōsen Kenkyū* (Geppō), No. 14 (February 25, 1963), pp. 16–23.

[56] Koh, "North Korea: Profile of a Garrison State," p. 18.

CONCLUSION

[1] Jerome D. Frank, *Sanity and Survival: Psychological Aspects of War and Peace* (New York: Random House, 1967), p. 187.

POSTSCRIPT

[1] Personnel data in the postscript are from the following sources: 1) Sekai Seikei Chōsa-kai (ed.) *Kankoku, Kita Chōsen Jinme Jiten* (Who's Who in South and North Korea) (Tokyo: Sekai Seikei Chōsa-kai, 1970); 2) "Puk-koe In'myŏng-rok" ("Who's Who in North Korea"), *Pukhan Ch'ongkam 1945–1968*, pp. 1019–1057; 3) *Translations on North Korea No. 42;* 4) "Korean Communist Who's Who" *Journal of Korean Affairs*, I, No. 2 (July, 1971), pp. 57–59; I, No. 3 (Oct. 1971), pp. 53–54; and II, No. 1 (April 1972), pp. 45–46; and 5) a few other sources.

[2] *Kim Il-sŏng Sŏnjip*, IV (1968), pp. 356–57. Also see *Nodong Shinmun*, December 16, 1962.

[3] *Nodong Shinmun*, October 6, 1966. See also *Kim Il-sŏng Sŏnjip*, IV (1968), pp. 363–65.

[4] Kim Il-sŏng, *Revolution and Social Construction in Korea: Selected Writings of Kim Il Sung* (New York: International Publishers, Co., Inc., 1971), p. 184. See also *Nodong Shinmun*, November 3, 1970.

[5] Kim Il-sŏng, *Revolution and Socialist Construction in Korea*, p. 164.

[6] *Kim Il-sŏng Sŏnjip*, III (1968), pp. 136–51. See also *Nodong Shinmun*, September 12, 1961.

[7] This lecture was addressed at the Ali Archam Academy of Social Sciences of Indonesia. For the full English text, see Kim Il-sŏng, *Revolution and Socialist Construction in Korea*, pp. 99–110.

[8] At the Fifth KWP Congress convened in November 1970, Kim Il-sŏng in his main speech, mentioned the futility of "peaceful unification" through South Korean leftist forces which had been responsive to P'yŏngyang's call for "peaceful unification" such as the Progressive Party, that was formed in 1955 but was dismantled by Syngman Rhee's regime in 1958, and the Socialist Mass Party, which appeared following the downfall of Syngman Rhee in April 1960 but was suppressed by the army that took over power after the *coup d'etat* on May 16, 1961. Kim continued that even after the military's take-over in Seoul, the Korean Workers' Party made every attempt to achieve "peaceful unification," but:

. . . the South Korean officials . . . ignored [our] proposals every time and opposed independent peaceful unification doggedly.

Kim Il-sŏng, *Chosŏn Nodongdang che 5 ch'a Taehoe esŏ'han Chung'ang Wi'wŏnhoe Sa'op Ch'onghwa Poko* (Report on the work of the Central Committee at the Fifth Korean Workers' Party Congress) (Tokyo: Federation of Korean Residents in Japan, 1970), pp. 90–95. Text of Kim's speech is also available in *Nodong Shinmun*, November 3, 1970.

[9] *Kim Il-sŏng Sŏnjip,* IV (1968), p. 393. Also see *Nodong Shinmun,* October 6, 1966.

[10] According to the *New York Times* of February 1, 1968, armed incidents involving North Koreans trained for infiltration rose from 50 in 1966 to 550 in 1967. The U. S. Ambassador to South Korea, William Porter, appearing before a Congressional hearing on June 8, 1971, gave the following statistics involving "the incidents from North to South Korea":

Number of incidents

	DMZ	Rear
1966	37	13
1967	452	277
1968	542	219

U. S. Congress, *Hearing Before the Subcommittee on Asian and Pacific Affairs of the Committee on Foreign Affairs House of Representatives,* Ninety-Second Congresss, First Session (Washington, D.C.: Government Printing Office, 1971), p. 11.

[11] *Tong A-Ilbo,* January 22, 1968.

[12] This was acknowledged during his answers made on March 1, 1969 to questions raised by North Korean educators in the previous April concerning economic issues. Kim Il-sŏng, *Revolution and Socialist Construction in Korea,* p. 164.

[13] *Pukhan Ch'ongkam 1945–1968,* pp. 233–34; and Joseph S. Chung, "The Six-Year Plan (1971–76) of North Korea: Targets, Problems and Prospects," *Journal of Korean Affairs,* I, No. 2 (July, 1971), p. 25.

[14] The economic burden stemming from the military programs was again admitted by Kim Il-sŏng at the Fifth Party Congress during his major report:

> Our national defense was accomplished with very heavy and costly prices. Frankly speaking, our defense expenditures became too big a burden considering the smallness of our population. Had we diverted even a very small portion from the national defense allotment to economic construction, our people's economy must have grown even faster and their living standard must have been much higher.

Nodong Shinmun, November 3, 1970. See also Kim Il-sŏng, *Chosŏn Nodongdang Che 5 ch'a Taehoe esŏ'han Chung'ang Wi'wŏnhoe Sa'op Ch'onghwa Poko,* pp. 31–32.

[15] *Kim Il-sŏng Sŏnjip,* IV (1968), p. 393.

[16] *Tong-A Ilbo,* January 25, 1968. Unlike the former three who had been engaged in underground political activities along the Korean-Manchurian border, Ko Hyŏk, born in eastern Manchuria, was a member of armed guerrilla troops commanded by Kim Il-sŏng in the 1930's. Ko became the Director of the party's Bureau of Culture and Arts in April 1964 and was appointed a Vice-Premier in the Cabinet in September 1966.

[17] At the 16th plenum of the Central Committee of the 4th period of the party convened June 28–July 3, 1967, by which time all the four persons are believed to have been purged, Kim Il-sŏng stated:

> The Representatives' Conference of the Party . . . proposed the great task to carry on economic construction and defense construction in parallel. This is a new revolutionary line of our Party . . . However, our experience did show that whenever a new party line is adopted there always emerges *shaky element, negative element, and conservative element, all of which obstruct its accomplishment.*

Kim Il-sŏng Sŏnjip, IV (1968), pp. 483, 486. Underline mine.

[18] *Pukhan Ch'ongkam,* 1945–1968, p. 116. Probably calling those who had just been purged a "shaky element," a "negative element," and a "conservative element," Kim Il-sŏng at the plenum of June 28–July 3, 1967 declared that "today these negative elements and shaky elements are not needed for us." *Kim Il-sŏng Sŏnjip,* IV (1968), p. 490.

[19] *Nodong Shinmun,* July 4, 1967.

[20] *Tong-A Ilbo,* November 6, 28, and December 16, 1968; and *New York Times,* March 22, 1969.

[21] *Tong-A Ilbo,* December 16, 1968; and *New York Times,* March 22, 1969.

[22] Though all the four held high positions in the party, none of them was ever known by any military rank in North Korea.

[23] *New York Times,* March 22, 1969, and November 22, 1970.

[24] *New York Times,* March 22, 1969.

[25] *Tong-A Ilbo,* January 25, 1968.

[26] *New York Times,* March 22, 1969.

[27] A *de facto* party congress was held in October 1966 in the form of the Party Representatives' Conference. But the Fifth Congress, which was attended by 1,871 delegates (1,734 voting delegates and 137 alternates), was the first party congress since the previous one convened in 1961, in spite of the stipulation of the party constitution that calls for a party congress every four years.

[28] For a full text of Kim Il-sŏng's speech, see *Nodong Shinmun,* November 3, 1970; or Kim Il-sŏng, *Chosŏn Nodongdang che 5 ch'a Taehoe esŏ'han Chung'ang Wi'wŏnhoe Sa'op Ch'onghwa Poko.*

[29] Roster of the central party leadership elected at the Fifth Party Congress appeared in *Nodong Shinmun,* November 14, 1970.

[30] *New York Times,* November 22, 1970.

[31] The six-member standing committee of the Politburo, which was created in October 1966, was not retained by the Fifth Congress.

BIBLIOGRAPHY

I. Primary Sources

A. DOCUMENTS, BOOKS, AND PAMPHLETS
1. In the Korean Language

Cho Ch'ae-son. *Chosŏn Minjuju'i Inmin Konghwaguk Sahoe Kyŏngje Jedo* (The Socio-Economic System in the Democratic People's Republic of Korea). P'yŏngyang: Korean Workers' Party, 1958.

Chosŏn Chung'ang Nyŏngam 1949–1968 (Korean Central Almanacs 1949–1968). P'yŏngyang: Korean Central News Agency, 1949–1968.

Chosŏn esŏui Miguk Ch'imryaekja dŭl ŭi Manhaeng ŭi kwanhan Munhŏnjip (Documents Regarding the Barbarous Activities of American Aggression in Korea). P'yŏngyang: Korean Workers' Party, 1954.

Chosŏn Minjuju'i Inmin Konghwanguk Hŏnpŏp (The Constitution of the Democratic People's Republic of Korea). Tokyo: Hak-u Sobang, 1960.

Chosŏn Minjuju'i Inmin Konghwaguk Hŏnpŏp mit Inmin Hoe'ŭi'isang'im Ui-wŏnhoe Jŏngryŏng-jip, 1948–1950 (Laws and Statutes of Democratic People's Republic of Korea and Collection of Edicts of the Supreme People's Assembly, 1948–1950). Tokyo: Hak-u Sobang, 1948–1950.

Chosŏn Nodongdang che Sach'a Taehoe Munhŏnjip (The Documents of the Fourth Korean Workers' Party Congress). P'yŏngyang: Kŭlloja-sa, 1961.

Chosŏn Nodongdang i kŏrŏ on Yŏngkwangsurŏun Kil (The Glorious Past of the Korean Workers' Party). Tokyo: Chosŏn Ch'ŏngnyŏnsa, 1965.

Chosŏn Nodongdang Kyuyak Haesŏl (Interpretation of Korean Workers' Party Regulations). Tokyo: Hak-u Sobang, 1960.

Chosŏn Nodongdang Kyuyak Haesŏl (Interpretation of Korean Workers' Party Regulations). Tokyo: Hak-u Sobang, 1963.

Chosŏn Nodongdang Ryŏksa Kyojae (Textbook for a History of Korean Workers' Party). P'yŏngyang: Korean Workers' Party, 1964.

Chung Kong ŏp Palchŏn ŭl wihan uridang'e Chŏngch'aek (Policy of Our Party For the Development of Heavy Industry). P'yŏngyang: Korean Workers' Party, 1961.

Democratic People's Republic of Korea, Academy of Science, Center For Historical Studies. *Chosŏn T'ongsa* (Outline of History of Korea). P'yŏngyang: Nodong Shinmun Press, 1958.

_____. *Chosŏn T'ongsa* (reprinted in Japan). Tokyo: Hak-u Sobang, 1961.

Han Im-hyŏk. *Kim Il-sŏng tongji e ŭihan Chosŏn Kongsandang Ch'angkŏn* (Establishment of Korean Communist Party by Comrade Kim Il-sŏng). P'yŏngyang: Korean Workers' Party, 1961.

Hang'il Palch'isan Ch'amkajadŭl'e Hoesangki, Vol. I - X (Memoirs of the Anti-Japanese Partisans, Vol. I - X). P'yŏngyang: Korean Workers' Party, 1960–1968.

Kim Han-ju. *Chosŏn Minjuju'i Inmin Konghwaguk ŭi Nongŏp Hyŏpptonghwa Undong ŭi Sŭngni* (The Victory of Agricultural Cooperative Movement in Democratic People's Republic of Korea). P'yŏngyang: Korean Workers' Party, 1959.

Kim Il-sŏng. *Chosŏn Nodongdang che sach'a Taehoe esŏ'han Chung'ang Wi'wŏnhoe Saŏp Poko* (Report on the Work of the Central Committee at the Fourth Korean Workers' Party Congress). P'yŏngyang: Korean Workers' Party, 1961.

_____. *Chosŏn Nodongdang che 5 ch'a Taehoe esŏ'han Chung'ang Wi'wŏn'hoe Sa'op Ch'onghwa Poko* (Report on the Work of the Central Committee at the Fifth Korean Workers' Party Congress). Tokyo: Federation of Korean Residents in Japan, 1970.

Kim Il-sŏng Jŏjak Sŏnjip (Selected Works of Kim Il-sŏng). P'yŏngyang: Korean Workers' Party, 1968.

Kim Il-sŏng Sŏnjip (Selected Works of Kim Il-sŏng). P'yŏngyang: Korean Workers' Party, 1960–1964.

Taejung Chŏngch'i Yong'ŏ Sajŏn (Everybody's Dictionary of Political Terms). P'yŏngyang: Korean Workers' Party, 1957.

Taejung Chŏngch'i Yong'ŏ Sajŏn. P'yŏngyang: Korean Workers' Party, 1964.

Yi Na-yŏng. *Chosŏn Minjok Haebang T'ujaengsa* (A History of Korean People's Struggle for Liberation). P'yŏngyang: Korean Workers' Party, 1958.

Yi Shin-hyong. *Kyŏngje Sangsik* (Economic Fundamentals). P'yŏngyang: Korean Workers' Party, 1960.

2. In the Japanese Language

Kin Nichisei Senshū (Selected Works of Kim Il-sŏng). Tokyo: Japanese Communist Party, 1964.

Kin Nichisei Senshū. Tokyo: Japanese Communist Party, 1966.

In the English Language

Baik Bong. *Kim Il Sung: Biography*, Vol. I, II, III (Translated from Korean into English by Committee for Translation of Kim Il Sung: Biography). Tokyo: Miraisha, 1969, 1970, 1970.

Documents of the Third Congress of the Korean Workers' Party, April 23–29, 1956. P'yŏngyang: Foreign Language Publishing House, 1956.

Documents of the Fourth Congress of the Korean Workers' Party. P'yŏngyang: Foreign Language Publishing House, 1961.

Facts About Korea. P'yŏngyang: Foreign Language Publishing House, 1961.
For Korea's Peaceful Unification. P'yŏngyang: Foreign Language Publishing House, 1961.
Kim Il-sŏng. *All For the Country's Unification and Independence and For Socialist Construction in the Northern Part of the Republic: Theses on the Character and Tasks of Our Revolution, April 1955.* P'yŏngyang: Foreign Language Publishing House, 1961.

————. *All For the Post-War Rehabilitation and Development of the National Economy,* P'yŏngyang: The New Korea Press, 1954.

————. *All For the Post-War Rehabilitation and Development of the National Economy: Report Delivered at the Sixth Plenum of the Central Committee of the Workers' Party of Korea, On August 5, 1953.* P'yŏngyang: The New Korea Press, 1954.

————. *The Great Liberation War of the Korean People for Freedom and Independence.* P'yŏngyang: Ministry of Culture and Propaganda, 1951.

————. *Revolution and Socialist Construction in Korea: Selected Writings of Kim Il Sung.* New York: International Publishers, Co., Inc., 1971.

B. ARTICLES AND PERIODICALS

1. In the Korean Language

Hŏ Il-hun. "Jippch'ejŏk Jido Wŏnch'ikŭi Jŏnghwakkhan Kwanch'ŏl ŭl wihan myŏtkaji Munje" ("Various Problems in the Correct Fulfillment of the Principle of Collective Leadership"), *Kŭlloja,* No. 12 (December, 1956), pp. 92–102.

Hwang Yŏng-sik. "Sahoe Chu'i wa Kaesŏng" ("Socialism and the Individuality"), *Kŭlloja,* No. 9 (May, 1964), pp. 21–28.

Kim Ch'ang-kyu. "Chosŏn Nodongdang che 2 ch'a Taehoe e Ryŏksajŏk Ŭi'i" ("The Historical Significance of the Second Congress of the Korean Workers' Party"), *Kŭlloja,* No. 6 (March, 1963), pp. 14–19.

Kim Ch'ang-man. "Chosŏn Nodongdang Yŏksa Yŏngu e cheki doenŭn myŏtkaji Munje" ("Several Problems Arising from Research in the History of the Korean Workers' Party"), *Kŭlloja,* No. 1 (January, 1960), pp. 10–21.

Kim Hyŏng-il. "Koekŭppsŏng kwa Inkansŏng" ("The Class Consciousness and Humanity"), *Kŭlloja,* No. 13 (July, 1963), pp. 12–16.

Kim Sŭng-il. "Kongsan Chu'i Kyoyang'e Yŏksajŏk Kwa'ŏp un Sŏngkwajŏk ŭro Haekyŏl tŏko itta" ("The Historical Task for Teaching Communism is Being Successfully Solved"). *Kŭlloja,* No. 4 (197) (April, 1962), pp. 73–80.

"Sahoe Chu'i Hyŏkmyongkwa Jaryŏk Kaengsaeng" ("Socialist Revolution and Self-Regeneration"), *Kŭlloja,* No. 19 (212) (November, 1962), pp. 2–7.

"Tangsŏng, Inkansŏng, Munhwasŏng" ("The Party Loyalty, Humanity and Culture"), *Kŭlloja,* No. 2 (February, 1962), pp. 11–17.

Yi Chong-hyŏn. "Kwangju Haksaeng Undong" ("Kwangju Student Movement"), *Yŏksa Kwahak*, No. 6 (December, 1959), pp. 1–10.

Yi Sŏk-shim. "Uri Naraesŏ Jaripjŏk Minjok Kyŏngje Kŏnsŏl" (Establishment of a Self-Supporting Economy in Our Country"), *Kŭlloja*, No. 19 (November, 1962), pp. 8–18.

In the Japanese Language

Atarashi Chōsen (New Korea, monthly periodical from P'yŏngyang), *Supplements*, March, 1958, No. 1; March, 1958, No. 2; March, 1958, No. 3; March, 1958, No. 4; April, 1958 (no number given); May, 1958 (no number given); June, 1958 (no number given); July, 1958 (1); July, 1958 (2); 1958, No. 25 (no month given); 1958, No. 26 (1) (no month given); and 1958, No. 26 (2) (no month given).

Kyōno Chōsen (Korea Today, monthly periodical from P'yŏngyang), *Supplements* (no months given in these supplements, here listed as they were issued), 1959, No. 34; 1959, No. 36 (1); 1959, No. 36 (2); 1959, No. 27 (1); 1959, No. 27 (2); 1959, No. 28 (1); 1959, No. 28; 1959, No. 33 (2); 1959, No. 33 (3); 1959, No. 33 (4); 1959, No. 29 (1); 1959, No. 29 (2); 1959, No. 29 (3); 1959, No. 29 (4); 1959, No. 30; 1959, No. 31; 1959, No. 32; 1959, No. 32 (1); 1959, No. 32 (2); 1959, No. 33 (1); and 1959, No. 38.

3. In the English Language

Han Shi-yoon. "Factory Trade Unions," *New Korea* (P'yŏngyang), No. 6 (June, 1958), pp. 34–35.

Kim Ch'ŏl-man. "Advance Again to the Homeland," *Korea* (P'yŏngyang), No. 4 (69) (August, 1962), pp. 32–33, 38.

Kim Il-sŏng. "Great October Socialist Revolution and National Liberation Struggle of Korean People," *For a Lasting Peace, For a People's Democracy*, No. 44 (156) (November 2, 1951), p. 4.

_____. "Lenin's Teaching—Our Guiding Star," *For a Lasting Peace, For a People's Democracy*, No. 15 (336) (April 15, 1955), pp. 3–4.

_____. "Report of Comrade Kim Il-sŏng at the Plenum of the Central Committee of the Workers' Party of Korea on the Work of the Party and Government Delegation which Attended Celebrations of the 40th Anniversary of the Great October Socialist Revolution and the Meetings of Representatives of the Communist and Workers' Parties of Various Countries in Moscow, December 5, 1957," *Supplement to New Korea*, No. 12 (December, 1957), pp. 2–16.

_____. "Report by Premier Kim Il-sŏng at the Celebration Meetings of the Tenth Anniversary of the Founding of the Democratic People's Republic of Korea, September 8, 1958," *New Korea*, No. 29 (September, 1958), pp. 3–29.

_____. "Text of Speech by Kim Il-sŏng to the Fourth Supreme People's Assembly on December 16, 1967, Presenting DPKR Government Political

[193]

Program," *North Korea Radio Broadcast,* December 17, 1967, cited in
Daily Report: Foreign Broadcast Information Service, Supplement (December 21, 1967) (FB 247/67/51S), pp. 1-39.
Korea (P'yŏngyang), No. 10 (October, 1957)
New Korea, No. 8 (August, 1957); No. 9 (September, 1957); No. 11 (November, 1957); No. 12, *Supplement* (December, 1957), No. 3 (March,
1958); No. 6 (June, 1958); No. 29 (September, 1958); and No. 30 (no
month given, 1958).

C. NEWSPAPERS

1. In the Korean Language

Minju Chosŏn (Democratic Korea, organ of the North Korean government),
July 24, 1962; and April 24, 1963.
Nodong Shinmun (Worker's Daily, organ of the Korean Workers' Party),
January 1, 1952—December 31, 1970.

D. NORTH KOREAN RADIO BROADCAST

February 27, 1958; January 15, 1959; and September 1, 1961—December
31, 1967 (contained in Daily Report: Foreign Broadcast Information Service,
February 1, 1958—January 15, 1968).

II. Secondary Sources

A. BOOKS AND PAMPHLETS

1. In the Korean Language

Bae Sŏng-yong. *Chaju Chosŏn e Jihang* (Direction of the Independent
Korea). Seoul: Kwangmun-sa, 1949.
Bang In-hu. *Pukhan "Chosŏn Nodongdang" ŭi Hyŏngsŏng kwa Palchŏn*
(North Korean "Korean Workers' Party," Its Formation and Develop-
ment). Seoul: Korea University Press, 1967.
Chang Pok-sŏng. *Chosŏn Kongsandang P'ajaengsa* (The History of the
Factional Struggle in the Korean Communist Party). Seoul: Taeryuk
Ch'ulp'ansa, 1949.
Chi Chung-se (ed.). *Chosŏn Sasangbŏm Kŏmkŏ Shilhwa-rok* (Collection of
Stories of Arrests of Korean Political Criminals). Seoul: Shin-kwang
Ch'ulp'an-sa, 1946.
Cho Yŏng-am. *Kodang, Cho Man-sik* (Biography of Cho Man-sik). Pusan:
Chŏngch'i Shinmun-sa, 1953.
Ch'oe Sang-dŏk. *Pukhan Goeroe Jiptan Chŏngch'e* (The Nature of North
Korean Puppet Regime). Seoul: Office of the Public Information, Repub-
lic of Korea, 1949.
Ch'oe Sŏk. *Hanguk T'ongil Munje e taehan Mosaek* (Search for the Unific-
ation of Korea). Seoul: Shin Munhwa-sa, 1967.

[194]

Chŏn Sŏk-tan. *Chosŏn Kyongjesa* (A History of Korean Economy). Seoul: Pakmun Ch'ulp'ansa, 1949.

Chŏngdang e Kiku Kinŭngkwa Chŏngkang Chŏngch'aek Tanghŏn (Structures, Functions, Platforms, and Constitutions of Various Political Parties). Seoul: Central Committee on Election Affairs, 1965.

Chosŏn Kwahakja Tongmaeng (ed.). *Chosŏn Haebang-sa* (An Emancipation History of Korea). Seoul: Mun-u In Sŏkwan, 1946.

Chosŏn Kyŏngje Nyŏnbo 1948 (Korean Economic Yearbook 1948). Seoul: Research Section, Bank of Korea, 1948.

Chosŏn Yŏng'am 1948 (Korean Annual 1948). Seoul: Chosŏn T'ongshin-sa, 1948.

Daehan Minguk Chŏngdangsa (A History of Korean Political Parties). Seoul: Central Committee on Election Affairs, 1964.

Han Ch'ŏl-yŏng. *Han'guk ŭi In-mul* (Notable Persons in Korea). Seoul: Munhwa Ch'un'ch'u-sa, 1952.

Han Jae-duk. *Hanguk e Kongsan Chu'i wa Pukhan Yŏksa* (Korean Communism and North Korean History). Seoul: Nae'oe Munhwasa, 1965.

_____. *Kim Il-sŏng kwa Pukkoe ŭi Silsang* (Kim Il-sŏng and the Actual Situation of North Korea). Seoul: Kongsankŏn Munje Yŏnguso, 1969.

_____. *Kim Il-sŏng ŭl Kobal Handa* (I Sue Kim Il-sŏng). Seoul: Nae'oe Munhwasa, 1965.

Han T'ae-su. *Hanguk Chŏngdangsa* (A History of Political Parties in Korea). Seoul: Shin T'ae-yang-sa, 1961.

Hanguk e issŏ sŏ ŭi Kongsanju'i (Communism in Korea). Seoul: The Office of Public Information, 1968.

Hyon Su. *Jŏkch'i Yuknyŏn e Pukhan Mundan* (Six Years of North Korean Literary World under the Red Rule). Seoul: Kukmin Sasang Jidowŏn, 1952.

Hyŏn-dae Han'guk Chŏng'ch'i-ka Kusipp-il-in-jip (Ninety-One Contemporary Korean Statesmen). Seoul: Shinjo-sa, 1957.

Jwa-ik Sakŏn Silrok, Vol. I, II, III (Records of Leftist Incidents, Vol. I, II, III), Seoul: Public Prosecutor's Office, 1965, 1968, 1969.

Kim Ch'ang-sun. *Pukhan Sip-o-Nyŏn-sa* (Fifteen Years of North Korean History). Seoul: Chimunkak, 1961.

_____. *Yŏksa ŭi Chŭng'in* (The Witness of History). Seoul: Hanguk Asea Pankong Yŏnmaeng, 1956.

Kim Chong-bŏm & Kim Tong-un. *Haebang Chŏnhu'ŭi Chosŏn Chinsang,* Vol. I & II (The Actual Situation of Korea Before and After Emancipation, Vol. I & II). Seoul: Chosŏn Chŏngkyŏng Yŏngusa, 1945.

Kim Jun-yŏp & Kim Ch'ang-sun. *Hanguk Kongsanchu'i Undongsa,* Vol. I & II (A History of the Korean Communist Movement, Vol. I & II). Seoul: Korea University Press, 1967, 1968.

Kim O-sŏng. *Jidoja-ron* (Discussion on Leadership). Seoul: Chosŏn Chŏngp'ansa, 1946.

Kim Sŭng-hak (ed.). *Hanguk Tongnip Undongsa* (A History of the Korean Independence Movement). Seoul: Tongnip Munhwasa, 1966.

Kim Tŭk-hwang. *Hanguk Sasangsa* (A History of Korean Thought). Seoul: Namsan-dang, 1958.

Kyŏngje Nyŏngam 1949, Part II (Economic Yearbook, Part II). Seoul: Research Section, Bank of Korea, 1949.

Lee Dong-jun. *Hwansangkwa Hyŏnsil: naŭi Kongsanju'i Kwan* (Fantasy and Fact: My Observation of Communism). Seoul: Tongbang T'ongsinsa, 1961.

Minju Chui Minjok Chŏnsŏn (ed.). *Chosŏn Haebang Nyŏnbo 1946* (Korean Emancipation Annual 1946). Seoul: Mun-u-in Sŏkwan, 1946.

Mun Ch'ang-chu. *Hanguk Chŏngch'i-ron* (Politics in Korea). Seoul: Ilcho-sa, 1965.

O Che-do. *Pulgun Gunsang, che il jip* (The Red Multitude, The First Series). Pusan: Namkwang Munhwa-sa, 1951.

O Yŏng-jin. *Han-e Chŭng-ŏn* (Eyewitness: North Korea under the Soviet Occupation). Seoul: Chungang Munhwa-sa, 1952.

Pak Ch'ŏl. *Puk Chosŏn Nosŏn Pip'an* (Criticism of the North Korean Course). Seoul: Shinjo-sa, 1961.

Pak Mun-ok. *Hanguk Chŏngbu Ron* (Korean Government). Seoul: Pukyongsa, 1963.

Pak Sang-hyŏk. *Chosŏn Minjokŭi Widaehan Chidoja* (The Great Leader of the Korean People). Tokyo: Chosŏn Shinbosa, 1964.

Pak T'ae-wŏn. *Yaksan kwa Uiyŏldan* (Yaksan and Uiyŏldan), Seoul: Paekyang-sa, 1947.

Pak Tong-un. *Pukhan T'ongch'i Kikuron* (The Government Structure in North Korea). Seoul: Korea University Press, 1964.

Park Dong-suh. *Hanguk Kwanryo Jedo ŭi Ryŏksadyok Dyonkae* (The Historical Development of the Bureaucracy in Korea). Seoul: The Korean Research Center, 1961.

Pukhan Ch'ongkam 1945–1968 (A Summary of Complete Facts About North Korea 1945–1968). Seoul: Kongsan Munje Yŏnguso, 1968.

Pukhan Kongsan Jipdan ŭi Hŭkp'i-sŏ (Story About the North Korean Leaders). Seoul: Nae'oe Munje Yŏnguso, 1961.

Puk Han Koeroe Shilchŏng, Chŏngch'ipyŏn (Real Situation of North Korean Political Affairs). Seoul: Date of publication and name of publisher are not given. It is classified as "top secret." Presumably it is a South Korean governmental document.

Pukhan Yoram (Concise Facts About North Korea). Seoul: The Office of Public Information, Republic of Korea, 1962.

Pukhan Yoram. Seoul: The Office of Public Information, 1968.

Suh Nam-won. *Pukhan Kyŏngje Chŏngch'aek kwa Saengsan Kwanri* (North Korean Economic Policy and Its Production Management). Seoul: Korea University Press, 1964.

Yang Ho-min. *Pukhan e Ideologi wa Chŏngch'i* (Ideology and Politics in North Korea). Seoul: Korea University Press, 1967.

Yi Hun-gu. *Manju wa Chosŏn-in* (Korean Immigrants in Manchuria). P'yŏngyang: Union Christian College Press, 1932.

Yi Ki-ha. *Hanguk Chŏngdang Paltalsa* (History of the Development of Korean Political Parties). Seoul: Uihoe Chŏngch'i-sa, 1961.

Yu Hŏn. *Pukhan Isip-nyŏn* (Twenty Years of North Korea). Seoul: Taehan Bankong Kyŏyukwon, 1966.

Yun Ki-jŏng. *Hanguk Kongsan chu'i Undong Pip'an* (Critique of the Korean Communist Movement). Seoul: T'ongil Ch'unch'u-sa, 1959.

_____. *Pukhan Hŭkmak* (Inside Story of North Korea). Seoul: T'ongil Ch'unch'u-sa, 1962.

2. In the Japanese Language

Chōsen Jijyō Kenkyū-sho (ed.). *Hokui Sanjū Hachidosen* (The 38th Parallel). Tokyo: Chōsen Jijyō Kenkyū-sho, 1948.

Chōsen sōtokufu, Hōmukyoku. *Chōsen Dokuritsu Shisō Undō no Hensen* (Changes in the Thoughts for the Korean Independence Movement). Keijō: Chōsen sōtokufu, 1931.

Foreign Ministry of Japan (ed.). *Chōsen Benran* (Summary Facts About Korea), Asian Series, No. 1. Tokyo: Foreign Ministry of Japan, 1964.

_____. (ed.). *Gendai Chūgoku Chōsen Jinmeikan* (Who's Who in Modern China and Korea). Tokyo: Foreign Ministry of Japan, 1953.

Foreign Ministry of Japan. *Sengo ni okeru Chōsen no Seijijyōsei* (Korean Politics in the Postwar Era). Tokyo: Foreign Ministry of Japan, 1948.

Fujishima Uuchi. *Gendai Chōsenron* (Discussion on Modern Korea). Tokyo: Keisō Shobō, 1966.

Hatano Kennichi (ed.). *Chūgoku Kyōsantō-shi* (History of the Chinese Communist Party). Tokyo: Jiji Tsūshin-sha, 1961.

Hayashi Takehiko. *Kankoku Gendaishi* (Modern History of Korea). Tokyo: Shiseidō, 1967.

Institute for Foreign Affairs (ed.). *Chōsen Yōran* (Survey of Korea). Tokyo: Musashi Shobō, 1960.

Kasumigaseki Kai (ed.). *Gendai Chōsen Jinmei Jiten* (Who's Who in Modern Korea). Tokyo: Kaikō Jihō-sha, 1960.

_____ (ed.). *Gendai Chōsen Jinmei Jiten* (Rev. Ed.) (Who's Who In Modern Korea). Tokyo: Sekai Jānaru-sha, 1962.

Kim Chong-myŏng (ed.). *Chōsen Dokuritsu Undō, Kyōsan Undō-hen*, Vol. IV, V (A History of the Korean Independence Movement, The Communist Movement, Vol. IV, V). Tokyo: Hara Shobō, 1967.

Kim Chong-myŏng. *Chōsen Shinminshushugi Kakumei-shi* (A History of the New Democratic Revolution in Korea). Tokyo: Gogatsu Shobō, 1953.

Kim Chong-myŏng *et al. Chōsen Kindai Kakumei Undō-shi* (History of Modern Korean Revolution). Tokyo: Shin Nippon Shuppan-sha, 1966.

Kim Sam-kyu. *Chōsen Gendai-shi* (Modern History of Korea). Tokyo: Tsukuma Shobō, 1963.

————. *Chōsen no Shinjitsu* (The Truth About Korea). Tokyo: Shiseido, 1960.

———— *Konnichi no Chōsen* (Korea Today). Tokyo: Kawade Shobō, 1956.

Kō-an Chyōsachyō (ed.). *Hokusen no Kaiho Undōshi* (A History of the North Korean Liberation Movement). Tokyo: Kō-an Chyōsachyō, 1957.

Maruo Itaru & Mura Tsuneo. *Bunretsu Kokka ni okeru Keizai Hatten no Futatsuno Ryūkei* (Two Patterns of Economic Development in the Divided Nations). Tokyo: Kokusai Mondai Kenkyū-sho, 1962.

Matsumoto Hirokazu. *Gekkidō suru Kankoku* (Turbulent Korea). Tokyo: Iwanami Shotten, 1963.

Rin Eiju *et al. Chōsen Sensōshi* (History of the Korean War). Tokyo: Koria Hyōronsha, 1967.

Sekai Seikei Chōsa-kai (ed.). *Kankoku, Kita Chōsen Jinmei Jiten* (Who's Who in South and North Korea). Tokyo: Sekai Seikei Chōsa-kai, 1966.

————(ed.). *Kankoku, Kita Chōsen Jinmei Jiten* (Who's Who in South and North Korea). Tokyo: Sekai Seikei Chōsa-kai, 1970.

Song-Chi-hak. *Chōsen Kyōiku-shi* (A History of Korean Education). Tokyo: Kuroshiyo Shuppan, 1960.

Tera-o Korō. *Sanjū Hachidosen-no Kita* (North of the 38th Parallel). Tokyo: Shin Nippon Shuppan-sha, 1959.

Tōitsu Chōsen Nenkan, 1967–68 (One-Korea Yearbook, 1967–68). Tokyo: Tōitsu Chōsen Shimbunsha, 1967.

Tsuboe Senji. *Chōsen Minzoku Dokuritsu Undō Hishi* (The Hidden Story of the Struggle of Korean People for Emancipation). Tokyo: Gennandō Shotten, 1966.

————. *Hokusen no Kaihō Jūnen* (Ten Years of Liberated North Korea). Tokyo: Nikkan Rōdō Tsūshin-sha, 1956.

————. *Nansen no Kaihō Jūnen* (Ten Years of Liberated South Korea). Tokyo: Rōdō Tsūshin-sha, 1956.

Yi Na-yōng. *Chōsen Minzok Kaihō Tōsōshi* (History of the Struggle for Korean National Emancipation). Tokyo: Shin Nippon Shuppan-sha, 1958.

Yu Ho-il. *Gendai Chōsen no Rekishi* (History of Modern Korea). Tokyo: San Ichi Shobō, 1953.

3. In the English Language

Allen, Richard C. *Korea's Syngman Rhee, An Unauthorized Portrait*. Rutland, Vermont: Charles E. Tuttle Company, 1960.

Beloff, Max. *Soviet Policy in the Far East, 1944–1951*. London: Oxford University Press, 1953.

Berger, Carl J. *The Korean Knot, A Military-Political History*. Philadelphia: University of Pennsylvania Press, 1957.

Black, Cyril E. & Thomas P. Thornton (eds.). *Communism and Revolution:*

The Strategic Uses of Political Violence. Princeton: Princeton University Press, 1964.

Burchett, Wilfred G. *Again Korea.* New York: International Publishers, 1968.

Burks, R. V. *The Dynamics of Communism in Eastern Europe.* Princeton, New Jersey: Princeton University Press, 1961.

Cho Soon-sung. *Korea in World Politics, 1940–1950.* Berkeley: University of California Press, 1967.

_____. "United States Policy Toward the Unification of Korea: 1943–50" (unpublished Ph.D. thesis). Ann Arbor: University of Michigan, 1960.

Chung, Henry. *The Russians Came to Korea.* Seoul: The Korean Pacific Press, 1947.

Chung In-t'aek. "The Korean Minority in Manchuria (1900–1937)" (unpublished Ph.D. thesis). Washington, D.C.: The American University, 1966.

Clark, Mark W. *From the Danube to the Yalu.* New York: Harper & Brothers, 1954.

Communist International. *First Congress of the Toilers of the Far East.* Petrograd: Communist International, 1922.

_____. *Fourth Congress of the Communist International.* London: Communist Party of Great Britain, 1922.

_____. *The Second Congress of the Communist International, as Reported and Interpreted by the Official Newspapers of Soviet Russia. Petrograd - Moscow, July 19–August 7, 1920.* Washington, D.C.: Government Printing Office, 1920.

Current Digest of the Soviet Press, Vol. I - XX (1949–1968). Washington: Joint Committee on Slavic Studies, 1949–1968.

Dallin, David J. *Soviet Russia and the Far East.* New Haven: Yale University Press, 1948.

Deutscher, Isaac. *Stalin, A Political Biography.* New York: Oxford University Press, 1967.

Dyakov, A. M. *et al. Crisis of the Colonial System: National Liberation Struggle of the Peoples of East Asia.* Bombay: People's Publishing House, LTD., 1951.

East-Asiatic Economic Investigation Bureau. *The Manchurian Year Book 1932–1933.* Tokyo: East-Asiatic Investigation Bureau, 1932.

Far Eastern Economic Review 1962.

Frank, Jerome D. *Sanity and Survival: Psychological Aspects of War and Peace.* New York: Random House, 1967.

George, Alexander L. *The Chinese Communist Army in Action: The Korean War and Its Aftermath.* New York: Columbia University Press, 1967.

Gitovich, Aleksandr I. & B. Bursov. *North of the 38th Parallel* (translated into English from Russian by George Leonof). Shanghai: Epoch Publishing Company, 1948.

Goodrich, Leland M. *Korea: A Study of United States Policy in the United Nations.* New York: Council on Foreign Relations, 1956.

Grajdanzev, Andrew J. *Modern Korea.* New York: Institute of Pacific Relations, 1944.

Griffith, William E. *Albania and the Sino-Soviet Rift.* Cambridge, Massachusetts: The Massachusetts Institute of Technology Press, 1963.

Groennings, Sven, E. W. Kelley, and Michael Leiserson (eds.). *The Study of Coalition Behavior: Theoretical Perspectives and Cases from Four Continents.* New York: Holt, Rinehart & Winston, Inc., 1970.

Hamm, Harry. *Albania—China's Beachhead in Europe* (translated by Victor Andersen). New York: Frederick A. Praeger, 1963.

Henderson, Gregory. *Korea, the Politics of the Vortex.* Cambridge, Massachusetts: Harvard University Press, 1968.

Isaak, Alan C. *Scope and Methods of Political Science: An Introduction to the Methodology of Political Inquiry.* Homewood, Illinois: The Dorsey Press, 1969.

Kennedy, Malcolm D. *A Short History of Communism in Asia.* New York: Frederick A. Praeger, 1957.

Kim San & Nym Wales *Song of Ariran: The Life Story of a Korean Rebel.* New York: The John Day Company, 1941.

Kolarz, Walter. *The Peoples of the Soviet Far East.* London: George Philip & Son Limited, 1954.

Lauterbach, R. E. *Danger from the East.* New York: Harper & Row, 1947.

Lee Chong-sik. *The Politics of Korean Nationalism.* Berkeley: University of California Press, 1963.

Lenin, V. I. *Selected Works, Vol. I–XII.* London: Laurence & Wishart LTD., 1936.

McCune, George M. *Korea Today.* Cambridge, Massachusetts: Harvard University Press, 1950.

McCune, Shannon. *Korea: Land of Broken Calm.* Princeton, N. J.: D. Van Nostrand Company, Inc., 1967.

_____. *Korea's Heritage: A Regional and Social Geography.* Tokyo: Charles E. Tuttle Co., 1960.

Meade, Edward G. *American Military Government in Korea.* London: Oxford University Press, 1951.

Merton, Robert K. *et al.* (eds.). *Reader in Bureaucracy.* New York: The Free Press, 1952.

Min, Benjamin. "North Korea's Foreign Policy in the Postwar Decade, 1953–1963: Its Strategy of Korean Unification and Relations with Moscow and Peking" (unpublished Ph.D. thesis). Amherst: University of Massachusetts, 1967.

North, Robert C. *Kuomintang and Chinese Communist Elites.* Stanford: Stanford University Press, 1952.

_____. *Moscow and the Chinese Communists.* Stanford: Stanford University Press, 1963.

Oliver, Robert T. *Korea: Forgotten Nation.* Washington, D. C.: Public Affairs Press, 1944.

Osgood, Cornelius G. *The Koreans and Their Culture.* New York: Ronald Press Company, 1951.

Paige, Glenn D. *The Korean People's Democratic Republic.* Stanford: The Hoover Institution, 1966.

Pauley, Edwin W. *Report on Japanese Assets in Soviet-Occupied Korea to the President of the United States.* Washington, D. C.: Government Printing Office, 1946.

Poats, Rutherford M. *Decision in Korea.* New York: The McBride Company, 1954.

The Research Institute for Internal and External Affairs. *North Korea under Communism: A Story of Suppression.* Seoul: The Research Institute for Internal and External Affairs, 1963.

Riker, William H. *The Theory of Political Coalitions.* New Haven, Connecticut: Yale University Press, 1962.

Riley, John W. (Jr.). & Wilbur Schramm. *The Reds Take a City: The Communist Occupation of Seoul with Eyewitness Accounts.* New Brunswick, N. J.: Rutgers University Press, 1951.

Rudolph, Philip. *North Korea's Political and Economic Structure.* New York: Institute of Pacific Relations, 1959.

Scalapino, Robert A. (ed.). *North Korea Today.* New York: Frederick A. Praeger, 1963.

Schurmann, Franz. *Ideology and Organization in Communist China.* Berkeley: University of California Press, 1966.

Shabshina, F. I. *et al. Crisis of the Colonial System: National Liberation Struggle of the Peoples of East Asia.* Bombay: People's Publishing House, LTD., 1951.

Shen Mo. *Japan in Manchuria, An Analytical Study of Treaties and Documents.* Manila: Grace Trading Co., Inc., 1960.

Simon, Sheldon W. *The Broken Triangle: Peking, Djakarta, and the PKI.* Baltimore: The John Hopkins Press, 1969.

Skilling, H. Gordon. *Communism, National and International: Eastern Europe After Stalin.* Toronto, Canada: University of Toronto Press, 1964.

Snow, Edgar. *The Other Side of the River: Red China Today.* New York: Random House, 1961.

Sorlin, Pierre. *The Soviet People and Their Society.* New York: Frederick A. Praeger, 1968.

Soviet Press Translations. Vol. I–IV. Seattle: Far Eastern Institute at University of Washington, 1946–1949.

Spanier, John W. *The Truman–MacArthur Controversy and the Korean War.* New York: W. W. Norton & Company, Inc., 1965.

[201]

Staar, Richard F. *The Communist Regimes in Eastern Europe: An Introduction*. Stanford, California: The Hoover Institution on War, Revolution and Peace, 1967.

Stalin, Joseph V. *Marxism and the National and Colonial Questions*. New York: International Publishers, 1935.

Suh Dae-sook. *The Korean Communist Movement 1918-1948*. Princeton: Princeton University Press, 1967.

Szulc, Tad. *Czechoslovakia Since World War II*. New York: The Viking Press, 1971.

United Nations. *Report of the United Nations Commission for the Unification and Rehabilitation of Korea*, General Assembly, Official Records: 6th Session, Supplement No. 12 (A/1881) (UNCURK Report), New York, 1951.

———. *Supplement to the Volume on Laws Concerning Nationality, 1954* (ST/LEG/SER/B/9) (New York, 1959), pp. 100-101.

United States, Commander-in-Chief, United States Army Forces, Pacific. *Summation of the United States Military Government Activities* (monthly), No. 7 (April, 1946)—No. 19 (April, 1947). Seoul.

United States Congress. *Hearings Before the Subcommittee on Asian and Pacific Affairs of the Committee on Foreign Affairs House of Representatives*, Ninety-Second Congress, First Session (June 8, 9, and 10, 1971). Washington, D. C.: Government Printing Office, 1971.

United States Joint Publications Research Service. *Translations on North Korea No. 42* (Biographical Data on Prominent North Koreans), JPRS 40950. Washington, D. C.: Government Printing Office, 1968.

United States State Department, *North Korea: A Case Study in the Technique of Takeover*, State Department Publication No. 7118, Far Eastern Series 103. Washington, D. C.: Government Printing Office, 1961.

———. *The Record on Korean Unification, 1943-1960: Narrative Summary with Principle Documents*, State Department Publication No. 7084, Far Eastern Series 101. Washington, D. C.: Government Printing Office, 1960.

Vatcher, William H. (Jr.). *Panmunjon: The Story of the Korean Military Armistice Negotiations*. New York: Frederick A. Praeger, Inc. 1958.

von Rauch, Georg. *A History of Soviet Russia*. New York: Frederick A. Praeger, Publishers, 1967.

Whiting, Allen S. *China Crosses the Yalu*. New York: The Macmillan Company, 1960.

Wu Yuan-le. *The Economy of Communist China*. New York: Frederick A. Praeger, Publishers, 1965.

B. ARTICLES AND PERIODICALS

1. In the Korean Language

Cho Seong-jik. "The Process of Abolishing Private Business in North Korea," *Studies on Communist Affairs* (Seoul), I, No. 1 (September, 1964), pp. 154-83. (Though written in Korean, titles were given in English.)

Choi Kwang-suk. "Ideological Education in North Korea: Its Forms and Contents," *Studies on Communist Affairs*, I, No. 2 (November, 1965), pp. 42–71. (Though written in Korean, titles were given in English.)

"Chosŏn Ŭiyong-gun Ch'ong Saryŏng Mu-Jŏng Chang-gun Ildae-ki" ("Biography of Commanding General of the Korean Volunteer Corps, General Mu-Jŏng"), *Shin Ch'ŏn-ji* (Seoul), I, No. 2 (March, 1946). pp. 238–41.

Han Jae-duk. "Problems of Kim Il-sŏng's 'Self-Dependence' and 'Self-Reliance'," *Studies on Communist Affairs*, I, No. 1 (September, 1964), pp. 26–59. (Although written in Korea, titles were given in English.)

Kang Dae-ho. "Mak-pu Sam-guk Oe'sang Hoe'i wa Chosŏn" ("The Moscow Three Foreign Ministers' Conference and Korea"), *Inmin* (People) (Seoul), II, No. 1 (January, 1946), pp. 66–72.

KYZ. "Sip'yŏng" ("Comments on Current Events"), *Inmin* (People) (Seoul), II, No. 1 (January, 1946), pp. 43–44.

"Kim Il-sŏng Changgun Pudae wa Chosŏn Ŭiyonggun ui Chunggyŏn Kanbu Chwadam-hoe" ("Roundtable Discussion of the Main Staff Members of the Kim Il-sŏng Company and the Korean Volunteer Corps"), *Shin Ch'ŏn-ji* (Seoul), I, No. 2 (March, 1946), pp. 230–37.

"Kim Tu-bong Chusŏk ŭi T'ujaeng-sa" ("Record of the Struggle of Chairman Kim Tu-bong"), *Shin Ch'ŏn-ji*, I, No. 2 (March, 1946), pp. 205–07.

Lee Ch'ŏl-chu. "Im Hwa e taehan Kisojang" ("Indictment Against Im Hwa"), *Sasangke* (Seoul), June, 1964, pp. 269–75.

———. "Pak Hŏn-yŏng kwa Yukyŏktae" ("Pak Hŏn-yŏng and the Partisans"), *Sasangke* (Seoul), May, 1964, pp. 237–43.

———. "Puk'e Shi'in kwa Unmyŏng" ("The Fate of a Poet in the North"), *Sasangke*, July, 1964, pp. 252–59.

———. "Pukke Chosŏn Nodongdang" ("The North Korean Communist Party"), *Shin Tong-a* (Seoul), May 1, 1965, pp. 260–97.

Ministry of Foreign Affairs, Republic of Korea. "Soryŏn nae'e in'nŭn Hangukin" ("Koreans in the Soviet Union"), *Oemu T'ongbo* (Seoul), No. 4 (September, 1954), pp. 88–100.

Pak Tal-hwan. "An Chae-hong ron" ("Discussion about Mr. An Chae-hong"), *Inmin* (People) (Seoul), II, No. 1 (January, 1946), pp. 51–57.

So Chin-chul. "How the International Communists Prepared the War in Korea," *Studies on Communist Affairs* (Seoul), I, No. 1 (September, 1964), pp. 1–25; and I, No. 2 (November, 1965), pp. 72–85. (Written in Korean but titles are given in English.)

Suh Nam-won. "North Korean Economic Policy, 1945–1960," *Studies on Communist Affairs* (Seoul), I, No. 1 (September, 1964), pp. 60–89. (Written in Korean but titles were given in English.)

"Tongnip Tongmaeng kŭp Ŭiyong-gun Yoin ŭi Yakyŏk" ("Short Biographies of the Important People of the Independence League and the Volunteer Corps"), *Shin Ch'ŏn-ji* (Seoul), I, No. 2 (March, 1946), pp. 242–44.

"Yi Chae-yu T'alch'ul-ki" ("The Jailbreak of Yi Chae-yu"), *Shin Ch'ŏn-ji* (Seoul), I, No. 3 (April, 1946), pp. 6–17; and II, No. 4 (May, 1946), pp. 54–63.

Yi Kang-kuk. "Rhee Pak-sa wa Chung'ang Hyŏp'i-hoe" ("Dr. Rhee and Central Consultative Association"), *Inmin* (People), II, No. 1 (January, 1946), pp. 11–15.

2. In the Japanese Language

Chōsen Kenkyū (Geppō) (Monthly Bulletin of Korean Studies) (issued by Nippon Chōsen Kenkyū-sho in Tokyo). No. 14 (February 25, 1963), pp. 16–23; No. 15 (March 25, 1963), pp. 1–6; No. 16 (April 25, 1963), pp. 1–21; No. 21 (September 25, 1963), pp. 1–21; No. 24 (December 25, 1963), pp. 1–5; No. 32 (August, 1964), pp. 25–37; No. 35 (December, 1964), pp. 1–4, 10–15; No. 36 (January, 1965), pp. 3–8, 16–22; No. 37 (February/March, 1965), pp. 17–23; No. 38 (April, 1965), pp. 17–35; No. 40 (June, 1965), pp. 34–36; No. 48 (March, 1966), pp. 13–18; No. 59 (February/March, 1967), pp. 12–15; No. 70 (February, 1968), pp. 2–28; No. 71 (March, 1968), pp. 5–12; and No. 77 (September, 1968), pp. 4–20.

"Chōsen no Kakumeiteki Rōdō Kumiai Undō no Ninmu" ("The Duty of the Revolutionary Labor Union Movement in Korea"), *Intanashonaru*, IV, No. 17 (December, 1930), pp. 1–8.

"Chōsen ni okeru Kyōsan Shugi Undō no Kinkyō" ("Recent Conditions of the Communist Movement in Korea"), *Shisō Ihō*, No. 5 (December, 1935), pp. 43–46.

"Chōsen ni okeru Shijisha ni atafuru Taiheiyō Rōdō Kumiai Shokikyoku no Kōkaijyō" ("The Open Letter from the Pan Pacific Labor Union Secretariat to the Supporters of Union in Korea"), *Intanashonaru*, VI, No. 8 (June, 1932), pp. 62–74.

"Chōsen no Kakumeiteki Rōdō Kumiai Undō no Ninmu" ("The Duty of the Revolutionary Labor Union Movement in Korea"), *Intanashonaru*, IV, No. 17 (December, 1930), pp. 1–8.

"Chōsen Shakaı Undō Gaikan" ("General Outlook of the Korean Socialist Movement"), *Intanashonaru*, II, No. 2 (February, 1928), pp. 63–70.

Ishii Toshio. "Kyōso Sai Saigu ni okeru Tōgaku shisō no rekishiteki tenkai" ("The Historical Development of Tonghak Thought by Founder Ch'oe Che-u"), *Rekishigaku Kenkyū*, II, No. 1 (January, 1941), pp. 17–60.

Itō Kenrō. "Chōsen Kyōsan-tō mebae no goro" ("The Embryonic Period of the Korean Communist Party"), *Kaizō*, XXXI, No. 10 (October, 1950), pp. 107–111.

"Kaizi Futei Senjin no Jyōkyō" ("Conditions of Recalcitrant Koreans Abroad"), *Tokkō Gaiji Geppō*, (April, 1938), pp. 95–97; (July, 1938), pp. 113–17; (August, 1938), pp. 88–92; and (October, 1938), pp. 134–42.

"Kwahoku Chōsen Seinen Rengōkai no Dōkō" ("The Activites of the North China Korean Youth Federation"), *Tokkō Geppō*, July, 1941, pp. 119–21.

"Shōwa Jūichinen do ni okeru Sennai Shisō Undō no Jyōkyō" ("The Conditions of the Thought Movement in Korea During 1936"), *Shisō Ihō*, No. 10 (March, 1937), pp. 27–41.

Smith, R. "Hokusen no akai Hoshi" ("Red Star of North Korea"), Kaizō, XXXIV, No. 9 (July, 1953), pp. 183–88.

Tō Kanbu no Chuihō to Shin Yakuin no Kaobure" ("Exile of the Party Leaders and the Faces of the New Officials"), *Soren Geppō*, No. 193 (August, 1953), pp. 870–73.

"Zai shi Futei Senjin no Anyaku ni kansuru Jyōhō" ("Information Concerning the Secret Maneuvers of the Recalcitrant Koreans in China"), *Shisō Ihō*, No. 14 (March, 1938), pp. 218–31.

3. In the English Language

An, Thomas. "New Winds in P'yŏngyang?," *Problems of Communism*, XV, No. 4 (July, 1960), pp. 68–71.

"Appeal of the Korean Supreme People's Assembly to Government of the USA and the Soviet Union," *Pravada*, September 14, 1948, in *Soviet Press Translations*, III, No. 16 (September 15, 1948), pp. 581–82.

"Away with Flunkeyism," *The Economist*, CCXX (August, 1960), p. 721.

Bradbury, John. "Sino-Soviet Competition in North Korea," *The China Quarterly*, II, No. 6 (April-June, 1961), pp. 15–28.

Cho Soon-sung. "Japan's Two Koreas Policy on the Problems of Korean Unification," *Asian Survey*, VII, No. 10 (October, 1967), pp. 703–25.

_____. "Politics of North Korea's Unification Policies," *World Politics*, XIX, No. 2 (January, 1967), pp. 218–41.

Cromley, Ray. "North Korea Sovietized," *The Wall Street Journal*, May 5, 1947, p. 4.

"Divided Korea," *The Economist*, CL, No. 5341 (January 5, 1946), pp. 5–6.

Dubin, Wilbert B. "The Political Evolution of the P'yongyang Government," *Pacific Affairs*, XXIII, No. 4 (December, 1950), pp. 381–92.

"The Factional Struggle Among the Korean Communists," *Inprecorr*, XIV No. 48 (September 14, 1934), pp. 1265–66.

Grajdanzev, Andrew J. "Korea Divided," *Far Eastern Survey*, XIV, No. 20 (October 10, 1945), pp. 281–83.

Guins, George C. "The Korean Plans of Russian Imperialism," *The American Journal of Economics and Sociology*, VI, No. 1 (October, 1946), pp. 71–86.

Houn, Franklin W. "The Eighth Central Committee of the Chinese Communist Party; A Study of an Elite," *The American Political Science Review*, LI, No. 2 (June, 1957), pp. 392–404.

Huggard, M. T. "North Korea's International Position," *Asian Survey*, V, No. 8 (August, 1965), pp. 375–88.

"Invitation to the Fourth World Congress of the Communist International," *Inprecorr*, II, No. 57 (July 17, 1922), p. 427.

Ivanov, P. "Elections in Northern Korea," *Izvestia*, November 16, 1946, in *Soviet Press Translations*, I, No. 4 (December 14, 1946), pp. 18-20.

Journal of Korean Affairs, Vol. I, No. 1 (April, 1971); Vol. I, No. 2 (July, 1971); Vol. I, No. 3 (October, 1971); Vol. I, No. 4 (January, 1972); and Vol. II, No. 1 (April, 1972).

Kalinov, Kyril. "An Ex-Soviet Officer Tells: How Russia Built the North Korean Army," *The Reporter*, III, No. 7 (September 26, 1950), pp. 4-8.

Kim Doo-yong. "Labor Legislation in North Korea," *Amerasia*, XI, No. 5 (May, 1947), pp. 156-60.

Kim Ilpyong J. "North Korea's Fourth Party Congress," *Pacific Affairs*, XXXV, No. 1 (Spring, 1962), pp. 37-50.

Kim Joungwon, A. "The Long March of North Korea's Kim," *The New York Times Magazine*, February 25, 1968, pp. 33, 107-11.

_____. "The 'Peak of Socialism' in North Korea: The Five and Seven Year Plans," *Asian Survey*, V, No. 5 (May, 1965), pp. 255-69.

Kim Kyu-sik, "The Asiatic Revolutionary Movement and Imperialism," *The Communist Review*, III, No. 3 (July, 1922), pp. 137-47.

Koh B. C. "North Korea and Its Quest for Autonomy," *Pacific Affairs*, XXXVIII, No. 3 (Fall & Winter, 1965-66), pp. 294-306.

_____. "North Korea: Profile of a Garrison State," *Problems of Communism*, XVIII, No. 1 (January, 1969), pp. 18-27.

_____. "North Korea and the Sino-Soviet Schism," *The Western Political Quarterly*, XXII, No. 4 (December, 1969), pp. 940-62.

"Korea—The Crossroads of Asia," *Amerasia*, IX, No. 17 (October, 1945), pp. 271-79.

"Korea, Past and Present," *The World Today*, II, No. 4 (April, 1946), pp. 175-92.

"The Korean People Welcome the Soviet Government Decision," *Izvestia*, September 25, 1948, in *Soviet Press Translations*, III, No. 19 (November 1, 1948), pp. 584-85.

Kurai Ryōzō. "Present Status of Japan-Communist China Relations," *The Japan Annual of International Affairs*," No. 1 (1961), pp. 91-157.

Latsinnik, N. "Industrial Scenes in the Korean Republic," *New Times*, No. 14 (March 30, 1949), pp. 26-30.

Lee Chong-sik. "Korean Communists and Yenan," *The China Quarterly*, No. 9 (January–March, 1962), pp. 182-92.

_____. "The 'Socialist Revolution' in the North Korean Countryside," *Asian Survey*, II, No. 8 (October, 1962), pp. 9-22.

Lee Chong-sik & Kim Nam-sik. "Control and Administrative Mechanism in the North Korean Countryside," *Journal of Asian Studies*, XXIX, No. 2 (February, 1970), pp. 309-26.

Lee Chong-sik & Oh Ki-wan. "The Russian Faction in North Korea," *Asian Survey*, VIII, No. 4 (April, 1968), pp. 270-88.

Lee Se-youl. "A Picture of North Korea's Industry," *Amerasia*, XI, No. 2 (February, 1947), pp. 61–62.

Li "B". "Renewed Wave of Japanese Terror in Korea," *Inprecorr*, XII, No. 39 (September 1, 1932), p. 820.

McCune, George M. "Korea: The First Year of Liberation," *Pacific Affairs*, XX, No. 1 (March, 1947), pp. 3–17.

McCune, Shannon. "Korea: Geographic Parallels, 1950–60," *The Journal of Geography*, LIX, No. 5 (May, 1960), pp. 201–06.

_____. "Physical Basis for Korean Boundaries," *The Far Eastern Quarterly*, V, No. 3 (May, 1946), pp. 272–88.

Noble, Harold J. "North Korean Democracy: Russian Style," *The New Leader*, XXX, No. 22 (May 31, 1947), Section 2, pp. 1–12.

"Nobody's Little Brother," *The Economist*, CCXVII (November, 1965), p. 600.

"North Korea Bites Moscow's Hand," *Atlas*, IX, No. 4 (April, 1965), p. 227.

Paige, Glenn D. "Korea and the Comintern, 1919–1935," *Bulletin of the Korean Research Center*, No. 13 (December, 1960), pp. 1–25.

Pak Tong-un. "The Basis of Thought and Organization of the Korean Workers' Party and the Operation of the Party Machinery," *Journal of Asiatic Studies*, VII, No. 4 (1964), pp. 83–86.

_____. "The Character of the Constitution of Communist North Korea and Its Establishment Process," *Journal of Asiatic Studies*, VI, No. 2 (December, 1963), pp. 25–28.

_____. "The Composition and Operation of the North Korean Supreme People's Assembly," *Journal of Asiatic Studies*, VII, No. 1 (1964), pp. 17–20.

Perlin, V. "Visit to North Korea," *New Times*, No. 2 (January 7, 1948), pp. 15–18.

Porter, Catherine & William L. Holland. "North Korea's Economic Development," *Far Eastern Survey*, XXIV, No. 11 (November, 1955), pp. 171–73.

"Resolution of the ECCI on the Korean Question, Adopted by the Polit-Secretariat of the ECCI on December 10, 1928," *Inprecorr*, IX, No. 8 (February 15, 1929), pp. 130–33.

Riley, John W. (Jr.), Wilbur Schramm & Frederick W. Williams. "Flight from Communism: A Report on Korean Refugees," *Public Opinion Quarterly*, No. 2 (summer, 1951), pp. 274–86.

Robinson, Joan. "Korean Miracle," *Monthly Review*, XIX, No. 9 (January, 1965), pp. 541–49.

Rudolph, Philip. "North Korea and the Path to Socialism," *Pacific Affairs*, XXXII, No. 2 (June, 1959), pp. 131–43.

"Save the Lives of the Korean Revolutionaries," *Inprecorr*, XIII, No. 57 (December 29, 1933), pp. 1305–06.

[207]

Scalapino, Robert A. "Moscow, Peking and the Communist Parties of Asia," *Foreign Affairs*, January, 1963, pp. 323–43.

Scalapino, Robert A. & Lee Chong-sik. "The Origins of the Korean Communist Movement (I)," *Journal of Asian Studies*, XX, No. 1 (November, 1960), pp. 19–31.

————. "The Origins of the Korean Communist Movement (II)," *Journal of Asian Studies*, XX, No. 2 (February, 1961), pp. 149–67.

Schram, Wilbur & John W. Riley (Jr.). "Communication in the Sovietized State, as Demonstrated in Korea," *American Sociological Review*, XVI, No. 6 (December, 1951), pp. 757–66.

Shii Motoyuki, "Flying Horseman," *Atlas*, XVII (June, 1969), pp. 48–49.

"The Situation in Korea," *Inprecorr*, XIII, No. 55 (December 15, 1933), p. 1246.

Smolensky, V. "The Situation in Korea," *Pravda*, November 16, 1946, in *Soviet Press Translations*, II, No. 5 (March 15, 1947), pp. 8–11.

"The Struggle of the Korean People for a United, Independent, Democratic Korea," *Bolshevik*, No. 11 (June 15, 1949), in *Soviet Press Translations*, IV, No. 18 (October 15, 1949), pp. 549–57.

Snow, Edgar, "China's Japanese Allies," *Asia*, XXXIX, No. 6 (June, 1939), pp. 340–44.

Thornton, Thomas P. "Foreign Relations of the Asiatic Communist Satellites," *Pacific Affairs*, XXXV, No. 4 (winter, 1962–1963), pp. 341–52.

Tralim, Hankum. "Land Reform in North Korea," *Amerasia*, XI, No. 2 (February, 1947), pp. 55–62.

"Trial of Case of Anti-State Espionage and Terrorist Center in Korean People's Democratic Republic," *Pravda*, August 8, 1953, in *Current Digest of the Soviet Korea*, V, No. 32 (September 19, 1953), pp. 18–19.

Wales, Nym. "Rebel Korea," *Pacific Affairs*, XV, No. 1 (March, 1942), pp. 25–43.

Washburn, John N. "Russia Looks at Northern Korea," *Pacific Affairs*, XX, No. 2 (June, 1947), pp. 152–60.

————. "Soviet Press Views North Korea," *Pacific Affairs*, XXII, No. 1 (March, 1949), pp. 53–58.

————. "Soviet Korea and the Korean Communist Party," *Pacific Affairs*, XXIII, No. 1 (March, 1950), pp. 59–64.

Yarovoy, B. "Korea: Forgotten Nation," *New Times* (Moscow), August 15, 1945, pp. 26–27.

C. NEWSPAPERS

1. In the Korean Language

Seoul Shinmun (Seoul Daily), November 30, 1945.

Tong-A Ilbo (Oriental Daily, Seoul), May 29, 1925; June 2, 4, 5 and 9, 1925; November 17, 1926; November 1 and 2, 1919; July 1, 2, and 4, 1932;

January 2, 3, 10 and 29, 1934; February 1, 3, 7, 17 and 28, 1934; March 2, 6, 7, 8, 9, 10, 17 and 30, 1934; June 5 (extra edition), 6 and 7, 1937; May 9, 1946; January 22 and 25, November 6 and 28, and December 16, 1968; and June 15, 1971.

2. In the Japanese Language

Nippon Keizai Shimbun (Japan Economy Newspaper), March 2, 1948.

(Osaka) *Asahi Shimbun*, May 1, 1928; November 2, 1929; June 1, 1930; July 16, 1930; July 3, 1932; September 3, 1932; December 29, 1932; February 25, 1937; June 6, 7 and 8, 1937; July 2, 1937; and July 4, 1961.

3. In the English Language

Jen Min Jih Pao (Peking), April 5, 1956.

New York Herald Tribune, November 2, 1945.

New York Times, October 27, 1945; May 11, 1946; October 18, 1949; January 13, 1950; June 28, 1950; September 15, 1950; December 1, 1950; August 19, 20 and 21, 1952; December 15, 1952; January 29, 1953; August 15 and 20, 1953; May 31, 1955; December 19, 1955; September 5, 1964; February 1, 23 and 27, 1968; March 22, 1969; and July 14, and November 22, 1970.

INDEX

[210]